Treasury *of* Home Baking

Over 400 recipes to warm your kitchen and their hearts

Publications International, Ltd.

Favorite Brand Name Recipes at www.fbnr.com

Microwave Cooking: Microwave ovens vary in wattage. Use the cooking times as
guidelines and check for doneness before adding more time.

Preparation/Cooking Times: Preparation times are based on the approximate amount
of time required to assemble the recipe before cooking, baking, chilling or serving.
These times include preparation steps such as measuring, chopping and mixing. The
fact that some preparations and cooking can be done simultaneously is taken into
account. Preparation of optional ingredients and serving suggestions is not included.

Contents

Rising to the Occasion
10

Bake Up Your Morning
38

Sweet & Savory Treats
64

Quick-As-Can-Be Breads
88

Oh My, Pie!
110

Bread Machine Marvels
136

Take the Cake
162

Start with a Mix
190

Cookie Jar Classics
214

Brownie Points
242

Dreamy Cheesecake
268

Crazy Kids' Stuff
290

Gatherings & Gifts
312

International Bake Shop
342

Acknowledgments
371

Index
372

Make Magic in Your Oven

Baking is the most magical sort of cooking, a unique mix of art and science. Take basic ingredients, flour and water, add the chemistry of yeast and they become loaves of bread. Mix together humble flour, butter and sugar and they can be transformed into hundreds of kinds of cookies, cakes or pies. The recipes for all these delicious miracles are here.

Treasury of Home Baking is written for beginning bakers as well as those with years of experience. Detailed instructions make even your very first yeast bread or layer cake virtually foolproof. If you already know your way around a kitchen, there's plenty of inspiration in recipes for extravagant desserts and international breads and cookies.

After all, the best thing about baking isn't turning out a perfect pie crust or cheesecake. It isn't even the fantastic aromas that waft through your house. The best thing is that baked goods, like the 400 in this book, are made to share with the ones you love.

Basic Baking Guidelines

• Always read through the entire recipe first to be sure you have the ingredients you need. That way you can also remove butter, margarine or cream cheese from the refrigerator to soften, if necessary.

• Check expiration dates on perishables in your cupboard like baking powder and yeast before you start so you won't have to run out for supplies at the last minute.

• Preheat your oven and check the temperature with an oven thermometer. It is not uncommon to have an oven that runs 25 degrees hotter or cooler than what it is set for. If you realize this ahead of time, you can adjust accordingly.

• Follow directions on adjusting oven racks, preparing baking sheets and choosing the size of baking pans. They can all make a real difference in your results.

• Measure ingredients accurately. This is the most important step in baking since chemistry plays a big part and recipes are "formulas" that are precisely crafted.

- Use glass or plastic measuring cups with spouts to measure liquids. Check the measurement at eye level.

- To measure dry ingredients, fill standard spoons and cups to overflowing, then level off with a spatula or flat edge of a knife. See the notes below on measuring flour.

- Bake with love. If you're angry, upset or rushed, recipes don't turn out as well. Just wait until a better time.

The Power of Flour

Wheat flour is the essential ingredient in all yeast breads because it contains an important protein called gluten. When mixed with liquid and stirred or kneaded, gluten stretches and forms a network of strands that catches the carbon dioxide bubbles produced by yeast. This network helps the dough rise and expand, giving the bread its structure. Baked goods that use baking powder or other leavening agents don't depend on this gluten network.

Bread flour is made from hard wheat that has a high protein content that works well in many yeast loaves. The gluten that makes it good for yeast breads will turn out a heavy unpalatable cake, however.

Cake flour is made from very soft wheat that is finely milled and low in gluten.

All-purpose flour is halfway between bread flour and cake flour in terms of gluten content, so it can be used for most any baking.

Bleached and unbleached flours may be used interchangeably. For the best results, always use the kind of flour recommended in the recipe, since that's the one that's been kitchen-tested.

The bran in *whole wheat flour* interferes with gluten development, so in whole grain breads it is usually combined with bread or all-purpose flour to avoid dense or poorly risen loaves.

Rye flour is low in gluten and must be combined with bread flour or all-purpose flour to produce a loaf that rises well.

Measuring Flour

Most flour is sold pre-sifted. To measure, stir the flour a bit to aerate it, and then spoon it into a measuring cup. Level off the excess with the straight edge of a knife or spatula. Do not bang the cup or press down on the flour since this will compact it and interfere with proper measuring. Because it is more finely milled, cake flour has a tendency to form lumps so it should always be sifted or strained before using.

Storing Flour

Flour is perishable. Store all-purpose, bread, cake, rye and self-rising flour in an airtight container in a cool, dry place for up to six months. Temperatures above 70°F encourage bug infestations and mold. For longer storage, refrigerate or freeze flour in moisture-proof wrapping. Whole wheat flour is more perishable than other types of flour, so purchase it in small amounts and store it in the freezer or in the refrigerator for up to three months. Allow chilled flour to return to room temperature before using.

Keeping it Light: Leaveners

Yeast 101

Yeast is a living, microscopic organism that produces carbon dioxide as it grows to make bread rise. While your grandmother may have used *compressed (cake) yeast*, it is highly perishable and must be refrigerated. Today most home bakers use packets of *active dry yeast*. To bring this dormant form of yeast back to life, it must come in contact with a warm liquid.

Active dry yeast is mixed with warm (105° to 115°F) liquid, which causes it to bubble into action. This is called proofing. The yeast mixture is then added to the other ingredients as directed in the recipe.

A newer kind of active dry yeast, *rapid-rise or quick-rise yeast* is made to mix with flour and other dry ingredients. It's best not to proof rapid rise yeast since that can use up too much of its energy ahead of time. Instead, warmer liquid (120° to 130°F) is usually added to the dry ingredients later.

Bread machine yeast is just what the name says—it's specially formulated to dissolve in your bread machine. For best results always use the yeast called for in each recipe and follow the directions given.

Baking Powder and Baking Soda Basics

Quick breads, biscuits, cookies and other non-yeast baked goods get most of their lightness from chemical leaveners.

Baking soda is also called sodium bicarbonate. When it is mixed with an acid ingredient like buttermilk, yogurt or molasses, it produces carbon dioxide bubbles that make baked goods, like quick breads and biscuits, have a light airy texture. Because it works immediately, you should make sure to place batter made with baking soda into the oven soon after it's mixed.

Baking powder is made of a combination of baking soda and an acid—usually cream of tartar. It is called "double acting" because some of its leavening power is released when it is mixed with wet ingredients and the rest occurs in the heat of the oven. Although they work in similar ways, baking soda and baking powder cannot be substituted for one another.

Choosing and Handling Chocolate

All chocolate comes from cocoa beans that have been fermented, roasted, crushed and ground into a paste called "chocolate liquor." Baking chocolate and cocoa come in many (sometimes confusing) varieties.

Unsweetened chocolate is pure chocolate liquor containing at least 50 percent cocoa butter and no added sugar. Various amounts of sugar are added to make *bittersweet, semisweet* and *dark chocolate*. Milk chocolate has dried milk powder, cocoa butter and sugar added. *White chocolate* is made with cocoa butter rather than chocolate liquor.

Unsweetened cocoa—not to be confused with the sweetened cocoa mixes used to make hot chocolate—is made from chocolate liquor with 75% of the cocoa butter extracted. The remaining paste is dried and ground. *Dutch process cocoa* is treated with an alkaline solution to produce a darker color and milder flavor.

Storing Chocolate

Keep baking chocolate well wrapped in a cool, dry, dark place—not the refrigerator, which is too damp. The grayish surface streaks and blotches that sometimes appear on chocolate are called "bloom." Don't worry, this is only an indication that some of the cocoa butter has separated from the solids. The chocolate is still fine to use.

Melting Chocolate

Because it is easy to scorch chocolate and ruin its flavor, it must always be melted over very low heat. The utensils you use must be completely dry since even a bit of moisture causes chocolate to "seize," which means it becomes stiff and grainy. If this happens, it can sometimes be corrected by immediately adding ½ teaspoon shortening (not butter) for each ounce of chocolate and stirring until smooth.

Double boiler method: Place the chocolate in the top of a double boiler or in a heatproof bowl over hot, not boiling, water; stir until smooth. Make sure that the water remains just below a simmer and is 1 inch below the bottom of the top pan. Be careful that no steam or water gets into the chocolate.

Direct heat method: Place the chocolate in a heavy saucepan and melt over very low heat, stirring constantly. Remove the chocolate from the heat as soon as it is melted. Be sure to watch it carefully because it is easily scorched when using this method.

Microwave oven method: Place 4 to 6 unwrapped 1-ounce squares of chocolate or 1 cup of chopped chocolate or chocolate chips in a small microwavable bowl. Microwave at HIGH 1 to 1½ minutes. Stir after 1 minute and at 30-second intervals after the first minute. The chocolate must be stirred because even when melted, the chocolate may retain its shape.

Weights and Measures

Dash = less than ⅛ teaspoon

½ tablespoon = 1½ teaspoons

1 tablespoon = 3 teaspoons

2 tablespoons = ⅛ cup

¼ cup = 4 tablespoons

⅓ cup = 5 tablespoons plus 1 teaspoon

½ cup = 8 tablespoons

⅔ cup = 10 tablespoons plus 2 teaspoons

¾ cup = 12 tablespoons

1 cup = 16 tablespoons

½ pint = 1 cup or 8 fluid ounces

1 pint = 2 cups or 16 fluid ounces

1 quart = 4 cups or 2 pints or 32 fluid ounces

1 gallon = 16 cups or 4 quarts

1 pound = 16 ounces

Substitution List

If you don't have:	Use:
1 teaspoon baking powder	¼ teaspoon baking soda + ½ teaspoon cream of tartar
½ cup firmly packed brown sugar	½ cup granulated sugar mixed with 2 tablespoons molasses
1 cup buttermilk	1 tablespoon lemon juice or vinegar plus milk to equal 1 cup (Stir; let mixture stand 5 minutes.)
1 ounce (1 square) unsweetened baking chocolate	3 tablespoons unsweetened cocoa + 1 tablespoon shortening
3 ounces (3 squares) semisweet baking chocolate	3 ounces (½ cup) semisweet chocolate morsels
½ cup corn syrup	½ cup granulated sugar + 2 tablespoons liquid
1 cup honey	1¼ cups granulated sugar + ¼ cup water
1 teaspoon freshly grated orange or lemon peel	½ teaspoon dried peel
1 teaspoon pumpkin pie spice	Combine: ½ teaspoon ground cinnamon, ¼ teaspoon ground nutmeg and ⅛ teaspoon *each* ground allspice and cardamom

Rising to the Occasion

Making and enjoying yeast bread is a simple and satisfying pleasure. Experience the soothing rhythm of kneading the dough, the magic of watching it rise and the wonderful aroma that fills your home. Whether it's simple Basic White Bread or savory Tomato-Peppercorn-Cheese Bread, nothing beats the taste of that first slice, still warm from the oven.

Honey Whole-Grain Bread

3 cups whole wheat bread flour, divided
2 cups warm (not hot) whole milk
¾ to 1 cup all-purpose flour, divided
¼ cup honey
2 tablespoons vegetable oil
1 package active dry yeast
¾ teaspoon salt

Slow Cooker Directions

1. Spray 1-quart casserole, soufflé dish or other high-sided baking pan that will fit in your slow cooker with nonstick cooking spray. Combine 1½ cups whole wheat flour, milk, ½ cup all-purpose flour, honey, oil, yeast and salt in large bowl. Beat at medium speed of electric mixer 2 minutes.

2. Add remaining 1½ cups whole wheat flour and ¼ cup to ½ cup all-purpose flour until dough is no longer sticky. (If mixer has difficulty mixing dough, mix in remaining flours with wooden spoon.) Transfer to prepared dish; place in slow cooker. Cover; cook on HIGH about 3 hours or until edges are browned.

3. Remove from slow cooker. Let stand 5 minutes. Unmold on wire rack to cool.

Makes 8 to 10 servings

Savory Summertime Oat Bread

Nonstick cooking spray

½ cup finely chopped onion

2 cups whole wheat flour

4¼ to 4½ cups all-purpose flour, divided

2 cups uncooked old-fashioned oats

¼ cup sugar

2 packages quick-rise active dry yeast

1½ teaspoons salt

1½ cups water

1¼ cups fat-free (skim) milk

¼ cup margarine

1 cup finely shredded carrots

3 tablespoons dried parsley leaves

1 tablespoon margarine, melted

1. Spray small nonstick skillet with cooking spray; heat over medium heat until hot. Cook and stir onion 3 minutes or until tender. Set aside.

2. Stir together whole wheat flour, 1 cup all-purpose flour, oats, sugar, yeast and salt in large mixer bowl. Heat water, milk and ¼ cup margarine in medium saucepan over low heat until mixture reaches 120° to 130°F. Add to flour mixture. Blend at low speed just until dry ingredients are moistened; beat 3 minutes at medium speed. Stir in carrots, onion, parsley and remaining 3¼ to 3½ cups all-purpose flour until dough is no longer sticky.

3. Knead dough on lightly floured surface 5 to 8 minutes or until smooth and elastic. Place in large bowl lightly sprayed with cooking spray; turn dough over. Cover and let rise in warm place about 30 minutes or until doubled in bulk.

4. Spray two 8×4-inch loaf pans with cooking spray. Punch dough down. Cover and let rest 10 minutes. Shape into 2 loaves; place in pans. Brush with melted margarine. Cover; let rise in warm place 30 minutes or until doubled in bulk. Meanwhile, preheat oven to 350°F.

5. Bake 40 to 45 minutes or until bread sounds hollow when tapped. Remove from pans; cool on wire racks.

Makes 2 loaves (24 slices)

Savory Summertime Oat Bread

Glazed Cocoa Batter Bread

2¾ cups all-purpose flour, divided
1 tablespoon plus 2 cups granulated sugar, divided
1 package active dry yeast
¾ cup milk
¼ cup water
¾ cup (1½ sticks) butter or margarine, softened
⅔ cup HERSHEY'S Cocoa
½ cup hot water
3 eggs, slightly beaten
1 teaspoon vanilla extract
1 teaspoon baking soda
¼ teaspoon salt
1 cup chopped pecans or walnuts
Powdered Sugar Frosting (recipe follows)
Chopped pecans or walnuts

1. Grease 10-inch tube pan.

2. Combine ¾ cup flour, 1 tablespoon sugar and yeast in large bowl. Heat milk and ¼ cup water in saucepan until lukewarm. Add to flour mixture; beat on low speed of mixer 2 minutes, scraping sides and bottom of bowl often. Add ¾ cup flour or enough flour to make soft dough; beat on medium speed 2 minutes. Cover; let rise in warm place (85°F), free from draft until mixture is light and spongy, about 45 minutes.

3. Meanwhile, beat butter with remaining 2 cups sugar; set aside. Stir together cocoa and hot water until smooth; let cool. Add butter and cocoa mixtures to yeast mixture. Beat in eggs, vanilla, remaining 1¼ cups flour, baking soda, salt and nuts. Pour into prepared pan. Let rise, uncovered, in warm place free from draft until doubled, about 2 hours. Heat oven to 350°F.

4. Bake 45 minutes or until bread sounds hollow when tapped. Cool on wire rack 10 minutes; remove from pan. Cool completely. Drizzle with Powdered Sugar Frosting; sprinkle additional nuts over top. Let stand 2 to 3 hours before slicing.

Makes 12 to 16 servings

Powdered Sugar Frosting

1 cup sifted powdered sugar
1 tablespoon milk
¼ teaspoon vanilla extract

Combine all ingredients in small bowl. Add additional milk, 1 teaspoon at a time, until frosting is smooth and of drizzling consistency.

Oven-Tested Tips

A batter bread is a yeast bread that is made without kneading. Instead, the dough is beaten vigorously, usually with an electric mixer. The first rise takes place in the mixing bowl, the second rise in the baking pan. Batter breads tend to have a coarser, more open texture than kneaded loaves.

Sage Buns

1½ cups milk
2 tablespoons shortening
3 to 4 cups all-purpose flour, divided
2 tablespoons sugar
1 package active dry yeast
2 teaspoons rubbed sage
1 teaspoon salt
1 tablespoon olive oil (optional)

1. Heat milk and shortening in small saucepan over medium heat, stirring constantly, until shortening is melted and temperature reaches 120° to 130°F. Remove from heat. Grease 13×9-inch pan; set aside.

2. Combine 2 cups flour, sugar, yeast, sage and salt in large bowl. Add milk mixture; beat vigorously 2 minutes. Add remaining flour, ¼ cup at a time, until dough begins to pull away from sides of bowl.

3. Turn out dough onto floured work surface. Knead 10 minutes or until dough is smooth and elastic, adding flour if necessary to prevent sticking.

4. Shape dough into ball. Place in large lightly oiled bowl; turn dough over once to oil surface. Cover with towel; let rise in warm place 1 hour or until doubled in bulk.

5. Turn out dough onto lightly oiled surface. Divide into 24 equal pieces. Form each piece into ball. Place evenly spaced in prepared pan. Cover with towel; let rise 45 minutes.

6. Preheat oven to 375°F. Bake 15 to 20 minutes or until golden brown. Immediately remove rolls from pan and cool on wire rack. Brush tops of rolls with olive oil for soft shiny tops, if desired.

Makes 24 rolls

Poppy Seed Breadsticks

1 cup hot milk (about 120°F)
¼ CRISCO® Stick or ¼ cup CRISCO® all-vegetable shortening
1 tablespoon sugar
1 teaspoon salt
1 package active dry yeast
3 to 3½ cups all-purpose flour, divided
1 egg
2 tablespoons water
Poppy seeds

1. Combine milk, ¼ cup shortening, sugar and salt. Cool slightly.

2. Combine yeast and 2½ cups flour in large bowl. Stir in milk mixture until well blended. Beat in enough remaining flour to make a stiff dough.

3. Turn dough onto lightly floured surface. Knead for 5 minutes or until smooth and elastic. Let rest for 5 minutes.

4. Cut dough into 72 equal pieces with sharp knife. Roll out each piece between palms of hands or on flat surface to make a 6-inch strip. Place on greased cookie sheets.

5. Combine egg and water. Brush breadsticks with egg mixture and sprinkle with poppy seeds. Cover; let rest for 20 minutes.

6. Heat oven to 300°F.

7. Bake at 300°F for 45 to 50 minutes or until golden brown. *Do not overbake.* Cool on racks.

Makes 72 breadsticks

Yeasty Cinnamon Loaves

1 package DUNCAN HINES®
    Bakery-Style Cinnamon Swirl
    Muffin Mix, divided
5 cups all-purpose flour
2 packages (¼ ounce each) quick-
    rise yeast
2 eggs, lightly beaten
¼ cup plus 2 tablespoons butter or
    margarine, melted, divided
2½ cups hot water (120° to 130°F),
    divided

1. Grease two 9×5×3-inch loaf pans.

2. Combine muffin mix, contents of crumb topping from Mix, flour and yeast in large bowl; set aside.

3. Combine contents of swirl packet from Mix, eggs, ¼ cup melted butter and ½ cup hot water in medium bowl. Stir well. Add remaining 2 cups hot water and stir until thoroughly blended. Add liquid ingredients to flour mixture; stir until thoroughly blended. Invert onto well-floured surface; let rest for 10 minutes. Knead for 10 minutes or until smooth, adding flour as necessary. Divide dough in half. Divide each half into 3 sections. Roll each section into 10-inch rope. Braid 3 ropes. Fold ends under. Place in greased pan. Repeat with remaining dough. Let rise 1 hour or until doubled in size.

4. Preheat oven to 375°F.

5. Bake at 375°F for 30 to 35 minutes or until bread is deep golden brown and sounds hollow when tapped. Brush with remaining 2 tablespoons melted butter. Cool in pans 5 minutes. Remove bread from pans to cooling racks. Cool completely.

Makes 2 loaves

Note: You may also braid loaves and bake free-form on greased baking sheets for 26 to 30 minutes.

Cinnamon Twists

Rolls

1 package DUNCAN HINES®
    Bakery-Style Cinnamon Swirl
    Muffin Mix, divided
2 cups all-purpose flour
1 package (¼ ounce) quick-rise
    yeast
1 egg, lightly beaten
1 cup hot water (120° to 130°F)
2 tablespoons butter or margarine,
    melted
1 egg white, lightly beaten
1 teaspoon water

Topping
1½ cups confectioners' sugar
2½ tablespoons milk

1. Grease 2 large baking sheets.

2. For rolls, combine muffin mix, flour and yeast in large bowl; set aside.

3. Combine contents of swirl packet from Mix, egg, hot water and melted butter in medium bowl. Stir until thoroughly blended. Pour into flour mixture; stir until thoroughly blended. Invert onto well-floured surface; let rest for 10 minutes. Knead for 10 minutes or until smooth, adding additional flour as necessary. Divide dough in half. Cut and shape 24 small ropes from each half. Braid 3 ropes to form small twist and place on greased baking sheet. Combine egg white and 1 teaspoon water in small bowl. Brush each twist with egg white mixture and sprinkle with contents of topping packet from Mix. Allow twists to rise 1 hour or until doubled in size.

4. Preheat oven to 375°F.

5. Bake at 375°F for 17 to 20 minutes or until deep golden brown. Remove to cooling racks.

6. For topping, combine confectioners' sugar and milk in small bowl. Stir until smooth. Drizzle over warm rolls. Serve warm or cool completely. *Makes 16 rolls*

Tip: For best results, let rolls rise in a warm, draft-free area. A slightly warm oven (130° to 140°F) is ideal.

From top to bottom: Yeasty Cinnamon Loaves and Cinnamon Twists

Anadama Bread

7¾ to 8¼ cups all-purpose flour, divided

2 packages (¼ ounce each) active dry yeast

1½ teaspoons salt

2¾ cups water

¾ cup molasses

¼ cup butter or margarine

1¼ cups yellow cornmeal

1. Combine 4 cups flour, yeast and salt in large bowl. Combine water, molasses and butter in 2-quart saucepan. Heat over low heat until mixture is 120° to 130°F. (Butter does not need to completely melt.)

2. Gradually beat water mixture into flour mixture with electric mixer at low speed. Increase speed to medium; beat 2 minutes. Beat in cornmeal and 2 cups flour at low speed. Increase speed to medium; beat 2 minutes.

3. Stir in enough additional flour, about 1¾ cups to make soft dough. Turn out dough onto floured surface. Knead dough 8 to 10 minutes or until smooth and elastic, adding remaining ½ cup flour to prevent sticking, if necessary.

4. Shape dough into a ball; place in large greased bowl. Turn dough over so that top is greased. Cover with towel; let rise in warm place about 1 hour or until doubled in bulk.

5. Punch down dough. Knead dough on well-floured surface 1 minute. Cut dough into halves. Cover with towel; let rest 10 minutes.

6. Grease 2 (1½-quart) soufflé or casserole dishes or 2 (9×5-inch) loaf pans. For soufflé dishes, shape each half of dough into a ball; place in prepared pans. For loaf pans, roll out one half of dough into 12×8-inch rectangle with well-floured rolling pin. Starting with one 8-inch side, roll up dough jelly-roll style. Pinch seam and ends to seal. Place loaf, seam side down, in prepared pan, tucking ends under. Repeat with remaining dough. Cover and let rise in warm place about 40 minutes or until doubled in bulk.

7. Preheat oven to 375°F. Bake 35 to 40 minutes or until loaves are browned and sound hollow when tapped. Immediately remove from soufflé dishes; cool on wire racks.

Makes 2 loaves

Golden Cheese Bread

1 package active dry yeast

¼ cup warm water (110° to 115°F)

1 cup cottage cheese, room temperature

1 egg

1 tablespoon sugar

1½ teaspoons salt

2¼ cups all-purpose flour

1 tablespoon butter, softened

Dissolve yeast in warm water. Beat together yeast mixture, cheese, egg, sugar and salt. Add flour gradually, stirring well after each addition. Cover dough and let rise in warm place until doubled in size, about 1 hour. Stir down dough; place in buttered 1½-quart casserole dish. Cover and let rise until almost doubled. Bake in preheated 350°F oven 40 to 50 minutes, until golden brown. Remove from pan and brush crust with butter.

Makes 1 loaf

Favorite recipe from **Wisconsin Milk Marketing Board**

Anadama Bread

Tomato-Peppercorn-Cheese Bread

1 cup boiling water

1 cup FIBER ONE® cereal

½ cup sun-dried tomatoes (not oil-packed), diced

2 packages regular or quick active dry yeast

1 tablespoon sugar

¼ cup warm water (105° to 115°F)

2 tablespoons vegetable oil

1 teaspoon salt

1 tablespoon black peppercorns, ground

1 cup (4 ounces) shredded Cheddar cheese

2¼ to 2½ cups GOLD MEDAL® all-purpose flour

1. Pour boiling water over cereal and tomatoes; let stand until mixture is lukewarm.

2. Dissolve yeast and sugar in warm water in large bowl. Stir in cereal mixture, oil, salt, ground peppercorns, cheese and enough of the flour to make a soft dough. Place dough on lightly floured surface. Knead about 5 minutes or until dough is smooth and springy. Place dough in large bowl greased with shortening, turning dough to grease all sides. Cover bowl tightly with plastic wrap and let rise in warm place 1 to 1½ hours or until doubled.

3. Grease large cookie sheet. Gently push fist into dough to deflate. Shape dough into 10-inch loaf. Place on cookie sheet. Cover and let rise in warm place 30 to 40 minutes or until almost doubled.

4. Heat oven to 350°F. Make ¼-inch-deep slits in top of loaf with sharp knife. Bake about 35 minutes or until loaf sounds hollow when tapped on bottom. Remove from cookie sheet to wire rack.

Makes 10 servings

Prep Time: 15 minutes
Knead Time: 5 minutes
Rise Time: 2 hours
Shape Time: 5 minutes
Bake Time: 35 minutes

Honey Wheat Brown-and-Serve Rolls

2 packages active dry yeast

1 teaspoon sugar

¾ cup warm water (105° to 115°F)

2 cups whole wheat flour

2 cups all-purpose flour

¼ cup vegetable shortening

¼ cup honey

1 teaspoon salt

1 egg

Additional ¼ to 1 cup all-purpose flour

1. Sprinkle yeast and sugar over warm water in small bowl; stir until yeast is dissolved. Let stand 5 minutes until mixture is bubbly.

2. Combine whole wheat flour and 2 cups all-purpose flour in medium bowl. Measure 1½ cups wheat flour mixture into large bowl. Add yeast mixture, shortening, honey, salt and egg. Beat with electric mixer at low speed until smooth. Increase mixer speed to medium; beat 2 minutes. Reduce speed to low; beat in 1 cup wheat flour mixture. Increase mixer speed to medium; beat 2 minutes. Stir in remaining wheat flour mixture and enough additional all-purpose flour, beginning with ¼ cup, to make a soft dough.

3. Turn dough out onto lightly floured surface. Knead 8 to 10 minutes or until smooth and elastic, adding more flour to prevent sticking, if necessary. Shape dough into a ball; place in large greased bowl. Turn once to grease surface. Cover with clean kitchen towel. Let rise in warm place (80° to 85°F) about 1½ hours or until doubled in bulk. Punch down dough. Turn dough onto lightly floured surface. Knead dough briefly; cover and let rest 15 minutes. Meanwhile, grease 24 muffin cups.

4. Divide dough into 24 pieces. Cut 1 piece into thirds. Roll each third into a ball. Place 3 balls in each muffin cup. Repeat with remaining dough. Cover and let rise in warm place about 30 minutes until doubled in bulk.

5. Preheat oven to 275°F.* Bake 20 to 25 minutes or until rolls are set but not brown. Immediately remove rolls from muffin cups and cool completely on wire racks. Store in resealable plastic food storage bags in refrigerator or freezer.

6. To bake rolls, thaw rolls if frozen. Preheat oven to 400°F. Grease large jelly-roll pan. Place rolls on jelly-roll pan. Bake 8 to 10 minutes or until golden brown.

Makes 24 rolls

*To bake and serve rolls immediately, preheat oven to 375°F. Bake 15 to 20 minutes or until golden brown. Immediately remove from pan. Serve warm.

Tomato-Peppercorn-Cheese Bread

Onion Buckwheat Bread

1 pound diced white onions

3 tablespoons olive oil

4½ teaspoons yeast

1½ cups water, at 90°F

½ cup milk

6½ cups unbleached bread flour

½ cup buckwheat flour

5 teaspoons sea salt

1 tablespoon finely chopped fresh rosemary

¾ cup (3 ounces) shredded Gouda or Cheddar cheese

Unbleached bread flour as needed for kneading

4 tablespoons poppy seeds or nigella seeds (onion seeds)

1. Sauté onions in olive oil in large skillet over medium-high heat until just browned, about 5 minutes. Set aside to cool.

2. Combine yeast with water in large bowl; let sit 10 minutes until bubbly.

3. Add milk to yeast mixture and stir to combine.

4. Gradually add bread flour, buckwheat flour, salt, rosemary and onions to yeast mixture.

5. When mixture is well combined, add cheese and blend. The dough will be slightly sticky.

6. Knead dough about 10 minutes on lightly floured surface, until smooth and elastic. Add additional bread flour as needed if dough is too soft.

7. Lightly oil clean bowl. Place dough in bowl; cover and let rise until doubled in bulk, 1½ to 2 hours.

8. Gently punch down dough and place on lightly floured surface. Cut dough in half and shape into two round loaves. Spritz top of each loaf with water, and press on poppy seeds or nigella seeds. Place on lightly floured baking sheet; cover and let rise until doubled in bulk, 45 minutes to 1 hour.

9. Preheat oven to 450°F. Slash tops of loaves with razor blade and place in oven. Bake 10 minutes. Add steam by placing two ice cubes in pan on bottom of oven. *Reduce heat to 400°F and bake an additional 35 to 40 minutes. Cool loaves completely on rack.*
Makes 2 (10-inch) round loaves

Favorite recipe from **National Onion Association**

Egg Twist

6 to 6½ cups all-purpose flour, divided

2 packages RED STAR® Active Dry Yeast or QUICK•RISE™ Yeast

3 tablespoons sugar

1 tablespoon salt

1 cup milk

½ cup water

¼ cup butter

4 eggs, lightly beaten (reserve 1 tablespoon)

1 tablespoon water

Sesame seeds

In large mixer bowl, combine 3 cups flour, yeast, sugar and salt; mix well. Heat milk, ½ cup water and butter until very warm (120° to 130°F); butter does not need to melt. Add to flour mixture. Add eggs. Blend at low speed until moistened; beat 3 minutes at medium speed. By hand, gradually stir in enough remaining flour to make a firm dough. Knead on floured surface until smooth and elastic, 5 to 8 minutes. Place in greased bowl, turning to grease top. Cover; let rise in warm place about 1 hour (40 minutes for Quick•Rise™ Yeast).

Punch down dough. On lightly floured surface, roll dough to 12-inch square. Cut into four 3-inch-wide strips. Twist 2 strips together; repeat with remaining strips. Place in greased 9×5-inch bread pans. Cover; let rise in warm place about 40 minutes (30 minutes for Quick•Rise™ Yeast). Preheat oven to 375°F. Combine reserved egg and 1 tablespoon water. Brush on loaves. Sprinkle with sesame seeds. Bake for 35 to 40 minutes until golden brown. Remove from pans; cool.   *Makes 2 loaves*

Onion Buckwheat Bread

Cajun Hot Tomato Bread

1 cup Bloody Mary mix
1 cup water
1 package active dry yeast
⅓ cup honey
¼ cup vegetable oil
¼ cup chopped green onion tops
¼ cup chopped parsley
1 clove garlic, pressed
1 teaspoon salt
5 to 6 cups all-purpose flour, divided

Combine Bloody Mary mix and water in small saucepan. Cook over low heat until mixture reaches 105° to 115°F; pour into large warm bowl. Add yeast; stir until dissolved. Add honey, oil, onion tops, parsley, garlic and salt; mix well. Add 1 cup flour and stir until smooth. Stir in remaining flour until firm dough is formed. Knead dough on lightly floured board about 5 minutes or until smooth and elastic. Shape dough into a ball. Place in greased large bowl; turn dough to grease all sides. Cover bowl and set in warm place to rise about 1 hour or until doubled in bulk.

Punch dough down and divide into two equal pieces. Roll each piece on lightly floured surface into rectangle. Roll up each piece tightly from short side, jelly-roll style. Pinch seam to seal; place in greased 9×5×3-inch loaf pan. Cover and set in warm place to rise about 1 hour or until doubled in bulk.

Bake in preheated 400°F oven about 30 minutes or until loaves sound hollow when tapped and crust is brown. Remove from pans and cool on wire racks.

Makes 2 loaves

Favorite recipe from **National Honey Board**

Whole Wheat Herb Bread

⅔ cup water
⅔ cup fat-free (skim) milk
2 teaspoons sugar
2 envelopes active dry yeast
3 egg whites, lightly beaten
3 tablespoons olive oil
1 teaspoon salt
½ teaspoon dried basil leaves
½ teaspoon dried oregano leaves
4 to 4½ cups whole wheat flour, divided

1. Bring water to a boil in small saucepan. Remove from heat; stir in milk and sugar. When mixture is warm (110° to 115°F), add yeast. Mix well; let stand 10 minutes or until bubbly.

2. Combine egg whites, oil, salt, basil and oregano in large bowl until well blended. Add yeast mixture; mix well. Add 4 cups flour, ½ cup at a time, mixing well after each addition, until dough is no longer sticky. Knead about 5 minutes adding enough remaining flour to make a smooth and elastic dough. Form into a ball. Cover and let rise in warm place about 1 hour or until doubled in bulk.

3. Punch dough down. On lightly floured surface, divide dough into 4 pieces and roll each piece into a ball. Spray baking sheet with cooking spray; Place dough balls on prepared baking sheet. Cover and set in warm place to rise 1 hour or until doubled in bulk.

4. Bake in preheated 350°F oven 30 to 35 minutes or until golden brown and loaves sound hollow when tapped.

Makes 4 loaves

Whole Wheat Herb Bread

Rising to the Occasion ◆ 25

Basic White Bread

2 packages active dry yeast

2 tablespoons sugar

2 cups warm water (105° to 115°F)

6 to 6½ cups all-purpose flour, divided

½ cup nonfat dry milk powder

2 tablespoons vegetable shortening

2 teaspoons salt

1. Combine yeast, sugar and water in large bowl. Let stand 5 minutes or until bubbly.

2. Add 3 cups flour, nonfat milk powder, shortening and salt. Beat with electric mixer at low speed until blended. Increase speed to medium; beat 2 minutes. Stir in enough remaining flour, about 3 cups, to make soft dough. Turn out dough onto lightly floured surface. Knead about 10 minutes adding enough remaining flour to make a smooth and elastic dough.

3. Shape dough into a ball; place in large greased bowl. Turn dough over so that top is greased. Cover with towel; let rise in warm place about 1 hour or until doubled in bulk.

4. Punch down dough; knead dough on lightly floured surface 1 minute. Cover with towel; let rest 10 minutes.

5. Grease 2 (8½×4½-inch) loaf pans; set aside. Divide dough in half. Roll out half of dough into 12×8-inch rectangle with lightly floured rolling pin. Starting with 1 short side, roll up dough jelly-roll style. Pinch seam and ends to seal. Place loaf, seam side down, in prepared pan, tucking ends under. Repeat with remaining dough.

6. Cover and let rise in warm place 1 hour or until doubled in bulk.

7. Preheat oven to 375°F. Bake 30 to 35 minutes or until loaves are golden brown and sound hollow when tapped.

Immediately remove from pans; cool completely on wire racks.

Makes 2 loaves

Refrigerator White Bread: Prepare and shape dough as directed in steps 1 through 5. Spray 2 sheets of plastic wrap with nonstick cooking spray. Cover dough with plastic wrap, greased side down. Refrigerate 3 to 24 hours. Dough should rise to top of pans during refrigeration. Remove loaves from refrigerator 20 minutes before baking. Preheat oven to 375°F. Remove plastic wrap. Bake 45 to 50 minutes or until loaves are golden brown and sound hollow when tapped. Immediately remove from pans; cool completely on wire racks.

Freezer White Bread: Prepare and shape dough as directed in steps 1 through 5. Spray 2 sheets of plastic wrap with nonstick cooking spray. Cover dough with plastic wrap, greased side down. Freeze about 5 hours or until firm. Remove loaves from pans. Wrap frozen loaves securely in plastic wrap; place in labeled plastic freezer bags. Freeze up to 1 month. To bake loaves, unwrap and place in greased loaf pans. Cover with towel; let stand in warm place 4 to 5 hours or until loaves are thawed and doubled in bulk. Preheat oven to 375°F. Bake 40 to 45 minutes or until loaves are golden brown and sound hollow when tapped. Immediately remove from pans; cool completely on wire racks.

French Bread

 2 packages active dry yeast
 1 tablespoon sugar
 2½ cups warm water, 105° to 115°F,
   divided
 6¾ to 7½ cups bread or all-purpose
   flour, divided
 2 teaspoons salt
 2 tablespoons yellow cornmeal
   Water

1. Combine yeast, sugar and ½ cup water in large bowl. Let stand 5 minutes or until bubbly. Add 2 cups flour, remaining 2 cups warm water and salt. Beat with electric mixer at low speed until blended. Increase speed to medium; beat 2 minutes. Stir in enough additional flour, about 4¾ cups, to make soft dough.

2. Turn out dough onto lightly floured surface. Knead about 10 minutes adding enough remaining flour to make a smooth and elastic dough. Shape dough into a ball; place in large greased bowl. Turn dough over so that top is greased. Cover with towel; let rise in warm place 1 to 1½ hours or until doubled in bulk.

3. Punch down dough. Knead dough in bowl 1 minute. Cover with towel; let rise in warm place about 1 hour or until doubled in bulk. Grease 2 (2-loaf) French bread pans or 2 large baking sheets. Sprinkle with cornmeal; set aside.

4. Punch down dough. Turn out dough onto lightly floured surface; knead several times to remove air bubbles. Cut dough into 4 pieces. Cover with towel; let rest 10 minutes. Roll each piece of dough back and forth, forming loaf about 14 inches long and 2 inches in diameter. Place loaves 4 inches apart on prepared baking sheets. Cut 3 (¼-inch-deep) slashes into each loaf with sharp knife. Brush loaves with water. Cover with towel; let rise in warm place about 35 minutes or until doubled in bulk.

5. Place small baking pan on bottom of oven. Preheat oven to 450°F. Place 2 ice cubes in pan on bottom of oven. Brush loaves with water; bake 10 minutes. Rotate pans top to bottom. Quickly spray loaves with cool water using spray mister. Reduce heat to 400°F; bake 10 to 15 minutes more or until loaves are golden brown. Remove from pans immediately; cool on wire racks. Serve warm. *Makes 4 loaves*

Wild Rice Three Grain Bread

 1 package active dry yeast
 ⅓ cup warm water (105° to 115°F)
 2 cups milk, scalded and cooled to
   105° to 115°F
 ½ cup honey
 2 tablespoons butter, melted
 2 teaspoons salt
 4 to 4½ cups bread flour or
   unbleached all-purpose flour,
   divided
 2 cups whole wheat flour
 ½ cup rye flour
 ½ cup uncooked rolled oats
 1 cup cooked wild rice
 1 egg, beaten with 1 tablespoon
   water
 ½ cup hulled sunflower seeds

In large bowl, dissolve yeast in water. Add milk, honey, butter and salt. Stir in 2 cups bread flour, whole wheat flour, rye flour and oats to make a soft dough. Add wild rice; cover and let rest 15 minutes. Stir in enough additional bread flour to make a stiff dough. Turn dough out onto board and knead 10 minutes. Add more flour as necessary to keep dough from sticking. Turn dough into lightly greased bowl; turn dough over to coat. Cover and let rise until doubled, about 2 hours. Punch down dough. Knead briefly on lightly oiled board. Divide dough into 3 portions; roll into long strands. Braid strands and place on greased baking sheet in wreath shape, or divide dough in half and place each half in greased 9½×5½- inch loaf pan. Let rise until doubled, about 45 minutes. Brush tops with egg mixture; slash loaves if desired. Sprinkle with sunflower seeds. Bake at 375°F 45 minutes or until loaves sound hollow when tapped.

Makes 1 braided wreath or 2 loaves

Favorite recipe from **Minnesota Cultivated Wild Rice Council**

French Bread

Cinnamon-Raisin Bread

1 package active dry yeast

½ cup plus 1 teaspoon sugar, divided

¼ cup warm water (105° to 115°F)

3 to 3½ cups all-purpose flour, divided

1 teaspoon salt

⅔ cup warm milk (105° to 115°F)

3 tablespoons butter or margarine, softened

1 whole egg

1 egg, separated

1 teaspoon vanilla

¾ cup raisins

1 tablespoon ground cinnamon

1 tablespoon butter or margarine, melted

1 tablespoon water

1. Combine yeast, 1 teaspoon sugar and water in small bowl. Let stand 5 minutes or until bubbly.

2. Combine 1½ cups flour, ¼ cup sugar and salt in large bowl. Gradually beat yeast mixture, warm milk and softened butter into flour mixture with electric mixer at low speed. Increase speed to medium.

3. Reduce speed to low. Beat in whole egg, egg yolk and vanilla. Increase speed to medium; beat 2 minutes. With wooden spoon stir in raisins and enough flour, about 1½ cups, to make soft dough.

4. Turn out dough onto lightly floured surface. Knead about 5 minutes adding enough remaining flour to make a smooth and elastic dough. Dough will be soft and slightly sticky. Shape dough into a ball; place in large greased bowl. Turn dough over so that top is greased. Cover with towel; let rise in warm place 1 to 1½ hours or until doubled in bulk.

5. Punch down dough. Knead on lightly floured surface 1 minute. Cover with towel; let rest 10 minutes. Grease 9×5-inch loaf pan; set aside. Combine remaining ¼ cup sugar and cinnamon. Set aside 1 tablespoon mixture in small cup.

6. Roll dough into 20×9-inch rectangle with lightly floured rolling pin. Brush with 1 tablespoon melted butter. Sprinkle cinnamon mixture evenly over butter. Starting with 9-inch side, roll up dough jelly-roll style. Pinch ends and seam to seal. Place loaf, seam side down, in prepared pan, tucking ends under. Cover with clean kitchen towel; let rise in warm place about 1¼ hours or until doubled in bulk. (Dough should rise to top of pan.)

7. Preheat oven to 350°F. Combine reserved egg white and 1 tablespoon water in small bowl. Brush loaf with egg white mixture; sprinkle with reserved 1 tablespoon cinnamon mixture.

8. Bake 40 to 45 minutes or until loaf sounds hollow when tapped. Immediately remove from pan; cool completely on wire rack.
Makes 1 loaf

Farmer-Style Sour Cream Bread

1 cup sour cream, at room
  temperature
3 tablespoons water
2½ to 3 cups all-purpose flour, divided
1 package active dry yeast
2 tablespoons sugar
1½ teaspoons salt
¼ teaspoon baking soda
  Vegetable oil or nonstick cooking
  spray
1 tablespoon poppy or sesame seeds

1. Stir together sour cream and water in small saucepan. Heat over low heat until temperature reaches 120° to 130°F. *Do not boil.* Combine 2 cups flour, yeast, sugar, salt and baking soda in large bowl. Spread sour cream mixture evenly over flour mixture with rubber spatula. Stir until well blended. Turn out dough onto lightly floured surface. Knead about 5 minutes adding enough remaining flour to make a smooth and elastic dough.

2. Grease large baking sheet. Shape dough into ball; place on prepared sheet. Flatten into 8-inch circle. Brush with oil. Sprinkle with poppy seeds. Invert large bowl over dough and let rise in warm place 1 hour or until doubled in bulk.

3. Preheat oven to 350°F. Bake 22 to 27 minutes or until golden brown. Remove immediately from baking sheet. Cool on wire rack. *Makes 8 to 12 servings*

Cinnamon-Raisin Bread

Spicy Cheese Bread

2 packages active dry yeast

1 teaspoon granulated sugar

½ cup warm water (110°F)

8¾ cups flour, divided

3 cups shredded Jarlsberg or Swiss cheese

2 tablespoons chopped fresh rosemary *or* 2 teaspoons dried rosemary

1 tablespoon salt

1 tablespoon TABASCO® brand Pepper Sauce

2 cups milk

4 large eggs, lightly beaten

Combine yeast, sugar and warm water. Let stand 5 minutes until foamy. Meanwhile, combine 8 cups flour, cheese, rosemary, salt, and TABASCO® Sauce in large bowl. Heat milk in small saucepan until warm (120° to 130°F).

Stir milk into flour mixture. Set aside 1 tablespoon beaten egg. Add remaining eggs to flour mixture with foamy yeast mixture; stir until soft dough forms.

Knead dough on lightly floured surface adding enough remaining flour to make a smooth and elastic dough, about 5 minutes. Shape dough into a ball; place in large greased bowl. Cover with towel and let rise in warm place until doubled, about 1½ hours.

Grease two large cookie sheets. Punch down dough and divide in half. Cut each half in three strips and braid. Place braided loaves on cookie sheets. Cover and let rise in warm place until almost doubled, 30 minutes to 1 hour. Preheat oven to 375°F. Brush loaves with reserved egg. Bake 45 minutes or until loaves sound hollow when tapped. Remove to wire racks to cool.   *Makes 2 loaves*

Bran and Honey Rye Breadsticks

1 package (¼ ounce) active dry yeast

1 teaspoon sugar

1½ cups warm water (110°F)

3¾ cups all-purpose flour, divided

1 tablespoon honey

1 tablespoon vegetable oil

½ teaspoon salt

1 cup rye flour

½ cup whole bran cereal

Milk

1. Combine yeast, sugar and water in large bowl. Let stand 5 minutes or until bubbly. Add 1 cup all-purpose flour, honey, oil and salt. Beat with electric mixer at medium speed 3 minutes. Stir in rye flour, bran cereal and 2 cups all-purpose flour or enough to make moderately stiff dough.

2. Turn out dough onto lightly floured surface. Knead about 10 minutes adding enough remaining flour to make a smooth and elastic dough. Place in greased bowl; turn over to grease surface. Cover and let rise in warm place 40 to 45 minutes or until doubled in bulk.

3. Spray 2 baking sheets with nonstick cooking spray. Punch dough down. Divide into 24 equal pieces on lightly floured surface. Roll each piece into an 8-inch rope. Place on prepared baking sheets. Cover with damp cloth; let rise in warm place 30 to 35 minutes or until doubled in bulk.

4. Preheat oven to 375°F. Brush breadsticks with milk. Bake 18 to 20 minutes or until breadsticks are golden brown. Remove from baking sheets. Cool on wire racks.
          Makes 24 breadsticks

Roasted Garlic Breadsticks

1 large head garlic (about 14 to
    16 cloves)
3 tablespoons olive oil, divided
3 tablespoons water, divided
1 tablespoon butter or margarine,
    softened
1 package active dry yeast
1 teaspoon sugar
1 cup warm water (105° to 115°F)
2½ to 3 cups all-purpose flour, divided
1 teaspoon salt
1 egg white
1 tablespoon sesame seeds

1. Preheat oven to 350°F. Remove outer
papery skin from garlic head. Place garlic in
10-ounce ovenproof custard cup. Drizzle
garlic with 1 tablespoon olive oil and
2 tablespoons water. Cover tightly with foil.
Bake 1 hour or until garlic cloves are tender.
Remove foil and let cool.

2. When garlic is cool enough to handle,
break into cloves. Squeeze skin of cloves
until garlic pops out. Finely chop garlic
cloves. Combine chopped garlic and butter
in small bowl. Cover; set aside.

3. Combine yeast, sugar and water in large
bowl. Let stand 5 minutes or until bubbly.
Beat 1½ cups flour, salt and remaining
2 tablespoons olive oil into yeast mixture
with electric mixer at low speed until
blended. Increase speed to medium; beat
2 minutes. Stir in enough additional flour,
about 1 cup, with wooden spoon to make
soft dough.

4. Turn out dough onto lightly floured
surface. Knead about 5 minutes adding
enough remaining flour to make a smooth
and elastic dough. Shape dough into a ball;
place in large greased bowl. Turn dough over
so that top is greased. Cover with clean
kitchen towel; let rise in warm place about
1 hour or until doubled in bulk.

5. Punch down dough; knead on lightly
floured surface 1 minute. Cover with towel;
let rest 10 minutes. Grease 2 large baking
sheets; set aside. Roll dough into 12-inch
square with lightly floured rolling pin.
Spread garlic mixture evenly over dough.
Fold square in half. Roll dough into
14×7-inch rectangle. Cut dough crosswise
into 7×1-inch strips.

6. Holding ends of each strip, twist 3 to
4 times. Place strips 2 inches apart on
prepared baking sheets, pressing both ends
to seal. Cover with clean kitchen towels; let
rise in warm place about 30 minutes or until
doubled in bulk.

7. Preheat oven to 400°F. Combine egg
white and remaining 1 tablespoon water in
small bowl. Brush sticks with egg white
mixture; sprinkle with sesame seeds. Bake
20 to 22 minutes or until golden. Serve
warm.   *Makes 12 breadsticks*

Pumpkin-Nut Bread

4½ to 4¾ cups all-purpose flour,
   divided
⅓ cup firmly packed brown sugar
2 envelopes FLEISCHMANN'S®
   RapidRise™ Yeast
1½ teaspoons salt
½ cup evaporated milk
¼ cup butter or margarine
1 cup canned pumpkin
2 large eggs
⅔ cup finely chopped pecans or
   walnuts, toasted
1½ teaspoons pumpkin pie spice
1 egg white
1 tablespoon water

In large bowl, combine 1½ cups flour, sugar, undissolved yeast and salt. Heat milk and butter until very warm (120° to 130°F); stir into dry ingredients. Beat 2 minutes at medium speed of electric mixer, scraping bowl occasionally. Stir in pumpkin, eggs and 1 cup flour. Beat 2 minutes at high speed. Stir in nuts, pumpkin pie spice and enough remaining flour to make soft dough. Knead on lightly floured surface until smooth and elastic, about 8 to 10 minutes. Cover; let rest 10 minutes.

Divide dough in half; roll each half to 12×7-inch rectangle. Roll up tightly from short end as for jelly roll; pinch seam and ends to seal. Place, seam sides down, in 2 greased 8½×4½-inch loaf pans.

Cover; let rise until doubled in size, about 1 hour. Brush with egg white mixed with water. Bake at 350°F for 25 to 30 minutes or until loaves sound hollow when tapped. Remove from pans and cool on wire rack.

Makes 2 loaves

Pumpkin-Nut Bread

Dinner Rolls

1¼ **cups milk**

½ **cup vegetable shortening**

3¾ **to** 4¼ **cups all-purpose flour, divided**

¼ **cup sugar**

2 **packages active dry yeast**

1 **teaspoon salt**

2 **eggs**

1. Stir milk and shortening in small saucepan over low heat until temperature reaches 120° to 130°F. (Shortening does not need to melt completely.)

2. Combine 1½ cups flour, sugar, yeast and salt in large bowl; set aside. Gradually beat milk mixture into flour mixture with electric mixer at low speed.

3. Beat in eggs and 1 cup flour. Increase speed to medium; beat 2 minutes. Stir in enough flour, about 1¼ cups, with wooden spoon to make soft dough.

4. Turn out dough onto lightly floured surface. Knead about 5 minutes adding enough of remaining flour to make a smooth and elastic dough. Shape dough into ball; place in large, lightly greased bowl. Turn dough over so top is greased. Cover with towel; let rise in warm place 1 hour or until doubled in bulk.

5. Punch down dough. Knead on lightly floured surface 1 minute. Cover with towel; let rest 10 minutes. Grease two 8-inch square baking pans. Cut dough into halves. Cut one half into 12 pieces, keeping remaining half covered with towel. Shape pieces into balls; place in rows in 1 prepared pan. Repeat with remaining dough. Cover pans with towels; let rise in warm place 30 minutes or until doubled in bulk.

6. Preheat oven to 375°F. Bake 15 to 20 minutes or until golden brown. Remove immediately from pans. Cool on wire racks. Serve warm. *Makes 24 rolls*

Dinner Rolls

Marble Swirl Bread

**2¾ to 3¼ cups all-purpose flour,
divided**

¼ cup sugar

1 package active dry yeast

1 teaspoon salt

**1⅓ cups plus 1 tablespoon water,
divided**

¼ cup butter or margarine

1 whole egg

2 tablespoons molasses

**2 teaspoons unsweetened cocoa
powder**

1 teaspoon instant coffee powder

1 to 1¼ cups rye flour

1 egg, separated

1. Combine 1½ cups all-purpose flour, sugar, yeast and salt in large bowl; set aside.

2. Heat 1⅓ cups water and butter in small saucepan until mixture is 120° to 130°F. (Butter does not need to completely melt.) Gradually beat water mixture into flour mixture with electric mixer at low speed. Increase speed to medium; beat 2 minutes.

3. Reduce speed to low; beat in 1 egg and ½ cup all-purpose flour. Increase speed to medium; beat 2 minutes. Reserve half of batter (about 1⅓ cups) in another bowl. Stir enough remaining all-purpose flour into remaining batter to make stiff dough; set aside.

4. To make darker dough, stir molasses, cocoa, coffee powder and enough rye flour into reserved batter to make stiff dough. Cover doughs with clean kitchen towels; let rise in warm place about 1 hour or until doubled in bulk.

5. Punch down doughs. Knead doughs separately on lightly floured surface 1 minute. Cover with towels; let rest

10 minutes. Grease large baking sheet. Roll out lighter dough into 12×9-inch rectangle with lightly floured rolling pin; set aside.

6. Roll out darker dough into 12×8-inch rectangle; place on top of lighter dough. Starting with 12-inch side, roll up doughs jelly-roll style. Pinch seam and ends to seal. Place loaf, seam side down, on prepared baking sheet, tucking ends under. Cover with clean kitchen towel; let rise in warm place about 45 minutes or until doubled in bulk.

7. Preheat oven to 350°F. Add remaining 1 tablespoon water to egg yolk; beat until just combined. Make 3 (½-inch-deep) slashes across top of loaf with sharp knife. Brush with egg yolk mixture.

8. Bake 35 to 40 minutes or until loaf is browned and sounds hollow when tapped. Immediately remove from baking sheet; cool on wire rack. *Makes 1 loaf*

Oven-Tested Tips

There are many warm places to let dough rise. Place it inside a gas oven warmed by a pilot light, or in an electric oven heated to 200°F for 1 minute and then turned off. Your microwave can also be used. Bring 2 cups of water to a boil in the microwave, then turn off the power, set the dough inside and close the door. You can even use a clothes dryer. Run it on the heat cycle for 1 minute, turn it off, place the dough inside and close the door.

Bake Up Your Morning

Nobody needs an alarm clock when they know breakfast includes luscious, home-baked goodies. They'll be at the table quicker than you can say "Chocolate Chunk Cinnamon Coffee Cake." Don't overlook savory recipes, like Ham-Broccoli Quiche and Bacon Cheese Muffins, either. They make elegant brunch fare or a tasty light dinner.

Bacon-Cheese Muffins

½ pound bacon (10 to 12 slices)
   Vegetable oil
1 egg, beaten
¾ cup milk
1¾ cups all-purpose flour
¼ cup sugar
1 tablespoon baking powder
1 cup (4 ounces) shredded Wisconsin Cheddar cheese
½ cup crunchy nutlike cereal nuggets

Preheat oven to 400°F. In large skillet, cook bacon over medium-high heat until crisp. Drain, reserving drippings. If necessary, add oil to drippings to measure ⅓ cup. In small bowl, combine dripping mixture, egg and milk; set aside. Crumble bacon; set aside.

In large bowl, combine flour, sugar and baking powder. Make well in center. Add egg mixture all at once to flour mixture, stirring just until moistened. Batter should be lumpy. Fold in bacon, cheese and cereal. Spoon into greased or paper-lined 2½-inch muffin cups, filling about ¾ full. Bake 15 to 20 minutes or until golden. Remove from pan. Cool on wire rack.

Makes 12 muffins

Favorite recipe from **Wisconsin Milk Marketing Board**

Apple Ring Coffee Cake

3 cups all-purpose flour
1 teaspoon baking soda
1 teaspoon salt
1 teaspoon ground cinnamon
1 cup walnuts, chopped
1½ cups granulated sugar
1 cup vegetable oil
2 eggs
2 teaspoons vanilla
2 medium tart apples, peeled, cored and chopped
Powdered sugar for garnish

1. Preheat oven to 325°F. Grease 10-inch tube pan.

2. Sift flour, baking soda, salt and cinnamon into large bowl. Stir in walnuts; set aside.

3. Combine granulated sugar, oil, eggs and vanilla in medium bowl. Stir in apples. Stir into flour mixture just until moistened.

4. Spoon batter into prepared pan, spreading evenly. Bake 1 hour or until toothpick inserted near center comes out clean. Cool cake in pan on wire rack 10 minutes. Loosen edges with metal spatula, if necessary. Remove from pan; cool completely on rack.

5. Transfer to serving plate. Sprinkle with powdered sugar and serve immediately. Store leftover cake in airtight container.

Makes 12 servings

Cinnamon Chip Filled Crescents

2 cans (8 ounces each) refrigerated quick crescent dinner rolls
2 tablespoons butter or margarine, melted
1⅔ cups (10-ounce package) HERSHEY'S Cinnamon Chips, divided
Cinnamon Chips Drizzle (recipe follows)

1. Heat oven to 375°F. Unroll dough; separate into 16 triangles.

2. Spread melted butter on each triangle. Sprinkle 1 cup cinnamon chips evenly over triangles; gently press chips into dough. Roll from shortest side of triangle to opposite point. Place, point side down, on ungreased cookie sheet; curve into crescent shape.

3. Bake 8 to 10 minutes or until golden brown. Drizzle with Cinnamon Drizzle. Serve warm.   *Makes 16 crescents*

Cinnamon Chips Drizzle: Place remaining ⅔ cup chips and 1½ teaspoons shortening (do not use butter, margarine, spread or oil) in small microwave-safe bowl. Microwave at HIGH (100%) 1 minute; stir until chips are melted.

Oven-Tested Tips

Always follow recipe directions when mixing batter. Many recipes call for ingredients to be mixed only until combined, or just until moistened. In these instances leaving some lumps in the batter is a good thing. Overmixing can produce tough, heavy baked goods.

Apple Ring Coffee Cake

Brunchtime Sour Cream Cupcakes

1 cup (2 sticks) butter, softened
2 cups plus 4 teaspoons sugar, divided
2 eggs
1 cup sour cream
1 teaspoon almond extract
2 cups all-purpose flour
1 teaspoon salt
½ teaspoon baking soda
1 cup chopped walnuts
1½ teaspoons ground cinnamon
⅛ teaspoon nutmeg

1. Preheat oven to 350°F. Insert paper liners into 18 muffin cups.

2. Beat together butter and 2 cups sugar in large bowl. Add eggs, one at a time, beating well after each addition. Blend in sour cream and almond extract.

3. Combine flour, salt and baking soda in medium bowl. Add to butter mixture and mix well.

4. Stir together remaining 4 teaspoons sugar, walnuts, cinnamon and nutmeg in small bowl.

5. Fill prepared muffin cups ⅓ full with batter; sprinkle with ⅔ of the walnut mixture.

6. Cover with remaining batter. Sprinkle with remaining walnut mixture.

7. Bake 25 to 30 minutes or until wooden toothpick inserted into centers comes out clean. Remove cupcakes from pan; cool on wire rack.   *Makes 1½ dozen cupcakes*

Blueberry Coffeecake

2 cups blueberries, fresh or frozen and partially thawed
1 tablespoon all-purpose flour
½ cup honey
2 tablespoons fresh lemon juice

Cake
1½ cups all-purpose flour
2 teaspoons baking powder
½ teaspoon baking soda
½ teaspoon salt
½ cup honey
2 eggs
¼ cup milk
2 tablespoons fresh lemon juice
1 teaspoon freshly grated lemon peel
1 teaspoon vanilla extract
6 tablespoons butter, melted

Place blueberries in bottom of greased 9-inch round cake pan; distribute evenly. Sprinkle with flour; drizzle with honey and lemon juice. Set aside.

In small bowl, combine flour, baking powder, baking soda and salt; set aside. In medium bowl, combine honey, eggs, milk, lemon juice, lemon peel and vanilla; beat with fork until well mixed. Add flour mixture; mix well. Stir in melted butter; mix well. Pour batter over blueberries in pan; spread to cover evenly. Bake at 350°F for 30 to 35 minutes, or until toothpick inserted in center of cake comes out clean. Cool in pan on wire rack 10 minutes. Invert cake onto large plate; cool.   *Makes 8 servings*

Favorite recipe from **National Honey Board**

Baked Doughnuts with Cinnamon Glaze

5 to 5½ cups all-purpose flour, divided

⅔ cup granulated sugar

2 packages active dry yeast

1 teaspoon salt

1 teaspoon grated lemon peel

½ teaspoon ground nutmeg

2 cups milk, divided

½ cup butter

2 eggs

2 cups sifted powdered sugar

½ teaspoon ground cinnamon

1. Combine 2 cups flour, granulated sugar, yeast, salt, lemon peel and nutmeg in large bowl. Combine 1¾ cups milk and butter in 1-quart saucepan. Heat over low heat until mixture is 120° to 130°F. (Butter does not need to completely melt.) Gradually beat milk mixture into flour mixture with electric mixer at low speed. Increase speed to medium; beat 2 minutes.

2. Beat in eggs and 1 cup flour at low speed. Increase speed to medium; beat 2 minutes.

Stir in enough additional flour, about 2 cups, to make soft dough. Cover with greased plastic wrap; refrigerate at least 2 hours or up to 24 hours.

3. Punch down dough. Turn out dough onto lightly floured surface. Knead dough about 1 minute or until dough is no longer sticky, adding remaining ½ cup flour to prevent sticking if necessary.

4. Grease 2 large baking sheets. Roll out dough to ½-inch thickness with lightly floured rolling pin. Cut dough with floured 2¾-inch doughnut cutter. Reroll scraps, reserving doughnut holes. Place doughnuts and holes 2 inches apart on prepared baking sheets. Cover with towels; let rise in warm place about 30 minutes or until doubled in bulk.

5. To prepare glaze, combine powdered sugar and cinnamon in small bowl. Stir in enough remaining milk, about ¼ cup, to make glaze of desired consistency. Cover; set aside.

6. Preheat oven to 400°F. Place pieces of waxed paper under wire racks to keep counter clean. Bake doughnuts and holes 8 to 10 minutes or until golden brown. Remove from pan; cool on wire racks 5 minutes. Dip warm doughnuts into glaze. Place right side up on racks, allowing glaze to drip down sides. Serve warm.

Makes 2 dozen doughnuts and holes

Baked Doughnuts with Cinnamon Glaze

Cherry and Almond Coffee Cake

1 sheet (½ of 17¼-ounce package) frozen puff pastry

1 package (3 ounces) cream cheese, softened

⅓ cup plus 2 tablespoons powdered sugar, divided

1 egg, separated

¼ teaspoon almond extract

1 tablespoon water

½ cup dried cherries or cranberries, coarsely chopped

½ cup sliced almonds, divided

1. Thaw pastry sheet according to package directions.

2. Preheat oven to 375°F. Spray baking sheet with nonstick cooking spray.

3. Combine cream cheese, ⅓ cup powdered sugar, egg yolk and almond extract in large bowl. Beat with electric mixer at medium speed until smooth; set aside. In separate small bowl, mix egg white and water; set aside.

4. On lightly floured board, roll out pastry into 14×10-inch rectangle. Spread cream cheese mixture over dough leaving 1-inch border. Sprinkle evenly with cherries. Reserve 2 tablespoons almonds; sprinkle remaining almonds over cherries.

5. Starting with long side, loosely roll up dough jelly-roll style. Place roll on baking sheet, seam side down. Form into circle, pinching ends together. Using scissors, cut at 1-inch intervals from outside of ring toward (but not through) center. Twist each section half a turn, allowing filling to show.

6. Brush top of ring with egg white mixture. Sprinkle with reserved almonds. Bake 25 to 30 minutes or until light brown. Using large spatula, carefully remove ring to wire rack. Cool 15 minutes; sprinkle with remaining 2 tablespoons powdered sugar.

Makes 1 (12-inch) coffee cake

Coffee Walnut Chocolate Chip Muffins

½ cup (1 stick) butter or margarine, softened

½ cup granulated sugar

½ cup packed light brown sugar

2 to 3 tablespoons powdered instant coffee

2 teaspoons vanilla extract

1¾ cups all-purpose flour

1 tablespoon baking powder

½ teaspoon salt

2 eggs

⅔ cup milk

1½ cups coarsely chopped walnuts

¾ cup HERSHEY'S Semi-Sweet Chocolate Chips

1. Heat oven to 350°F. Line twelve muffin cups (2½ inches in diameter) with paper bake cups.

2. Beat butter, granulated sugar, brown sugar, coffee and vanilla in large bowl until creamy. Stir together flour, baking powder and salt. Beat together eggs and milk; add alternately with flour mixture to butter mixture, stirring just to combine. Stir in walnuts and chocolate chips. Fill muffin cups ½ full with batter.

3. Bake 20 to 25 minutes. Cool 5 minutes; remove from pans to wire rack. Cool completely.

Makes 12 muffins

Cherry and Almond Coffee Cake

Sour Cream Coffee Cake with Brandy-Soaked Cherries

Streusel Topping (recipe follows)
3¼ cups all-purpose flour, divided
1 cup dried sweet or sour cherries
½ cup brandy
1½ cups sugar
¾ cup butter
3 eggs
1 container (16 ounces) sour cream
1 tablespoon vanilla
2 teaspoons baking powder
2 teaspoons baking soda
¼ teaspoon salt

1. Prepare Streusel Topping; set aside.

2. Preheat oven to 350°F. Grease 10-inch tube pan with removable bottom. Sprinkle ¼ cup flour into pan, rotating pan to evenly coat bottom and sides of pan. Discard any remaining flour.

3. Bring cherries and brandy to a boil in small saucepan. Cover; remove from heat. Let stand 20 to 30 minutes or until cherries are tender. Drain; discard any remaining brandy.

4. Beat sugar and butter in large bowl with electric mixer at medium speed until light and fluffy. Add eggs, 1 at a time, beating until thoroughly blended. Beat in sour cream and vanilla.

5. Add remaining 3 cups flour, baking powder, baking soda and salt. Beat with electric mixer at low speed until just blended. Stir in cherries.

6. Spoon ½ of batter into prepared tube pan. Sprinkle with ½ of Streusel Topping. Repeat with remaining batter and Streusel Topping. Bake 1 hour or until toothpick inserted into center comes out clean.

7. Cool in pan on wire rack 10 minutes. Remove from pan. Serve warm or at room temperature. Garnish as desired.

Makes 16 servings

Streusel Topping

1 cup chopped walnuts or pecans
½ cup packed brown sugar
1 teaspoon ground cinnamon
½ teaspoon ground nutmeg
2 tablespoons butter or margarine melted

Combine nuts, brown sugar, cinnamon and nutmeg in small bowl. Drizzle mixture with butter and toss with fork until evenly mixed.

Oven-Tested Tips

To grease and flour cake pans, use a paper towel, waxed paper or your fingers to apply a thin, even layer of shortening. Sprinkle flour into the greased pan; rotate and tilt the pan until sides and bottom have a fine coating. Hold the pan upside down over the sink and tap it gently until any excess flour falls away.

Ham-Broccoli Quiche

1 cup sliced fresh mushrooms

1 clove garlic, minced

2 teaspoons butter or margarine

½ cup shredded Swiss cheese

1 (9-inch) pastry shell

1½ cups (8 ounces) chopped CURE 81® ham

1 cup cooked, chopped broccoli

3 eggs

1 cup milk

2 teaspoons all-purpose flour

¼ teaspoon white pepper

Dash ground nutmeg

2 tablespoons grated Romano or Parmesan cheese

Heat oven to 350°F. In skillet over medium-high heat, sauté mushrooms and garlic in butter until tender. Sprinkle Swiss cheese in pastry shell. Top with mushroom mixture, ham and broccoli. In bowl, beat together eggs, milk, flour, white pepper and nutmeg; pour into pastry shell. Sprinkle with Romano or Parmesan cheese. Bake 35 to 40 minutes or until knife inserted near center comes out clean. Let stand 10 minutes before serving.

Makes 6 servings

Ham-Broccoli Quiche

Chocolate Chunk Cinnamon Coffee Cake

1 package (12 ounces) BAKER'S®
Semi-Sweet Chocolate Chunks

¾ cup chopped nuts

2 cups sugar, divided

1½ teaspoons cinnamon

2⅔ cups flour

1½ teaspoons baking soda

¾ teaspoon CALUMET® Baking
Powder

½ teaspoon salt

¾ cup (1½ sticks) butter or
margarine, softened

1 teaspoon vanilla

3 eggs

1½ cups BREAKSTONE'S® or
KNUDSEN® Sour Cream

HEAT oven to 350°F. Grease 13×9-inch
baking pan.

MIX chocolate, nuts, ⅔ cup of the sugar
and cinnamon; set aside. Mix flour, baking
soda, baking powder and salt; set aside.

BEAT butter, remaining 1⅓ cups sugar and
vanilla in large bowl with electric mixer on
medium speed until light and fluffy. Add
eggs, 1 at a time, beating well after each
addition. Add flour mixture alternately with
sour cream, beating after each addition until
smooth. Spoon ½ of the batter into
prepared pan. Top with ½ of the chocolate-
nut mixture. Repeat layers.

BAKE 40 to 45 minutes or until toothpick
inserted in center comes out clean. Cool in
pan on wire rack. *Makes 16 servings*

Prep Time: 30 minutes
Bake Time: 45 minutes

Breakfast Cookies

1 Butter Flavor CRISCO® Stick or
1 cup Butter Flavor CRISCO®
all-vegetable shortening

1 cup JIF® Crunchy Peanut Butter

¾ cup granulated sugar

¾ cup firmly packed brown sugar

2 eggs, beaten

1½ cups all-purpose flour

1 teaspoon baking powder

1 teaspoon baking soda

1 teaspoon ground cinnamon

1¾ cups quick oats, uncooked

1¼ cups raisins

1 medium Granny Smith apple,
finely grated, including juice

⅓ cup finely grated carrot

¼ cup flake coconut (optional)

1. Heat oven to 350°F. Place sheets of foil
on countertop for cooling cookies.

2. Combine 1 cup shortening, peanut butter
and sugars in large bowl. Beat at medium
speed with electric mixer until blended.
Beat in eggs.

3. Combine flour, baking powder, baking
soda and cinnamon. Add gradually to
creamed mixture at low speed. Beat until
blended. Stir in oats, raisins, apple, carrot
and coconut, if desired. Drop by measuring
tablespoonfuls onto ungreased baking sheet.

4. Bake for 9 to 11 minutes or until just
brown around edges. *Do not overbake.* Cool
2 minutes on baking sheet. Remove cookies
to foil to cool completely.
Makes 5 to 6 dozen cookies

Hint: Freeze cookies between sheets of waxed
paper in sealed container. Use as needed for
breakfast on-the-run or as a nutritious snack.

Chocolate Chunk Cinnamon Coffee Cake

Spinach Quiche

1 medium leek

¼ cup butter or margarine

2 cups finely chopped cooked chicken

½ package (10 ounces) frozen chopped spinach or broccoli, cooked and drained

1 unbaked ready-to-use pie crust (10 inches in diameter)

1½ cups (6 ounces) shredded Swiss cheese

1 tablespoon all-purpose flour

4 eggs

1½ cups half-and-half or evaporated milk

2 tablespoons brandy

½ teaspoon salt

¼ teaspoon black pepper

¼ teaspoon ground nutmeg

1. Preheat oven to 375°F. Cut leek in half lengthwise; wash and trim, leaving about 2 inches of green tops intact. Cut leek halves crosswise into thin slices. Place in small saucepan; add enough water to cover. Bring to a boil over high heat; reduce heat and simmer 5 minutes. Drain; reserve leek.

2. Melt butter in large skillet over medium heat. Add chicken; cook until chicken is golden, about 5 minutes. Add spinach and leek to chicken mixture; cook 1 to 2 minutes longer. Remove from heat.

3. Spoon chicken mixture into pie crust. Sprinkle cheese and flour over chicken mixture. Combine eggs, half-and-half, brandy, salt, pepper and nutmeg in medium bowl. Pour egg mixture over cheese.

4. Bake 35 to 40 minutes or until knife inserted into center comes out clean. Let stand 5 minutes. Serve hot or cold.

Makes 6 servings

Orange Brunch Muffins

3 cups all-purpose baking mix

¾ cup all-purpose flour

⅔ cup granulated sugar

2 large eggs, lightly beaten

½ cup plain yogurt

½ cup orange juice

1 tablespoon grated orange peel

2 cups (12-ounce package) NESTLÉ® TOLL HOUSE® Premier White Morsels, *divided*

½ cup chopped macadamia nuts or walnuts

PREHEAT oven to 375°F. Grease or paper-line 18 muffin cups.

COMBINE baking mix, flour and sugar in large bowl. Add eggs, yogurt, juice and orange peel; stir just until blended. Stir in 1⅓ cups morsels. Spoon into prepared muffin cups, filling ¾ full. Sprinkle with nuts.

BAKE for 18 to 22 minutes or until wooden pick inserted into centers comes out clean. Cool in pans for 10 minutes; remove to wire racks to cool slightly.

MICROWAVE *remaining* morsels in small, *heavy-duty* plastic bag on MEDIUM-HIGH (70%) power for 1 minute; knead bag. Microwave at additional 10- to 20-second intervals, kneading until smooth. Cut tiny corner from bag; squeeze to drizzle over muffins. Serve warm. *Makes 18 muffins*

Orange Streusel Coffeecake

Cocoa Streusel (recipe follows)

¾ cup (1½ sticks) butter or margarine, softened

1 cup sugar

3 eggs

1 teaspoon vanilla extract

½ cup dairy sour cream

3 cups all-purpose flour

2 teaspoons baking powder

1 teaspoon baking soda

1 cup orange juice

2 teaspoons grated orange peel

½ cup orange marmalade or apple jelly

1. Prepare Cocoa Streusel. Heat oven to 350°F. Grease 12-cup fluted tube pan.

2. Beat butter and sugar in large bowl until well blended. Add eggs and vanilla; beat well. Add sour cream; beat until blended. Stir together flour, baking powder and baking soda; add alternately with orange juice to butter mixture, beating until well blended. Stir in orange peel.

3. Spread marmalade in bottom of prepared pan; sprinkle half of streusel over marmalade. Pour half of batter into pan, spreading evenly. Sprinkle remaining streusel over batter; spread remaining batter evenly over streusel.

4. Bake 1 hour or until toothpick inserted in center of cake comes out clean. Loosen cake from side of pan with metal spatula; immediately invert onto serving plate.

Makes 12 servings

Cocoa Streusel: Combine ⅔ cup packed light brown sugar, ½ cup chopped walnuts, ¼ cup HERSHEY'S Cocoa and ½ cup MOUNDS® Sweetened Coconut Flakes, if desired.

Oven-Baked French Toast

12 slices cinnamon bread or cinnamon raisin bread

1 pint (16 ounces) half and half or light cream

2 large eggs

6 tablespoons I CAN'T BELIEVE IT'S NOT BUTTER!® Spread, melted

2 tablespoons firmly packed brown sugar

2 teaspoons vanilla extract

1 teaspoon grated orange peel (optional)

¼ teaspoon ground cinnamon

⅛ teaspoon ground nutmeg (optional)

Preheat oven to 350°F.

In lightly greased 13×9-inch baking pan, arrange bread slices in two layers.

In large bowl, with wire whisk, blend remaining ingredients. Evenly pour over bread slices, pressing bread down until some liquid is absorbed and bread does not float. Bake 45 minutes or until center reaches 160°F. and bread is golden brown. Serve hot and sprinkle, if desired, with confectioners' sugar.

Makes 6 servings

Tip: Freeze leftover French toast in airtight container. To reheat, let come to room temperature, then arrange on baking sheet and bake at 350°F. until hot.

Apple Sauce Cinnamon Rolls

Rolls

- **4 cups all-purpose flour, divided**
- **1 package active dry yeast**
- **1 cup MOTT'S® Natural Apple Sauce, divided**
- **½ cup skim milk**
- **⅓ cup plus 2 tablespoons granulated sugar, divided**
- **2 tablespoons margarine**
- **½ teaspoon salt**
- **1 egg, beaten lightly**
- **2 teaspoons ground cinnamon**

Icing

- **1 cup sifted powdered sugar**
- **1 tablespoon skim milk**
- **½ teaspoon vanilla extract**

1. To prepare Rolls, in large bowl, combine 1½ cups flour and yeast. In small saucepan, combine ¾ cup apple sauce, ½ cup milk, 2 tablespoons granulated sugar, margarine and salt. Cook over medium heat, stirring frequently, until mixture reaches 120° to 130°F and margarine is almost melted (milk will appear curdled). Add to flour mixture along with egg. Beat with electric mixer on low speed 30 seconds, scraping bowl frequently. Beat on high speed 3 minutes. Stir in 2¼ cups flour until soft dough forms.

2. Turn out dough onto lightly floured surface; flatten slightly. Knead 3 to 5 minutes or until smooth and elastic, adding remaining ¼ cup flour to prevent sticking if necessary. Shape dough into ball; place in large bowl sprayed with nonstick cooking spray. Turn dough over so that top is greased. Cover with towel; let rise in warm place about 1 hour or until doubled in bulk.

3. Spray two 8- or 9-inch round baking pans with nonstick cooking spray.

4. Punch down dough; turn out onto lightly floured surface. Cover with towel; let rest 10 minutes. Roll out dough into 12-inch square. Spread remaining ¼ cup apple sauce over dough, to within ½ inch of edges. In small bowl, combine remaining ⅓ cup granulated sugar and cinnamon; sprinkle over apple sauce. Roll up dough jelly-roll style. Moisten edge with water; pinch to seal seam. Cut roll into 12 (1-inch) slices with sharp floured knife. Arrange 6 rolls ½ inch apart in each prepared pan. Cover with towel; let rise in warm place about 30 minutes or until nearly doubled in bulk.

5. Preheat oven to 375°F. Bake 20 to 25 minutes or until lightly browned. Cool on wire rack 5 minutes. Invert each pan onto serving plate.

6. To prepare Icing, in small bowl, combine powdered sugar, 1 tablespoon milk and vanilla until smooth. Drizzle over tops of rolls. Serve warm.   *Makes 12 servings*

Oven-Tested Tips

Cinnamon can vary in flavor depending on where it is grown. Some of the world's sweetest and strongest comes from China and Vietnam. Like most spices, ground cinnamon will lose its strength over time, so if yours has been in the cabinet for a while, sniff or taste it before using it to make sure it is still flavorful.

Cranberry Streusel Coffee Cake

1 egg
½ cup plus 3 tablespoons sugar, divided
½ cup milk
1 tablespoon vegetable oil
1 tablespoon orange juice
1 teaspoon grated orange peel
¼ teaspoon almond extract
1½ cups all-purpose flour, divided
2 teaspoons baking powder
½ teaspoon salt
8 ounces (2 cups) fresh cranberries
2 tablespoons butter

1. Preheat oven to 375°F.

2. Beat egg in large bowl. Add ½ cup sugar, milk, oil, orange juice, orange peel and almond extract; mix thoroughly. Combine 1 cup flour, baking powder and salt; add to egg mixture and stir, being careful not to overmix. Pour into 8×8×2-inch pan sprayed with nonstick cooking spray.

3. Chop cranberries in blender or food processor; spoon over batter. Mix remaining ½ cup flour and remaining 3 tablespoons sugar. Cut in butter with pastry blender or 2 knives until mixture resembles coarse crumbs; sprinkle over cranberries.

4. Bake 25 to 30 minutes. Serve warm.

Makes 9 servings

Apple Sauce Cinnamon Roll

Apricot-Filled Coffee Cake

Coffee cakes

  1 cup sugar

  1 teaspoon cinnamon

  ½ cup butter

  1 can (12 ounces) evaporated milk

  1½ teaspoons salt

  2 packages active dry yeast

  ¼ cup warm water (105° to 115°F)

  ½ cup sour cream

  3 eggs

  6 to 7 cups all-purpose flour, divided

Filling

  2¼ to 2¾ cups water

  1 package (6 ounces) dried apricots
    (2 cups)

  1 egg, lightly beaten

  2 tablespoons milk

  Additional sugar

1. For coffee cakes, combine sugar and cinnamon in medium saucepan; stir in butter, evaporated milk and salt. Cook over medium heat 5 to 8 minutes or until butter is melted, stirring occasionally. Remove from heat; let cool slightly.

2. Dissolve yeast in ¼ cup water in large bowl; stir in warm milk mixture, sour cream, 3 eggs and 3 cups flour. Beat at medium speed with electric mixer 1 to 2 minutes or until smooth. Stir in enough remaining flour, by hand, to make dough easy to handle. Turn dough out onto lightly floured surface; knead about 5 minutes or until smooth and elastic. Place dough in greased bowl; turn dough over so that top is greased. Cover and let rise in warm place 1 to 1½ hours or until double in size.

3. For filling, combine 2¼ cups water and apricots in medium saucepan. Cook over low heat about 45 minutes or until apricots are tender and mixture has thickened. Add small amounts of additional water if necessary. Stir occasionally.

4. Punch down dough and divide in half; let rest 10 minutes. Roll half of dough on lightly floured surface into 20×9-inch rectangle; cut into 3 (3-inch-wide) strips. Spread each strip with ¼ cup apricot mixture to within ½ inch of edges. Bring 20-inch sides up together; pinch sides and ends tightly to seal well. Gently braid filled strips together. Place on large greased cookie sheet. Form into wreath; pinch ends to seal well. Repeat with remaining dough and apricot mixture. Cover and let rise in warm place 30 minutes.

5. Preheat oven to 350°F. Bake 25 to 30 minutes or until lightly browned. (Cover with aluminum foil if coffee cakes brown too quickly.) Blend beaten egg and milk in small bowl. Brush coffee cakes with egg mixture; sprinkle with additional sugar. Continue baking 5 to 10 minutes or until golden brown. Remove from cookie sheets; cool on wire racks.   *Makes 2 coffee cakes*

Oven-Tested Tips

Place a damp towel under the board to keep it from sliding around when you knead bread. Too much added flour makes baked goods dry and dense. So remember to dust the board lightly. If dough or flour builds up on your hands, rub them together over the sink or wastebasket, so dried particles don't get kneaded back into the dough.

Apricot-Filled Coffee Cake

Tuscan Brunch Torta

    3 cups all-purpose flour
    ¾ teaspoon salt
    1 cup unsalted butter
    6 to 8 tablespoons ice water
    1 egg, separated
    4 eggs
    1 container (15 ounces) ricotta or
        light ricotta cheese
    1 package (10 ounces) frozen
        chopped spinach, thawed and
        well drained
    ½ cup freshly grated Parmesan
        cheese
    ½ teaspoon red pepper flakes
    ⅛ teaspoon ground nutmeg
    8 ounces sliced proscuitto or smoked
        ham
    ½ cup prepared pesto
    1 jar (7 ounces) roasted red peppers,
        rinsed, drained and patted dry
    4 ounces sliced provolone cheese
    1 tablespoon milk

1. Combine flour and salt in medium bowl. Cut in butter with pastry blender or 2 knives until mixture forms pea-sized pieces.

2. Add water, 1 tablespoon at a time, until dough forms a soft ball. Shape ⅔ of dough into disk; shape ⅓ of dough into another disk. Wrap each in plastic wrap; refrigerate 30 minutes or until firm enough to roll out.

3. Preheat oven to 375°F. Turn out large disk of dough onto lightly floured surface. Roll dough into 13-inch round. Transfer to 10-inch deep-dish pie plate; trim to ¼ inch beyond rim. Reserve scraps.

4. Pierce dough with fork about 40 times. Brush lightly with beaten egg white. Bake 10 minutes; cool on wire rack.

5. Beat 4 eggs lightly in large bowl. Add ricotta cheese, spinach, Parmesan cheese, red pepper flakes and nutmeg; mix well. Layer half of proscuitto over cooled crust; spread spinach mixture over proscuitto. Layer remaining proscuitto, pesto, roasted red peppers and provolone cheese over top.

6. Roll out remaining dough to 12-inch round. Place over filling; trim to ½ inch beyond rim and flute edge. Reroll pastry scraps; cut into decorative shapes and place over pastry. Cut several slits on top of pastry to allow steam to escape.

7. Beat egg yolk and milk in small bowl with wire whisk; brush evenly over pastry. Place pie plate on baking sheet; bake 1 hour or until golden brown. Let cool on wire rack 15 minutes. Serve warm.

Makes 12 servings

Green Onion Cream Cheese Breakfast Biscuits

    2 cups all-purpose flour
    1 tablespoon baking powder
    1 tablespoon sugar
    ¾ teaspoon salt
    1 package (3 ounces) cream cheese
    ¼ cup shortening
    ½ cup finely chopped green onions
    ⅔ cup milk

1. Preheat oven to 450°F.

2. Combine flour, baking powder, sugar and salt in medium bowl. Cut in cream cheese and shortening with pastry blender or two knives until mixture resembles coarse crumbs. Stir in green onions.

3. Make well in center of flour mixture. Add milk; stir until mixture forms soft dough that clings together and forms a ball.

4. Turn out dough onto well-floured surface. Knead dough gently 10 to 12 times.

5. Roll or pat dough to ½-inch thickness. Cut out dough with floured 3-inch biscuit cutter.

6. Place biscuits 2 inches apart on ungreased large baking sheet. Bake 10 to 12 minutes or until tops and bottoms are golden brown. Serve warm. *Makes 8 biscuits*

Tuscan Brunch Torta

Raspberry-Applesauce Coffee Cake

1½ cups fresh or frozen raspberries
¼ cup water
7 tablespoons sugar, divided
2 tablespoons cornstarch
½ teaspoon ground nutmeg, divided
1¾ cups all-purpose flour, divided
3 tablespoons margarine
1 tablespoon finely chopped walnuts
1½ teaspoons baking powder
½ teaspoon baking soda
⅛ teaspoon ground cloves
2 egg whites
1 cup unsweetened applesauce

1. Preheat oven to 350°F. Spray 8-inch square baking pan with nonstick cooking spray.

2. Combine raspberries and water in small saucepan; bring to a boil over high heat. Reduce heat to medium. Combine 2 tablespoons sugar, cornstarch and ¼ teaspoon nutmeg in small bowl. Stir into raspberry mixture. Cook and stir until mixture boils and thickens. Cook and stir 2 minutes more.

3. Combine ¾ cup flour and remaining 5 tablespoons sugar in medium bowl. Cut in margarine with pastry blender until mixture resembles coarse meal. Set aside ½ cup mixture for topping; stir walnuts into remaining crumb mixture.

4. Add remaining 1 cup flour, baking powder, baking soda, remaining ¼ teaspoon nutmeg and cloves to walnut mixture; mix well. Stir in egg whites and applesauce; beat until well combined. Spread half of batter into prepared pan. Spread raspberry mixture over batter. Drop remaining batter in small mounds on top. Sprinkle with reserved topping.

5. Bake 40 to 45 minutes or until edges start to pull away from sides of pan. Serve warm or cool. *Makes 9 servings*

Quick Crumb Coffee Cake

2 cups all-purpose flour
1½ cups sugar
2 teaspoons baking powder
¼ teaspoon salt
¾ CRISCO® Stick or ¾ cup CRISCO® all-vegetable shortening
2 eggs
½ cup milk
1 teaspoon vanilla
½ cup chopped pecans

1. Heat oven to 350°F. Grease two 8×1½-inch round cake pans; set aside.

2. Combine flour, sugar, baking powder and salt in a medium mixing bowl. Cut in shortening until crumbly. Reserve 1 cup crumb mixture for topping.

3. Stir together eggs, milk and vanilla. Add to remaining crumb mixture. Stir just until moistened. (Batter will be slightly lumpy.) Spread batter evenly in prepared pans.

4. Combine reserved crumbs and chopped nuts. Sprinkle evenly over batter. Bake at 350°F about 25 minutes or until edges are lightly browned and toothpick inserted in center comes out clean. *Do not overbake.* Cool on wire rack. Serve warm or cool. *Makes 16 servings*

Raspberry-Applesauce Coffee Cake

Bake Up Your Morning ◆ 61

Wild Rice Breakfast Bread

¼ cup extra-light margarine, softened
¼ cup packed brown sugar
4 egg whites
1 teaspoon vanilla extract
1½ cups well-cooked wild rice
½ cup chopped pecans
¾ cup whole wheat flour
¾ cup all-purpose flour
1 teaspoon baking powder
1 teaspoon salt
2 teaspoons ground cinnamon
¾ cup skim milk
Maple Butter (recipe follows), optional

Preheat oven to 325°F. Grease 8×4-inch loaf pan.

Beat margarine and brown sugar in large bowl until creamy. Add egg whites and beat until fluffy. Add vanilla. Stir in rice and pecans. Combine flours, baking powder, salt and cinnamon. Add flour mixture alternately with milk to rice mixture; stir just until flour mixture is moistened. Pour into prepared pan.

Bake about 55 minutes or until wooden pick inserted in center comes out clean. Serve with Maple Butter, if desired.

Makes 10 servings

Maple Butter

½ cup butter, softened
¼ cup maple syrup

Beat butter in small bowl until light and fluffy. Thoroughly blend in maple syrup.

Favorite recipe from **Minnesota Cultivated Wild Rice Council**

Egg and Sausage Breakfast Strudel

1 pound BOB EVANS® Original Recipe Roll Sausage
¾ cup finely grated Parmesan cheese
1 (10¾-ounce) can condensed cream of mushroom soup
2 hard-cooked eggs, cut into ¼-inch cubes
½ cup thinly sliced green onions
¼ cup chopped fresh parsley
1 (16-ounce) package frozen phyllo dough, thawed according to package directions
Butter-flavored nonstick cooking spray or ½ cup melted butter or margarine

Crumble and cook sausage in medium skillet until browned. Drain off any drippings; place in medium bowl. Add cheese, soup, eggs, green onions and parsley; stir gently until blended. Cover and chill at least 4 hours.

Preheat oven to 375°F. Layer 4 sheets of phyllo dough, coating each sheet with cooking spray or brushing with melted butter before stacking. Cut stack in half lengthwise. Shape ⅓ cup filling into log and place at bottom end of 1 stack. Fold in sides to cover filling; roll up phyllo dough and filling jelly roll style. Seal edges and spray roll with cooking spray or brush with butter. Repeat with remaining phyllo dough and filling. Place rolls on ungreased baking sheet, seam sides down. Bake 15 to 20 minutes or until golden brown. Serve hot. Refrigerate leftovers.

Makes 10 strudels

Note: Unbaked strudels can be wrapped and refrigerated up to 24 hours, or frozen up to 1 month. If frozen, allow additional baking time.

Good Morning Bread

¼ cup water

1 cup mashed ripe banana (about 3 medium)

3 tablespoons vegetable oil

1 teaspoon salt

2¼ cups bread flour

¾ cup whole wheat flour

¾ cup chopped pitted dates

½ cup uncooked old-fashioned oats

¼ cup nonfat dry milk powder

1 teaspoon grated orange peel (optional)

1 teaspoon ground cinnamon

2 teaspoons active dry yeast

1. Measuring carefully, place all ingredients in bread machine pan in order specified by owner's manual.

2. Program basic cycle and desired crust setting; press start. Immediately remove baked bread from pan; cool on wire rack.

Makes 1 (1½-pound) loaf

Note: This recipe produces a moist, slightly dense loaf that has a lower volume than other loaves. The banana flavor is more prominent when the bread is toasted.

Good Morning Bread

Sweet & Savory Treats

Biscuits, muffins and scones are a baker's best friends. Quick and easy to make, they turn even a simple meal into a feast. Start preheating that oven! From plain old-fashioned biscuits to new-fangled combinations like Mocha-Macadamia Nut Muffins, there's inspiration here for every cook and every occasion.

English-Style Scones

3 eggs
½ cup heavy cream
1½ teaspoons vanilla
2 cups all-purpose flour
2 teaspoons baking powder
¼ teaspoon salt
¼ cup (½ stick) cold butter
¼ cup finely chopped pitted dates
¼ cup golden raisins or currants
1 teaspoon water
6 tablespoons no-sugar-added orange marmalade fruit spread
6 tablespoons softly whipped cream or crème fraîche

Preheat oven to 375°F. Beat 2 eggs with cream and vanilla; set aside. Combine flour, baking powder and salt in medium bowl. Cut in butter with pastry blender or two knives until mixture resembles coarse crumbs. Stir in dates and raisins. Add egg mixture; mix just until dry ingredients are moistened. With floured hands, knead dough four times on lightly floured surface. Place dough on greased cookie sheet; pat into 8-inch circle. With sharp wet knife, gently score dough into six wedges, cutting ¾ of the way into dough. Beat remaining egg with water; brush lightly over dough. Bake 18 to 20 minutes or until golden brown. Cool 5 minutes on wire rack. Cut into wedges. Serve warm with marmalade and whipped cream.   *Makes 6 scones*

Gingerbread Streusel Raisin Muffins

1 cup raisins

½ cup boiling water

⅓ cup margarine or butter, softened

¾ cup GRANDMA'S® Molasses (Unsulphured)

1 egg

2 cups all-purpose flour

1½ teaspoons baking soda

½ teaspoon salt

1 teaspoon cinnamon

1 teaspoon ginger

Topping

⅓ cup all-purpose flour

¼ cup firmly packed brown sugar

¼ cup chopped nuts

3 tablespoons margarine or butter

1 teaspoon cinnamon

Preheat oven to 375°F. Grease bottoms only of 12 muffin cups or line with paper baking cups. In small bowl, cover raisins with boiling water; let stand 5 minutes. In large bowl, beat ⅓ cup margarine and molasses until fluffy. Add egg; beat well. Stir in 2 cups flour, baking soda, salt, 1 teaspoon cinnamon and ginger. Blend just until dry ingredients are moistened. Gently stir in raisins and water. Fill prepared muffin cups ¾ full. For topping, combine all ingredients in small bowl. Sprinkle over muffins.

Bake 20 to 25 minutes or until toothpick inserted in centers comes out clean. Cool 5 minutes; remove from pan. Serve warm.

Makes 12 muffins

Cherry-Up Biscuits

1½ cups all-purpose flour

1 tablespoon baking powder

1½ teaspoons granulated sugar

¼ cup shortening

½ teaspoon salt

½ teaspoon cream of tartar

½ cup milk

½ cup butter, melted

¼ cup packed brown sugar

1 can (21 ounces) tart cherry pie filling

1. Preheat oven to 425°F. Place flour, baking powder, granulated sugar, shortening, salt and cream of tartar in food processor fitted with metal blade. Process using on/off pulsing action until mixture resembles coarse crumbs, about 10 seconds.

2. Pour milk over flour mixture. Process on/off 4 to 6 times, or just until mixture is blended and dough is soft.

3. Turn dough onto lightly floured surface. Knead gently a few times. Roll or pat dough out until ½ inch thick. Cut dough into 2½-inch circles using floured cutter.

4. Put 1 teaspoon butter, 1 teaspoon brown sugar and 1 heaping tablespoon pie filling in each of 12 ungreased muffin cups. Place 1 biscuit in each cup. Brush with remaining butter. Bake until biscuits are golden brown, 12 to 15 minutes. Invert and unmold biscuits. Serve warm.

Makes 1 dozen biscuits

Gingerbread Streusel Raisin Muffins

Bayou Yam Muffins

1 cup flour
1 cup yellow cornmeal
¼ cup sugar
1 tablespoon baking powder
1¼ teaspoons ground cinnamon
½ teaspoon salt
2 eggs
1 cup mashed yams or sweet
    potatoes
½ cup very strong cold coffee
¼ cup butter or margarine, melted
½ teaspoon TABASCO® brand
    Pepper Sauce

Preheat oven to 425°F. Grease 12 (3×1½-inch) muffin cups. Combine flour, cornmeal, sugar, baking powder, cinnamon and salt in large bowl. Beat eggs in medium bowl; stir in mashed yams, coffee, butter and TABASCO® Sauce. Make a well in center of dry ingredients; add yam mixture and stir just to combine. Spoon batter into prepared muffin cups. Bake 20 to 25 minutes or until cake tester inserted in center of muffin comes out clean. Cool 5 minutes on wire rack. Remove from pans. Serve warm or at room temperature.   *Makes 12 muffins*

Microwave Directions: Prepare muffin batter as directed above. Spoon approximately ⅓ cup batter into each of 6 paper baking cup-lined 6-ounce custard cups or microwave-safe muffin pan cups. Cook uncovered on High (100% power) 4 to 5½ minutes or until cake tester inserted in center of muffin comes out clean; turn and rearrange cups or turn muffin pan ½ turn once during cooking. Remove muffins with small spatula. Cool 5 minutes on wire rack. Remove from pans. Repeat procedure with remaining batter. Serve warm or at room temperature.

Bayou Yam Muffins

Honey Currant Scones

Honey Currant Scones

2½ **cups all-purpose flour**

2 **teaspoons grated orange peel**

1 **teaspoon baking powder**

½ **teaspoon baking soda**

½ **teaspoon salt**

½ **cup cold butter or margarine**

½ **cup currants**

½ **cup sour cream**

⅓ **cup honey**

1 **egg, slightly beaten**

Preheat oven to 375°F. Grease baking sheet; set aside.

Combine flour, orange peel, baking powder, baking soda and salt in large bowl. Cut in butter with pastry blender or 2 knives until mixture resembles coarse crumbs. Add currants. Combine sour cream, honey and egg in medium bowl until well blended. Stir into flour mixture until soft dough forms. Turn out dough onto lightly floured surface. Knead dough 10 times. Shape dough into 8-inch square. Cut into 4 squares; cut each square diagonally in half, making 8 triangles. Place triangles 1 inch apart on prepared baking sheet.

Bake 15 to 20 minutes or until golden brown and wooden pick inserted in center comes out clean. Remove from baking sheet. Cool on wire rack 10 minutes. Serve warm or cool completely.

Makes 8 scones

Favorite recipe from **National Honey Board**

Angel Biscuits

⅓ cup warm water (110°F)
1 package (¼ ounce) active dry yeast
5 cups all-purpose flour
3 tablespoons sugar
1 tablespoon baking powder
1 teaspoon baking soda
1 teaspoon salt
1 cup shortening
2 cups buttermilk

1. Preheat oven to 450°F. Pour warm water into small bowl. Sprinkle yeast over water and stir until dissolved. Let stand 10 minutes or until small bubbles form.

2. Combine flour, sugar, baking powder, baking soda and salt in large bowl. Add shortening. With fingers, pastry blender or 2 knives, rub or cut in shortening until mixture resembles fine crumbs. Make a well in center. Pour in yeast mixture and buttermilk; stir with fork until mixture forms dough.

3. Turn dough out onto lightly floured board. Knead 30 seconds or until dough feels light and soft but not sticky. Roll out desired amount of dough to ½-inch thickness. Cut biscuit rounds with 2-inch cutter. Place biscuits close together (for soft sides) or ½ inch apart (for crispy sides) on ungreased baking sheet. Bake 15 to 18 minutes or until tops are lightly browned.

4. Place remaining dough in airtight bag; refrigerate up to 3 days. Or roll out and cut remaining dough into rounds; place on baking sheet and freeze. Transfer frozen rounds to airtight bags; return to freezer. At baking time, place frozen rounds on ungreased baking sheet. Let stand 20 minutes or until thawed before baking. Bake as directed.

Makes about 5 dozen biscuits

Red Devil Biscuits: Prepare Angel Biscuits but add 2 tablespoons mild red chili powder to flour mixture. Cut biscuits regular size to serve as a hot bread. To serve as an appetizer, cut biscuits miniature size. Serve with your favorite cheese spread or with softened butter and thinly sliced roast beef or turkey.

Biscuits

2 cups sifted all-purpose flour
3 teaspoons baking powder
1 teaspoon salt
⅓ CRISCO® Stick or ⅓ cup CRISCO® all-vegetable shortening
¾ cup milk

1. Heat oven to 425°F. Combine flour, baking powder and salt in bowl. Cut in ⅓ cup shortening using pastry blender (or 2 knives) until mixture resembles coarse meal. Add milk; stir with fork until blended.

2. Transfer dough to lightly floured surface. Knead gently 8 to 10 times. Roll dough ½ inch thick. Cut with floured 2-inch-round cutter.

3. Bake at 425°F 12 to 15 minutes. *Do not overbake.*

Makes 12 to 16 (2-inch) biscuits

Oven-Tested Tips

The secret to making flaky, tender biscuits is to cut chilled shortening into the dry ingredients just until the mixture forms coarse crumbs. Don't worry about leaving some chunks of shortening; they'll melt and help make layers. Don't overwork the dough either.

Pesto Surprise Muffins

2 cups all-purpose flour

3 tablespoons grated Parmesan
    cheese, divided

1 tablespoon baking powder

½ teaspoon salt

1 cup milk

¼ cup vegetable oil

1 egg

¼ cup prepared pesto sauce

1. Preheat oven to 400°F. Grease or paper-line 12 (2½-inch) muffin cups.

2. Combine flour, 2 tablespoons cheese, baking powder and salt in large bowl. Whisk together milk, oil and egg in small bowl until blended. Stir into flour mixture just until moistened. Spoon into prepared muffin cups, filling ⅓ full. Stir pesto sauce; spoon 1 teaspoon sauce into each muffin cup. Spoon remaining batter evenly over pesto sauce. Sprinkle remaining 1 tablespoon cheese evenly over muffins.

3. Bake 25 to 30 minutes or until toothpick inserted into centers comes out clean. Cool in muffin pan on wire rack 5 minutes. Remove from pan and cool on wire rack 10 minutes. *Makes 12 muffins*

Pesto Surprise Muffins

Chocolate Popovers

¾ **cup plus 2 tablespoons all-purpose flour**

¼ **cup granulated sugar**

2 **tablespoons unsweetened cocoa powder**

¼ **teaspoon salt**

4 **eggs**

1 **cup milk**

2 **tablespoons butter, melted**

½ **teaspoon vanilla**

   Powdered sugar

1. Position rack in lower third of oven. Preheat oven to 375°F. Grease 6-cup popover pan or 6 (6-ounce) custard cups. Set custard cups in jelly-roll pan for easier handling.

2. Sift flour, granulated sugar, cocoa and salt into medium bowl; set aside. Beat eggs in large bowl with electric mixer at low speed 1 minute. Beat in milk, butter and vanilla. Beat in flour mixture until smooth. Pour batter into prepared pan. Bake 50 minutes.

3. Place pieces of waxed paper under wire rack to keep counter clean. Immediately remove popovers to wire rack. Place powdered sugar in fine-mesh sieve; sprinkle generously over popovers. Serve immediately. *Makes 6 popovers*

Oven-Tested Tips

Popovers are leavened only by eggs and steam. Be sure the oven is fully preheated and do not peek during baking because letting in cold air may cause popovers to collapse.

Apple Cheddar Scones

1½ **cups all-purpose flour**

½ **cup toasted wheat germ**

3 **tablespoons sugar**

2 **teaspoons baking powder**

½ **teaspoon salt**

2 **tablespoons butter**

1 **small Washington Rome apple, cored and chopped**

¼ **cup shredded Cheddar cheese**

1 **large egg white**

½ **cup low-fat (1%) milk**

1. Heat oven to 400°F. Grease an 8-inch round cake pan. In medium-size bowl, combine flour, wheat germ, sugar, baking powder and salt. With two knives or pastry blender, cut in butter until the size of coarse crumbs. Toss chopped apple and cheese in flour mixture.

2. Beat together egg white and milk until well combined. Add to flour mixture, mixing with fork until dough forms. Turn dough out onto lightly floured surface and knead 6 times.

3. Spread dough evenly in cake pan and score deeply with knife into 6 wedges. Bake 25 to 30 minutes or until top springs back when gently pressed. Let stand 5 minutes; remove from pan. Cool before serving. *Makes 6 scones*

Favorite recipe from **Washington Apple Commission**

Chocolate Popovers

Cocoa Applesauce Raisin Muffins

1¼ cups all-purpose flour
½ cup whole-wheat flour
¾ cup packed light brown sugar
¼ cup HERSHEY'S Cocoa
1 tablespoon baking powder
½ teaspoon baking soda
½ teaspoon salt
⅛ teaspoon ground cinnamon
⅛ teaspoon ground nutmeg
⅓ cup butter or margarine, melted
1 cup chunky applesauce
¼ cup milk
1 egg
¾ cup raisins
Cinnamon Butter (recipe follows)

1. Heat oven to 400°F. Grease bottoms of or line muffin cups (2½ inches in diameter) with paper bake cups.

2. Stir together all-purpose flour, whole-wheat flour, brown sugar, cocoa, baking powder, baking soda, salt, cinnamon and nutmeg in large bowl. Stir together butter, applesauce, milk and egg in small bowl until well blended; add to dry ingredients. Stir just until dry ingredients are moistened. Stir in raisins. Fill muffin cups about ¾ full with batter.

3. Bake 20 to 22 minutes or until wooden pick inserted in center comes out clean. Remove from pans to wire racks. Cool slightly.

4. Meanwhile, prepare Cinnamon Butter. Serve with warm muffins.

Makes about 15 muffins

Cinnamon Butter

½ cup (1 stick) butter or margarine, softened
2 tablespoons powdered sugar
⅛ to ¼ teaspoon ground cinnamon

1. Beat butter, powdered sugar and cinnamon in small bowl until well blended.

Grandma's® Bran Muffins

2½ cups bran flakes, divided
1 cup raisins
1 cup boiling water
½ cup canola oil
1 cup GRANDMA'S® Molasses
2 eggs, beaten
2 cups buttermilk
2¾ cups all-purpose flour
2½ teaspoons baking soda
½ teaspoon salt

Heat oven to 400°F. In medium bowl, mix 1 cup bran flakes, raisins and water. Set aside. In large bowl, combine remaining ingredients. Mix in bran-raisin mixture. Pour into greased muffin pan cups. Fill ⅔ full and bake for 20 minutes. Remove muffins and place on rack to cool.

Makes 48 muffins

Grandma's® Bran Muffins

Zesty Parmesan Biscuits

4 cups all-purpose flour

½ cup grated Parmesan cheese

2 tablespoons baking powder

2 teaspoons sugar

1 teaspoon baking soda

6 tablespoons cold butter, cut into pieces

6 tablespoons cold solid vegetable shortening

1 cup plus 2 tablespoons buttermilk, divided

½ cup *Frank's® RedHot®* Cayenne Pepper Sauce

Sesame seeds (optional)

1. Preheat oven to 450°F. Place flour, cheese, baking powder, sugar and baking soda in blender or food processor.* Cover; process 30 seconds. Add butter and shortening; process, pulsing on and off, until fine crumbs form. Transfer to large bowl.

2. Add 1 cup buttermilk and *Frank's RedHot* Sauce all at once. Stir together just until mixture starts to form a ball. (Dough will be dry. Do not over mix.)

3. Turn dough out onto lightly floured board. With palms of hands, gently knead 8 times. Using floured rolling pin or hands, roll dough to ¾-inch thickness. Using 2½-inch round biscuit cutter, cut out 16 biscuits, re-rolling dough as necessary.

4. Place biscuits 2-inches apart on large foil-lined baking sheet. Brush tops with remaining 2 tablespoons buttermilk; sprinkle with sesame seeds, if desired. Bake 12 to 15 minutes or until golden.

Makes 16 biscuits

*Or, place dry ingredients in large bowl. Cut in butter and shortening until fine crumbs form using pastry blender or 2 knives. Add buttermilk and Frank's RedHot Sauce; mix just until moistened. Continue with step 3.

Prep Time: 30 minutes
Cook Time: 12 minutes

White Chocolate Chunk Muffins

2½ cups all-purpose flour

1 cup packed brown sugar

⅓ cup unsweetened cocoa powder

2 teaspoons baking soda

½ teaspoon salt

1⅓ cups buttermilk

6 tablespoons butter, melted

2 eggs, beaten

1½ teaspoons vanilla

1½ cups chopped white chocolate

1. Preheat oven to 400°F. Grease 12 (3½-inch) large muffin cups; set aside.

2. Combine flour, sugar, cocoa, baking soda and salt in large bowl. Blend buttermilk, butter, eggs and vanilla in small bowl. Stir into flour mixture just until moistened. Fold in white chocolate. Spoon into prepared muffin cups, filling half full.

3. Bake 25 to 30 minutes or until toothpick inserted in center comes out clean. Cool in pan on wire rack 5 minutes. Remove from pan. Cool on wire rack 10 minutes. Serve warm or cool completely.

Makes 12 jumbo muffins

Peachy Oat Bran Muffins

1½ cups oat bran
½ cup all-purpose flour
⅓ cup firmly packed brown sugar
2 teaspoons baking powder
1 teaspoon cinnamon
½ teaspoon salt
¾ cup lowfat milk
1 egg, beaten
¼ cup vegetable oil
1 can (15 ounces) DEL MONTE® LITE® Yellow Cling Sliced Peaches, drained and chopped
⅓ cup chopped walnuts

1. Preheat oven to 425°F. Combine oat bran, flour, brown sugar, baking powder, cinnamon and salt; mix well.

2. Combine milk, egg and oil. Add to dry ingredients; stir just enough to blend. Fold in fruit and nuts.

3. Fill greased muffin cups with batter. Sprinkle with granulated sugar, if desired.

4. Bake 20 to 25 minutes or until golden brown. *Makes 12 medium muffins*

Hint: Muffins can be frozen and reheated in microwave or toaster oven.

Prep Time: 10 minutes
Cook Time: 25 minutes

Zesty Parmesan Biscuits

Broccoli & Cheddar Muffins

3 cups buttermilk baking and
  pancake mix
2 eggs, lightly beaten
⅔ cup milk
1 teaspoon dried basil
1 cup (4 ounces) shredded Cheddar
  cheese
1 box (10 ounces) BIRDS EYE®
  frozen Chopped Broccoli,
  thawed and drained

• Preheat oven to 350°F. Combine baking mix, eggs, milk and basil. Mix until moistened. (Do not overmix.)

• Add cheese and broccoli; stir just to combine. Add salt and pepper to taste.

• Spray 12 muffin cups with nonstick cooking spray. Pour batter into muffin cups. Bake 25 to 30 minutes or until golden brown.

• Cool 5 minutes in pan. Loosen sides of muffins with knife; remove from pan and serve warm. *Makes 1 dozen large muffins*

Southwestern Corn Muffins: Prepare 1 box corn muffin mix according to package directions; add ⅔ cup BIRDS EYE® frozen Corn and 1 teaspoon chili powder to batter. Mix well; bake according to package directions.

Prep Time: 5 to 10 minutes
Bake Time: 25 to 30 minutes

Pumpkin-Ginger Scones

½ cup sugar, divided
2 cups all-purpose flour
2 teaspoons baking powder
1 teaspoon ground cinnamon
½ teaspoon baking soda
½ teaspoon salt
4 tablespoons cold butter
1 egg
½ cup solid pack pumpkin
¼ cup sour cream
½ teaspoon grated fresh ginger
1 tablespoon butter, melted

1. Preheat oven to 425°F.

2. Reserve 1 tablespoon sugar. Combine remaining sugar, flour, baking powder, cinnamon, baking soda and salt in large bowl. Cut in 4 tablespoons butter with pastry blender or 2 knives until mixture resembles coarse crumbs. Beat egg in small bowl. Add pumpkin, sour cream and ginger; beat until well combined. Stir pumpkin mixture into flour mixture until it forms soft dough that leaves side of bowl.

3. Turn dough out onto well-floured surface. Knead 10 times. Roll dough using floured rolling pin into 9×6-inch rectangle. Cut dough into 6 (3-inch) squares. Cut each square diagonally in half, making 12 triangles. Place triangles, 2 inches apart, on ungreased baking sheets. Brush tops of triangles with melted butter and sprinkle with reserved sugar.

4. Bake 10 to 12 minutes or until golden brown. Cool 10 minutes on wire racks. Serve warm. *Makes 12 scones*

Spiced Brown Bread Muffins

2 cups whole wheat flour
⅔ cup all-purpose flour
⅔ cup packed brown sugar
2 teaspoons baking soda
1 teaspoon pumpkin pie spice
2 cups buttermilk
¾ cup raisins

Preheat oven to 350°F. Grease 6 large (4-inch) muffin cups. Combine flours, sugar, baking soda and pumpkin pie spice in large bowl. Stir in buttermilk just until flour mixture is moistened. Fold in raisins. Spoon into muffin cups. Bake 35 to 40 minutes until wooden pick inserted in center comes out clean. Remove from pan.

Makes 6 large muffins

Country Recipe Biscuits

2 cups all-purpose flour
1 tablespoon baking powder
½ cup prepared HIDDEN VALLEY® The Original Ranch® Dressing
½ cup buttermilk

Preheat oven to 425°F. In small bowl, sift together flour and baking powder. Make a well in flour mixture; add salad dressing and buttermilk. Stir with fork until dough forms a ball. Drop by rounded spoonfuls onto ungreased baking sheet. Bake until lightly browned, 12 to 15 minutes.

Makes 12 biscuits

Broccoli & Cheddar Muffin

Cranberry Scones

1½ cups all-purpose flour
½ cup oat bran
¼ cup plus 1 tablespoon sugar, divided
2 teaspoons baking powder
½ teaspoon baking soda
½ teaspoon salt
5 tablespoons cold margarine or butter
¾ cup dried cranberries
⅓ cup milk
1 egg
¼ cup sour cream
1 tablespoon uncooked old-fashioned or quick oats (optional)

1. Preheat oven to 425°F. Combine flour, oat bran, ¼ cup sugar, baking powder, baking soda and salt in large bowl. Cut in margarine with pastry blender or 2 knives until mixture resembles coarse crumbs. Stir in cranberries.

2. Lightly beat milk and egg in small bowl. Reserve 2 tablespoons milk mixture; set aside. Stir sour cream into remaining milk mixture. Stir into flour mixture until soft dough forms.

3. Turn out dough onto well-floured surface. Gently knead 10 to 12 times. Roll out into 9×6-inch rectangle. Cut dough into 6 (3-inch) squares using floured knife; cut diagonally into halves, forming 12 triangles. Place 2 inches apart on ungreased baking sheets. Brush triangles with reserved milk mixture. Sprinkle with oats, if desired, and remaining 1 tablespoon sugar.

4. Bake 10 to 12 minutes or until golden brown. Remove from baking sheets and cool on wire racks 10 minutes. Serve warm.

Makes 12 scones

Freezer Buttermilk Biscuits

3 cups all-purpose flour
1 tablespoon baking powder
1 tablespoon sugar
1 teaspoon baking soda
½ teaspoon salt
⅔ cup shortening
1 cup buttermilk*

*You may substitute soured fresh milk. To sour milk, place 1 tablespoon lemon juice plus enough milk to equal 1 cup in 2-cup measure. Stir; let stand 5 minutes before using.

1. Combine flour, baking powder, sugar, baking soda and salt in large bowl. Cut in shortening with pastry blender or 2 knives until mixture resembles fine crumbs. Stir buttermilk into flour mixture until mixture forms soft dough that leaves side of bowl.

2. Turn out dough onto well-floured surface. Knead 10 times; roll into 8-inch square. Cut dough into 16 (2-inch) squares.** Place squares on baking sheet lined with plastic wrap. Freeze about 3 hours or until firm. Remove squares and place in airtight freezer container. Freeze up to 1 month.

3. When ready to prepare, preheat oven to 400°F. Place frozen squares 1½ inches apart on ungreased baking sheets. Bake 20 to 25 minutes or until golden brown. Serve warm.

Makes 16 biscuits

**To bake immediately, preheat oven to 450°F. Place squares 1½ inches apart on ungreased baking sheets. Bake 10 to 12 minutes or until golden brown. Serve warm.

Chocolate Chunk Sour Cream Muffins

½ cup milk

2 tablespoons MAXWELL HOUSE® Instant Coffee, any variety

1½ cups flour

½ cup sugar

1½ teaspoons CALUMET® Baking Powder

½ teaspoon cinnamon

¼ teaspoon salt

2 eggs

½ cup BREAKSTONE'S® Sour Cream or plain yogurt

¼ cup (½ stick) butter or margarine, melted

1 teaspoon vanilla

1 package (4 ounces) BAKER'S® GERMAN'S® Sweet Baking Chocolate, chopped

HEAT oven to 375°F.

STIR milk and instant coffee in small bowl until well blended; set aside. Mix flour, sugar, baking powder, cinnamon and salt in large bowl. Beat eggs in small bowl; stir in coffee-milk mixture, sour cream, butter and vanilla until well blended. Add to flour mixture; stir just until moistened. Stir in chopped chocolate.

SPOON batter into greased or paper-lined muffin pan, filling each cup ⅔ full.

BAKE for 30 minutes or until toothpick inserted into center comes out clean. Serve warm.   *Makes 12 muffins*

Prep Time: 15 minutes
Bake Time: 30 minutes

Herb Biscuits

¼ cup hot water (130°F)

1½ teaspoons (½ package) quick-rise active dry yeast

2½ cups all-purpose flour

3 tablespoons sugar

1½ teaspoons baking powder

½ teaspoon baking soda

½ teaspoon salt

5 tablespoons cold butter or margarine, cut into pieces

2 teaspoons finely chopped fresh parsley *or* ½ teaspoon dried parsley flakes

2 teaspoons finely chopped fresh basil *or* ½ teaspoon dried basil leaves

2 teaspoons finely chopped fresh chives *or* ½ teaspoon dried chives

¾ cup buttermilk

1. Preheat oven to 425°F. Spray cookie sheet with nonstick cooking spray.

2. Combine hot water and yeast in small cup; let stand 2 to 3 minutes. Combine flour, sugar, baking powder, baking soda and salt in medium bowl; cut in butter using pastry blender or 2 knives until mixture resembles coarse crumbs. Mix in parsley, basil and chives. Stir in buttermilk and yeast mixture to make soft dough. Turn dough out onto lightly floured surface. Knead 15 to 20 times.

3. Roll to ½-inch thickness. Cut hearts or other shapes with 2½-inch cookie cutter. Place biscuits on prepared cookie sheet. Bake 12 to 15 minutes or until browned. Cool on wire racks. Serve immediately.
Makes 18 biscuits

Mocha-Macadamia Nut Muffins

1¼ cups all-purpose flour

⅔ cup sugar

2½ tablespoons unsweetened cocoa
powder

1 teaspoon baking soda

¼ teaspoon salt

⅔ cup buttermilk*

3 tablespoons butter, melted

1 egg, beaten

1 tablespoon instant coffee granules,
dissolved in 1 tablespoon hot
water

¾ teaspoon vanilla

½ cup coarsely chopped macadamia
nuts

Powdered sugar (optional)

*You may substitute soured fresh milk. To sour milk, place 2 teaspoons lemon juice plus enough milk to equal ⅔ cup in 2-cup measure. Stir, let stand 5 minutes before using.

1. Preheat oven to 400°F. Grease or paper-line 12 (2½-inch) muffin cups.

2. Combine flour, sugar, cocoa powder, baking soda and salt in large bowl. Whisk together buttermilk, butter, egg, coffee mixture and vanilla in small bowl until blended. Stir into flour mixture just until moistened. Fold in macadamia nuts. Spoon evenly into prepared muffin cups.

3. Bake 13 to 17 minutes or until toothpick inserted into centers comes out clean. Cool in pan on wire rack 5 minutes. Remove from pan and cool on wire rack 10 minutes. Sprinkle with powdered sugar, if desired.

Makes 12 muffins

Oven-Tested Tips

When making muffins, don't grease any cups that won't be filled since the fat will burn and make the pan hard to clean. Add two or three tablespoons of water to any empty cups to keep the pan from heating unevenly and warping in the oven.

Mocha-Macadamia Nut Muffin

Lemon Poppy Seed Muffins

3 cups all-purpose flour
1 cup sugar
3 tablespoons poppy seeds
1 tablespoon grated lemon peel
2 teaspoons baking powder
1 teaspoon baking soda
½ teaspoon salt
1 container (16 ounces) plain low-fat yogurt
½ cup fresh lemon juice
2 eggs, beaten
¼ cup vegetable oil
1½ teaspoons vanilla

1. Preheat oven to 400°F. Grease 12 (3½-inch) large muffin cups; set aside.

2. Combine flour, sugar, poppy seeds, lemon peel, baking powder, baking soda and salt in large bowl. Combine yogurt, lemon juice, eggs, oil and vanilla in small bowl until well blended. Stir into flour mixture just until moistened.

3. Spoon into prepared muffin cups, filling two-thirds full. Bake 25 to 30 minutes or until toothpick inserted in center comes out clean. Cool in pans on wire racks 5 minutes. Remove from pans. Cool on wire racks 10 minutes. Serve warm or cool completely.
Makes 12 jumbo muffins

Lemon Poppy Seed Muffins

Crisp Cheese Popovers

Nonstick cooking spray

1 cup sifted all-purpose flour, plus additional for dusting pan

1 cup fat-free (skim) milk

1 tablespoon melted margarine

¼ teaspoon salt

½ cup egg substitute *or* 2 eggs beaten

1¼ cups (5 ounces) shredded JARLSBERG LITE™ cheese

All ingredients should be at room temperature. Preheat oven to 450°F.

Spray 9 cups in muffin tin with cooking spray. Lightly flour prepared muffin cups, tapping out excess flour. (If there are unfilled cups in muffin tin, fill each with ½ inch water to prevent burning.)

Place milk and margarine in blender or mixing bowl. Add 1 cup flour and salt; blend until smooth, scraping down sides of blender if necessary. Gradually add egg substitute and blend until smooth.

Working quickly to ensure batter will rise, pour 1 tablespoon batter into each prepared muffin cup and top with 2 tablespoons cheese. Pour in remaining batter, dividing evenly (about 2 tablespoons per cup). Muffin cups should be ⅔ full.

Bake immediately. After 20 minutes, without opening oven door, *reduce oven temperature to 350°F* and bake 15 minutes for medium-soft or 20 minutes for crisper popovers. Popovers are done when sides are firm.   *Makes 9 popovers*

Chive Whole Wheat Drop Biscuits

1¼ cups whole wheat flour

¾ cup all-purpose flour

3 tablespoons toasted wheat germ, divided

1 tablespoon baking powder

1 tablespoon chopped fresh chives *or* 1 teaspoon dried chives

2 teaspoons sugar

3 tablespoons cold margarine

1 cup fat-free (skim) milk

½ cup shredded low-fat process American cheese

1. Preheat oven to 450°F. Spray baking sheet with nonstick cooking spray. Combine whole wheat flour, all-purpose flour, 2 tablespoons wheat germ, baking powder, chives and sugar in medium bowl. Cut in margarine with pastry blender or two knives until mixture resembles coarse meal. Add milk and American cheese; stir until just combined.

2. Drop dough by rounded teaspoonfuls onto prepared baking sheet about 1 inch apart. Sprinkle with remaining 1 tablespoon wheat germ. Bake 10 to 12 minutes or until golden brown. Remove immediately from baking sheet. Serve warm.   *Makes 12 servings*

Tropical Treat Muffins

2 cups all-purpose flour

⅓ cup plus 1 tablespoon sugar, divided

1 tablespoon baking powder

1 teaspoon grated lemon peel

½ teaspoon salt

¾ cup (4 ounces) finely diced, dried papaya

½ cup coarsely chopped banana chips

½ cup chopped macadamia nuts

¼ cup flaked coconut

½ cup milk

½ cup butter, melted

¼ cup sour cream

1 egg, beaten

1. Preheat oven to 400°F. Grease or paperline 12 (2½-inch) or 6 (4-inch) large muffin cups.

2. Combine flour, ⅓ cup sugar, baking powder, lemon peel and salt in large bowl. Combine papaya, banana chips, macadamia nuts and coconut in small bowl; stir in 1 tablespoon flour mixture until well coated.

3. Combine milk, butter, sour cream and egg in another small bowl until blended; stir into flour mixture just until moistened. Fold in fruit mixture. Spoon evenly into prepared muffin cups. Sprinkle remaining 1 tablespoon sugar over tops of muffins.

4. Bake 15 to 20 minutes for regular-size muffins, 25 to 30 minutes for muffins, or until toothpick inserted in centers comes out clean. Remove from pan. Cool on wire rack.

Makes 12 regular-size or 6 large muffins

Streusel-Topped Blueberry Muffins

1½ cups plus ⅓ cup all-purpose flour, divided

½ cup plus ⅓ cup sugar, divided

1 teaspoon ground cinnamon

3 tablespoons cold butter, cut into small pieces

2 teaspoons baking powder

½ teaspoon salt

1 cup milk

¼ cup butter, melted and slightly cooled

1 egg, beaten

1 teaspoon vanilla

1 cup fresh blueberries

1. Preheat oven to 375°F. Grease or paper-line 12 (2½-inch) muffin cups; set aside.

2. Combine ⅓ cup flour, ⅓ cup sugar and cinnamon in small bowl. Cut in 3 tablespoons butter with pastry blender until mixture resembles coarse crumbs; set aside. Combine remaining 1½ cups flour, ½ cup sugar, baking powder and salt in large bowl.

3. Combine milk, ¼ cup melted butter, egg and vanilla in small bowl. Stir into flour mixture just until moistened. Fold in blueberries. Spoon evenly into prepared muffin cups. Sprinkle reserved topping over top of each muffin.

4. Bake 20 to 25 minutes or until toothpick inserted in center comes out clean. Remove from pan; cool completely.

Makes 12 muffins

Orange Coconut Muffins

¾ cup all-purpose flour
¾ cup whole wheat flour
⅔ cup toasted wheat germ
½ cup sugar
½ cup flaked coconut
1½ teaspoons baking soda
½ teaspoon salt
1 cup dairy sour cream
2 eggs
1 can (11 ounces) mandarin oranges, drained
½ cup chopped nuts

Preheat oven to 400°F. Butter 12 (2½-inch) muffin cups.

Combine flours, wheat germ, sugar, coconut, baking soda and salt in large bowl. Blend sour cream, eggs and oranges in small bowl; stir into flour mixture just until moistened. Fold in nuts. Spoon into prepared muffin cups, filling ¾ full.

Bake 18 to 20 minutes or until toothpick inserted in center comes out clean. Remove from pan. Cool on wire rack.

Makes 12 muffins

Favorite recipe from **Wisconsin Milk Marketing Board**

Orange Coconut Muffins

Quick-As-Can-Be Breads

No need to knead, or set aside time for rising, these breads are mixed together in a matter of minutes and popped right into your oven. Even in our hurry-up world, there's time for delectable Tex-Mex Corn Bread or Lemon Poppy Seed Tea Loaf. Serve them for breakfast, a snack, or dessert. Many taste even better the next day—that is, if they don't get devoured first.

Date Nut Bread

2 cups all-purpose flour
½ cup packed light brown sugar
1 tablespoon baking powder
½ teaspoon salt
¼ cup (½ stick) butter
1 cup toasted chopped walnuts
1 cup chopped dates
1¼ cups milk
1 egg
½ teaspoon grated lemon peel

1. Preheat oven to 375°F. Spray 9×5-inch loaf pan with nonstick cooking spray; set aside.

2. Combine flour, sugar, baking powder and salt in large bowl. Cut in butter with pastry blender or 2 knives until mixture resembles fine crumbs. Add walnuts and dates; stir until coated. Beat milk, egg and lemon peel in small bowl with fork. Add to flour mixture; stir just until moistened. Pour into prepared pan.

3. Bake 45 to 50 minutes or until toothpick inserted into center comes out clean. Cool in pan on wire rack 10 minutes. Remove from pan and cool completely on wire rack. *Makes 12 servings*

Buttermilk Corn Bread Loaf

1½ cups all-purpose flour
1 cup yellow cornmeal
⅓ cup sugar
2 teaspoons baking powder
1 teaspoon salt
½ teaspoon baking soda
½ cup vegetable shortening
1⅓ cups buttermilk*
2 eggs

Or, substitute soured fresh milk. To sour milk, place 4 teaspoons lemon juice plus enough milk to equal 1⅓ cups in 2-cup measure. Stir; let stand 5 minutes before using.

1. Preheat oven to 375°F. Grease 8½×4½-inch loaf pan; set aside.

2. Combine flour, cornmeal, sugar, baking powder, salt and baking soda in medium bowl. Cut in shortening with pastry blender or 2 knives until mixture resembles coarse crumbs.

3. Whisk together buttermilk and eggs in small bowl. Make well in center of dry ingredients. Add buttermilk mixture; stir until mixture forms stiff batter. (Batter will be lumpy.) Turn into prepared pan; spread mixture evenly, removing any air bubbles.

4. Bake 50 to 55 minutes or until toothpick inserted in center comes out clean. Cool in pan on wire rack 10 minutes. Remove from pan; cool on rack 10 minutes more. Serve warm. *Makes 1 loaf*

Morning Glory Bread

2½ cups all-purpose flour
2 teaspoons baking powder
1 teaspoon baking soda
½ teaspoon salt
½ teaspoon ground cinnamon
¼ teaspoon ground nutmeg
¼ teaspoon ground allspice
¾ cup granulated sugar
¾ cup firmly packed light brown sugar
½ cup MOTT'S® Chunky Apple Sauce
3 egg whites
1 tablespoon vegetable oil
1 tablespoon GRANDMA'S® Molasses
¾ cup finely shredded carrots
½ cup raisins
⅓ cup drained crushed pineapple in juice
¼ cup shredded coconut

1. Preheat oven to 375°F. Spray 8½×4½-inch loaf pan with nonstick cooking spray.

2. In large bowl, combine flour, baking powder, baking soda, salt, cinnamon, nutmeg and allspice.

3. In medium bowl, combine granulated sugar, brown sugar, apple sauce, egg whites, oil and molasses.

4. Stir apple sauce mixture into flour mixture just until moistened. Fold in carrots, raisins, pineapple and coconut. Spread into prepared pan.

5. Bake 45 to 50 minutes or until toothpick inserted in center comes out clean. Cool in pan 10 minutes. Invert onto wire rack; turn right side up. Cool completely. Cut into 16 slices. *Makes 16 servings*

Buttermilk Corn Bread Loaf

Lemon Poppy Seed Tea Loaf

Tea Loaf

2½ **cups all-purpose flour**

¼ **cup poppy seeds**

1 **tablespoon grated lemon peel**

2 **teaspoons baking powder**

½ **teaspoon baking soda**

½ **teaspoon salt**

1 **cup sugar**

⅔ **cup MOTT'S® Natural Apple Sauce**

1 **whole egg**

2 **egg whites, lightly beaten**

2 **tablespoons vegetable oil**

1 **teaspoon vanilla extract**

⅓ **cup skim milk**

Lemon Syrup

¼ **cup sugar**

¼ **cup lemon juice**

1. Preheat oven to 350°F. Spray 9×5-inch loaf pan with nonstick cooking spray.

2. To prepare Tea Loaf, in large bowl, combine flour, poppy seeds, lemon peel, baking powder, baking soda and salt.

3. In medium bowl, combine 1 cup sugar, apple sauce, whole egg, egg whites, oil and vanilla.

4. Stir apple sauce mixture into flour mixture alternately with milk. Mix until thoroughly moistened. Spread batter into prepared pan.

5. Bake 40 to 45 minutes or until toothpick inserted in center comes out clean. Cool in pan 10 minutes. Invert onto wire rack; turn right side up.

6. To prepare Lemon Syrup, in small saucepan, combine ¼ cup sugar and lemon juice. Cook, stirring frequently, until sugar dissolves. Cool slightly.

7. Pierce top of loaf in several places with metal skewer. Brush lemon syrup over loaf. Let stand until cool. Cut into 16 slices.

Makes 16 servings

Grandma's® Gingerbread

½ **cup shortening or butter**

½ **cup sugar**

1 **cup GRANDMA'S® Molasses**

2 **eggs**

2½ **cups all-purpose flour**

1 **teaspoon salt**

2 **teaspoons baking powder**

½ **teaspoon baking soda**

1 **teaspoon ground ginger**

2 **teaspoons ground cinnamon**

½ **teaspoon ground cloves**

1 **cup hot water**

Heat oven to 350°F. In medium bowl, blend shortening with sugar, add molasses and eggs. Beat well. Sift dry ingredients, add alternately with water to molasses mixture. Bake in greased 9-inch square pan, about 50 minutes.

Makes 8 servings

Oven-Tested Tips

Always measure baking powder and baking soda carefully. Too much leavening gives quick bread a dry texture and a bitter aftertaste. Too little leavening produces bread with a dense, heavy texture.

Southern Spoon Bread

4 eggs, separated

3 cups milk

1 cup yellow cornmeal

3 tablespoons butter or margarine

1 teaspoon salt

¼ teaspoon black pepper *or*
   ⅛ teaspoon ground red pepper

1 teaspoon baking powder

1 tablespoon grated Parmesan cheese
   (optional)

1. Preheat oven to 375°F. Spray 2-quart round casserole with nonstick cooking spray; set aside. Beat egg yolks in small bowl; set aside.

2. Heat milk almost to a boil in medium saucepan over medium heat. Gradually beat in cornmeal using wire whisk. Cook 2 minutes, stirring constantly. Whisk in butter, salt and pepper. Beat about ¼ cup cornmeal mixture into egg yolks. Beat egg yolk mixture into remaining cornmeal mixture; set aside.

3. Beat egg whites in large bowl with electric mixer at high speed until stiff peaks form. Stir baking powder into cornmeal mixture. Stir about ¼ cup egg whites into cornmeal mixture. Gradually fold in remaining egg whites. Pour into prepared casserole; sprinkle with cheese, if desired.

4. Bake 30 to 35 minutes or until golden brown and toothpick inserted into center comes out clean. Serve immediately.

Makes 6 servings

Southern Spoon Bread

Tex-Mex Quick Bread

1½ cups all-purpose flour
1 cup (4 ounces) shredded Monterey Jack cheese
½ cup cornmeal
½ cup sun-dried tomatoes, coarsely chopped
1 can (about 4 ounces) black olives, drained and chopped
¼ cup sugar
1½ teaspoons baking powder
1 teaspoon baking soda
1 cup milk
1 can (about 4 ounces) green chilies, drained and chopped
¼ cup olive oil
1 large egg, beaten

1. Preheat oven to 325°F. Grease 9×5-inch loaf pan or four 5×3-inch loaf pans; set aside.

2. Combine flour, cheese, cornmeal, tomatoes, olives, sugar, baking powder and baking soda in large bowl.

3. Combine remaining ingredients in small bowl. Add to flour mixture; stir just until combined. Pour into prepared pan. Bake 9×5-inch loaf 45 minutes and 5×3-inch loaves 30 minutes or until toothpick inserted near center of loaf comes out clean. Cool in pan 15 minutes. Remove from pan and cool on wire rack.

Makes 1 large loaf or 4 small loaves

Muffin Variation: Preheat oven to 375°F. Spoon batter into 12 well-greased muffin cups. Bake 20 minutes or until toothpick inserted near center of muffin comes out clean. Makes 12 muffins.

Lots o' Chocolate Bread

⅔ cup packed light brown sugar
½ cup butter, softened
2 cups miniature semisweet chocolate chips, divided
2 eggs
2½ cups all-purpose flour
1½ cups applesauce
1 teaspoon baking soda
1 teaspoon baking powder
½ teaspoon salt
1½ teaspoons vanilla
1 tablespoon shortening (do not use butter, margarine, spread or oil)

Preheat oven to 350°F. Grease 5 (5½×3-inch) mini loaf pans. Beat brown sugar and butter in large bowl with electric mixer until creamy. Melt 1 cup chocolate chips; cool slightly and add to sugar mixture with eggs. Add flour, applesauce, baking soda, baking powder, salt and vanilla; beat until well mixed. Stir in ½ cup chocolate chips. Spoon batter into prepared pans; bake 35 to 40 minutes or until center crack is dry to the touch. Cool 10 minutes before removing from pans.

Place remaining ½ cup chocolate chips and shortening in small microwavable bowl. Microwave at HIGH 1 minute; stir. If necessary, microwave at HIGH an additional 15 seconds at a time, stirring after each heating. Drizzle warm loaves with glaze. Cool completely.

Makes 5 mini loaves

Chocolate Chip Lemon Loaf

¾ cup granulated sugar
½ cup vegetable shortening
2 eggs, lightly beaten
1⅔ cups all-purpose flour
1½ teaspoons baking powder
¼ teaspoon salt
¾ cup milk
½ cup chocolate chips
   Grated peel of 1 lemon
   Juice of 1 lemon
¼ to ½ cup powdered sugar
   Melted chocolate (optional)

Slow Cooker Directions

1. Grease 2-quart soufflé dish or 2-pound coffee can; set aside. Beat granulated sugar and shortening until blended. Add eggs, one at a time, mixing well after each addition.

2. Sift together flour, baking powder and salt. Add flour mixture and milk alternately to shortening mixture. Stir in chocolate chips and lemon peel.

3. Spoon batter into prepared dish. Cover with greased foil. Place in preheated slow cooker. Cook, covered, with slow cooker lid slightly ajar to allow excess moisture to escape, on HIGH 1¾ to 2 hours or on LOW 3 to 4 hours or until edges are golden and knife inserted in center of loaf comes out clean. Remove dish from slow cooker; remove foil. Place loaf on wire rack to cool completely.

4. Combine lemon juice and ¼ cup powdered sugar in small bowl. Add more sugar as needed to reach desired sweetness. Pour glaze over loaf. Drizzle loaf with melted chocolate, if desired. *Makes 8 servings*

Golden Apple Buttermilk Bread

1½ cups unsifted all-purpose flour
1 cup whole wheat flour
½ cup natural bran cereal
1 teaspoon baking soda
½ teaspoon baking powder
¼ teaspoon ground ginger
1⅓ cups buttermilk
¾ cup sugar
¼ cup vegetable oil
1 large egg
1 teaspoon grated orange peel
1 cup chopped Washington Golden Delicious apples

1. Heat oven to 350°F. Grease 9×5-inch loaf pan. In medium bowl, combine flours, bran, baking soda, baking powder and ginger. In large bowl, beat together buttermilk, sugar, oil, egg and orange peel.

2. Add flour mixture to buttermilk mixture, stirring just until combined. Fold in apples. Spread batter in prepared pan and bake 45 to 50 minutes or until wooden toothpick inserted in center comes out clean. Cool bread in pan 10 minutes. Remove from pan and cool on wire rack.

Makes 1 loaf (8 servings)

Favorite recipe from **Washington Apple Commission**

Chocolate Chip Lemon Loaf

Coconut Date Nut Quick Bread

2 cups all-purpose flour

2 teaspoons baking powder

½ teaspoon baking soda

½ teaspoon salt

2 eggs

¾ cup thawed frozen unsweetened apple juice concentrate

¼ cup (½ stick) butter, melted

¼ cup fat-free (skim) milk

2 teaspoons vanilla

1 cup chopped pitted dates

½ cup chopped walnuts or pecans

⅓ cup unsweetened flaked coconut*

Cream cheese (optional)

Unsweetened flaked coconut is available in health food stores.

1. Preheat oven to 350°F. Combine dry ingredients in medium bowl; set aside.

2. Beat eggs in separate medium bowl. Blend in apple juice concentrate, butter, milk and vanilla. Add to dry ingredients; mix just until moistened.

3. Stir in dates, walnuts and coconut. Spread into greased 9×5-inch loaf pan.

4. Bake 45 minutes or until toothpick inserted in center comes out clean. Cool 10 minutes in pan on wire rack. Remove from pan; cool completely. Slice and serve at room temperature, or toast slices and spread with cream cheese, if desired.

Makes 12 servings

Walnut Cheddar Apple Bread

½ cup (1 stick) butter, softened

1 cup packed light brown sugar

2 eggs

1 teaspoon vanilla

2 cups all-purpose flour

2 teaspoons baking powder

1 teaspoon baking soda

¼ teaspoon salt

1 cup sour cream

¼ cup milk

1 cup (4 ounces) shredded Cheddar cheese

1 cup diced dried apples

½ cup coarsely chopped walnuts

1. Preheat oven to 350°F. Grease 9×5-inch loaf pan.

2. Beat butter and sugar in large bowl with electric mixer on medium speed until light and fluffy. Beat in eggs and vanilla until blended.

3. Combine flour, baking powder, baking soda and salt in small bowl. Add flour mixture to butter mixture on low speed alternately with sour cream and milk, beginning and ending with flour mixture. Mix well after each addition. Stir in cheese, apples and walnuts. Spoon batter into prepared pan.

4. Bake 50 to 55 minutes or until toothpick inserted in center comes out clean. Cool in pan 15 minutes. Remove from pan and cool completely on wire rack. Store tightly wrapped in plastic wrap at room temperature.

Makes 1 loaf

Onion-Wheat Pan Bread

⅓ cup wheat germ, divided
1¾ cups all-purpose flour
2 tablespoons sugar
1¾ teaspoons baking powder
½ teaspoon salt
1 cup milk
⅓ cup finely chopped green onions
⅓ cup vegetable oil
1 egg
2 tablespoons grated Parmesan
    cheese
1 tablespoon toasted sesame seeds

1. Preheat oven to 400°F. Spray 9-inch cast iron skillet with nonstick cooking spray.* Heat skillet in oven 5 minutes. Reserve 1 tablespoon wheat germ; set aside.

2. Combine remaining wheat germ, flour, sugar, baking powder and salt in large bowl. Beat milk, onions, oil and egg in medium bowl with fork. Add to flour mixture; stir just until moistened. Spoon into preheated skillet. Sprinkle with reserved wheat germ, cheese and sesame seeds.

3. Bake 15 minutes or until golden brown and toothpick inserted into center comes out clean. Cool in pan on wire rack 15 minutes. Serve warm.

Makes 12 servings

Or, substitute 9-inch round pan sprayed with nonstick cooking spray. Do not preheat pan in oven. Increase baking time 5 minutes for a total of 20 minutes.

Spiced Kahlúa® Loaf

1¼ cups all-purpose flour
1 cup whole wheat flour
¾ cup sugar
2 teaspoons baking powder
1 teaspoon salt
¾ teaspoon baking soda
½ teaspoon cinnamon
¼ teaspoon ginger
3 eggs
⅓ cup KAHLÚA® Liqueur
¾ cup oil
1½ cups grated carrots, lightly packed
½ cup finely chopped hazelnuts
    Kahlúa® Glaze (recipe follows)
    Chopped nuts (optional)

Stir together flours, sugar, baking powder, salt, baking soda, cinnamon and ginger in large bowl. Beat eggs well in medium bowl. Beat in Kahlúa® and oil; blend egg mixture into flour mixture. Add carrots and nuts; mix well. Divide batter between two well-greased loaf pans (7½×3¾×2¼-inches) or one pan (9×5×3-inches). Bake in 350°F oven 40 minutes for small loaves or about 60 minutes for larger loaf, until wooden toothpick inserted in centers of loaves comes out clean. Cool in pan 10 minutes; turn out onto wire rack to cool completely. Brush Kahlúa® Glaze over top of cooled loaves. Sprinkle with chopped nuts, if desired, before glaze sets.

Makes 2 small or 1 large loaf

Kahlúa® Glaze: Combine 2 cups powdered sugar, 2 tablespoons Kahlúa® and 1 tablespoon heavy cream in large bowl; beat until smooth.

Onion-Wheat Pan Bread

Peanut Butter Chocolate Chip Loaves

3 cups all-purpose flour
1½ teaspoons baking powder
1 teaspoon baking soda
1 teaspoon salt
1 cup creamy peanut butter
½ cup granulated sugar
½ cup packed light brown sugar
½ cup butter, softened
2 eggs
1½ cups buttermilk*
2 teaspoons vanilla
1 cup miniature semisweet chocolate chips

*You may substitute soured fresh milk. To sour milk, place 4½ teaspoons lemon juice plus enough milk to equal 1½ cups in 2-cup measure. Stir; let stand 5 minutes before using.

1. Preheat oven to 350°F. Spray two 8½×4½-inch loaf pans with nonstick cooking spray; set aside.

2. Sift flour, baking powder, baking soda and salt into large bowl. Beat peanut butter, granulated sugar, brown sugar and butter in second large bowl with electric mixer at medium speed until light and fluffy. Beat in eggs, one at a time. Beat in buttermilk and vanilla. Gradually add flour mixture. Beat at low speed until blended. Stir in chocolate chips. Divide batter evenly between prepared pans.

3. Bake 45 minutes or until toothpick inserted into centers comes out clean. Cool in pans on wire racks 10 minutes. Remove from pans and cool completely on wire racks. *Makes 2 loaves*

Variation: Stir in ¾ cup chocolate chips before baking; sprinkle with remaining ¼ cup after baking.

Peanut Butter Chocolate Chip Loaf

Boston Brown Bread

Boston Brown Bread

3 (16-ounce) cleaned and emptied
   vegetable cans
½ cup rye flour
½ cup yellow cornmeal
½ cup whole wheat flour
3 tablespoons sugar
1 teaspoon baking soda
¾ teaspoon salt
½ cup chopped walnuts
½ cup raisins
1 cup buttermilk*
⅓ cup molasses

*Soured fresh milk may be substituted. To sour,
place 1 tablespoon lemon juice plus enough milk to
equal 1 cup in 2-cup measure. Stir; let stand
5 minutes before using.

Slow Cooker Directions

1. Spray vegetable cans and 1 side of three
6-inch-square pieces of foil with nonstick
cooking spray; set aside. Combine rye flour,
cornmeal, whole wheat flour, sugar, baking
soda and salt in large bowl. Stir in walnuts
and raisins.

2. Whisk buttermilk and molasses in
medium bowl until blended. Add buttermilk
mixture to dry ingredients; stir until well
mixed. Spoon mixture evenly into prepared
cans. Place 1 piece of foil, greased side
down, on top of each can. Secure foil with
rubber bands or cotton string.

3. Place filled cans in slow cooker. Pour
boiling water into slow cooker to come
halfway up sides of cans. (Make sure foil
tops do not touch boiling water.) Cover;
cook on LOW 4 hours or until skewer
inserted in centers comes out clean. To
remove bread, lay cans on side; roll and tap
gently on all sides until bread releases. Cool
completely on wire racks.   *Makes 3 loaves*

Breadstick Sampler

1 can (11 ounces) refrigerated
    breadstick dough (8 breadsticks)
1 tablespoon grated Parmesan cheese
⅛ teaspoon ground red pepper
½ teaspoon dried basil leaves
½ teaspoon dried oregano leaves
½ teaspoon dried thyme leaves
2 tablespoons olive oil
1 tablespoon garlic powder, divided

1. Preheat oven to 350°F. Separate and unroll strips of dough. Twist each breadstick several times and place on greased cookie sheet about 1 inch apart. Press ends firmly onto pans to anchor.

2. Combine cheese and pepper in small bowl. Combine basil, oregano and thyme in another small bowl.

3. Brush all 8 breadsticks with olive oil. Sprinkle 2 breadsticks with a teaspoon each of garlic powder. Sprinkle two breaksticks with a teaspoon each of cheese-pepper mixture. Sprinkle 2 breadsticks with ½ teaspoon each of herb mixture. For the last pair of breadsticks, sprinkle each with remaining garlic powder, cheese-pepper mixture and herb mixture.

4. Bake 15 minutes or until golden brown. Transfer to wire rack to cool 5 minutes. Serve warm. *Makes 8 breadsticks*

Cook's Notes: You can easily adapt this recipe by sprinkling on your favorite toppings. Try sesame or poppy seeds, seasoned salt, onion powder or cinnamon and sugar.

Apricot Carrot Bread

1¾ cups all-purpose flour
1 teaspoon baking powder
¼ teaspoon baking soda
¼ teaspoon salt
½ cup granulated sugar
½ cup finely shredded carrots
½ cup MOTT'S® Natural Apple
    Sauce
1 egg, beaten lightly
2 tablespoons vegetable oil
⅓ cup dried apricots, snipped into
    small bits
½ cup powdered sugar
2 teaspoons MOTT'S® Apple Juice

1. Preheat oven to 350°F. Spray 8×4-inch loaf pan with nonstick cooking spray.

2. In large bowl, combine flour, baking powder, baking soda and salt.

3. In small bowl, combine granulated sugar, carrots, apple sauce, egg and oil.

4. Stir apple sauce mixture into flour mixture just until moistened. (Batter will be thick.) Fold in apricots. Spread batter into prepared pan.

5. Bake 45 to 50 minutes or until toothpick inserted in center comes out clean. Cool in pan 10 minutes. Invert onto wire rack; turn right side up. Cool completely. For best flavor, wrap loaf in plastic wrap or foil; store at room temperature overnight.

6. Just before serving, in small bowl, combine powdered sugar and apple juice until smooth. Drizzle over top of loaf. Cut into 12 slices. *Makes 12 servings*

Quick Pumpkin Bread

1 cup packed light brown sugar
⅓ cup cold butter, cut into 5 pieces
2 eggs
1 cup canned pumpkin
1½ cups all-purpose flour
½ cup whole wheat flour
1½ teaspoons pumpkin pie spice
1 teaspoon baking soda
¾ teaspoon salt
½ teaspoon baking powder
¼ teaspoon ground cardamom (optional)
½ cup dark raisins or chopped, pitted dates
½ cup chopped pecans or walnuts

1. Preheat oven to 350°F. Fit processor with steel blade. Measure sugar and butter into work bowl. Process until smooth, about 10 seconds.

2. Turn on processor and add eggs one at a time through feed tube. Add pumpkin, flours, pie spice, baking soda, salt, baking powder and cardamom, if desired. Process just until flour is moistened, about 5 seconds. *Do not overprocess.* Batter should be lumpy.

3. Sprinkle raisins and nuts over batter. Process using on/off pulsing action 2 or 3 times or just until raisins and nuts are mixed into batter.

4. Turn batter into greased 9×5-inch loaf pan or 3 greased 5¾×3¼-inch loaf pans. Bake until wooden pick inserted in center comes out clean, about 1 hour for larger loaf or 30 to 35 minutes for smaller loaves. Cool bread 15 minutes in pan. Remove from pan and cool on wire rack.

Makes 1 large or 3 small loaves

Chocolate-Chocolate Chip Bread

⅔ cup sugar
⅓ cup Dried Plum Purée (recipe follows) or prepared dried plum butter
2 egg whites
¼ cup semisweet miniature chocolate chips, melted
½ cup nonfat milk
1 teaspoon vanilla
1⅓ cups all-purpose flour
½ teaspoon baking powder
½ teaspoon salt
¼ teaspoon baking soda
⅓ cup semisweet miniature chocolate chips

Preheat oven to 350°F. Coat 8½×4½×2¾-inch loaf pan with vegetable cooking spray. In mixer bowl, beat sugar, dried plum purée, egg whites and melted chocolate chips until well blended. Mix in milk and vanilla. In medium bowl, combine flour, baking powder, salt and baking soda; stir into sugar mixture just until blended. Stir in chocolate chips. Spoon batter into prepared pan. Bake in center of oven 40 to 45 minutes until springy to the touch and pick inserted into center comes out clean. Cool in pan 5 minutes; remove from pan to wire rack. Cool completely before slicing.

Makes 1 loaf (12 slices)

Dried Plum Purée: Combine 1⅓ cups (8 ounces) pitted dried plums and 6 tablespoons hot water in container of food processor or blender. Pulse on and off until dried plums are finely chopped and smooth. Store leftovers in covered container in refrigerator for up to two months. Makes 1 cup.

Favorite recipe from **California Dried Plum Board**

Irish Soda Bread

4 cups all-purpose flour

¼ cup sugar

1 tablespoon baking powder

1 teaspoon baking soda

1 teaspoon salt

1 tablespoon caraway seeds

⅓ cup vegetable shortening

1 cup raisins or currants

1 egg

1¼ cups buttermilk*

Or, substitute soured fresh milk. To sour milk, place 2 tablespoons lemon juice plus enough milk to equal 1¾ cups in 2-cup measure. Stir; let stand 5 minutes before using.

1. Preheat oven to 350°F. Grease large baking sheet; set aside.

2. Sift flour, sugar, baking powder, baking soda and salt into large bowl. Stir in caraway seeds. Cut in shortening with pastry blender or 2 knives until mixture resembles coarse crumbs. Stir in raisins. Beat egg in medium bowl using fork. Add buttermilk; beat until well combined. Add buttermilk mixture to flour mixture; stir until mixture forms soft dough that clings together and forms a ball.

3. Turn dough out onto well-floured surface. Knead dough gently 10 to 12 times. Place dough on prepared baking sheet. Pat dough into 7-inch round. Score top of dough with tip of sharp knife, making an "X" about 4 inches long and ¼ inch deep.

4. Bake 55 to 60 minutes or until toothpick inserted in center comes out clean. Immediately remove from baking sheet; cool on wire rack.** Bread is best eaten the day it is made.   *Makes 12 servings*

**For a sweet crust, combine 1 tablespoon sugar and 1 tablespoon water in custard cup. Brush over hot loaf.*

Irish Soda Bread

Banana Bread

1 cup FIBER ONE® cereal

1½ cups mashed ripe bananas (3 to 4 medium)

⅔ cup milk

1 teaspoon vanilla

1¼ cups sugar

½ cup margarine,* softened

2 eggs

2½ cups GOLD MEDAL® all-purpose flour

3 teaspoons baking powder

1 teaspoon ground cinnamon

½ teaspoon salt

If you substitute a spread for the margarine, for best results, use one with at least 65% vegetable oil.

1. Place oven rack in lowest position. Heat oven to 350°F. Grease bottoms only of two 8½×4½×2½-inch loaf pans or one 9×5×3-inch loaf pan.

2. Crush cereal.** Stir together cereal, bananas, milk and vanilla; let stand about 5 minutes or until cereal is softened.

3. Stir together sugar and margarine in large bowl. Stir in eggs until well blended. Beat in banana mixture thoroughly with fork. Stir in remaining ingredients just until moistened. Pour into prepared pans.

4. Bake 8-inch loaves 40 to 50 minutes (9-inch loaf 50 to 60 minutes) or until toothpick inserted in centers comes out clean. Cool 10 minutes. Loosen sides of loaves; remove from pans to wire racks. Cool completely before slicing.

Makes two 8-inch loaves (12 slices each) or one 9-inch loaf (24 slices)

**Place cereal in plastic bag or between sheets of waxed paper and crush with rolling pin. Or, crush in blender or food processor.*

Prep Time: 15 minutes
Bake Time: 60 minutes

Rosemary Breadsticks

⅔ cup reduced-fat (2%) milk

¼ cup finely chopped fresh chives

2 teaspoons baking powder

1 teaspoon finely chopped fresh rosemary *or* ½ teaspoon dried rosemary

¾ teaspoon salt

½ teaspoon black pepper

¾ cup whole wheat flour

¾ cup all-purpose flour

Nonstick cooking spray

1. Combine milk, chives, baking powder, rosemary, salt and pepper in large bowl; mix well. Stir in flours, ½ cup at a time, until blended. Turn onto floured surface and knead dough about 5 minutes or until smooth and elastic, adding more flour if dough is sticky. Let stand 30 minutes at room temperature.

2. Preheat oven to 375°F. Spray baking sheet with cooking spray. Divide dough into 12 balls, about 1¼ ounces each. Roll each ball into long thin rope; place on prepared baking sheet. Lightly spray breadsticks with cooking spray. Bake about 12 minutes or until bottoms are golden brown. Turn breadsticks over; bake about 10 minutes more or until golden brown.

Makes 12 breadsticks

Oven-Tested Tips

Store quick breads in plastic bags or wrapped in plastic at room temperature for up to three days. Freeze them in plastic bags or tightly wrapped in heavy-duty foil for up to three months.

Banana Bread

Oh My, Pie!

Getting your piece of the pie has never been easier or more fun. Try recipes for double-crust fruit pies, fancy tarts, chocolate pies, pecan pies and much more. Every one is guaranteed to rate "oohs" and "aahs" from family and friends. Nothing makes a kitchen feel more like home than a pie cooling on the counter.

Apple Cranberry Pie

1 package (8 ounces) PHILADELPHIA® Cream Cheese, softened
½ cup firmly packed brown sugar, divided
1 egg
1 unbaked pastry shell (9 inch)
2 cups sliced apples
½ cup halved cranberries
1 teaspoon ground cinnamon, divided
⅓ cup flour
⅓ cup old-fashioned or quick-cooking oats, uncooked
¼ cup (½ stick) butter or margarine
¼ cup chopped PLANTER'S® Walnuts

BEAT cream cheese and ¼ cup of the sugar with electric mixer on medium speed until well blended. Blend in egg. Pour into pastry shell.

TOSS apples, cranberries and ½ teaspoon of the cinnamon. Spoon over cream cheese mixture in pastry shell.

MIX flour, oats, remaining ¼ cup sugar and remaining ½ teaspoon cinnamon. Cut in butter until mixture resembles coarse crumbs. Stir in walnuts. Spoon over fruit mixture.

BAKE at 375°F for 40 to 45 minutes or until lightly browned. Cool slightly before serving.

Makes 8 to 10 servings

Prep Time: 15 minutes
Bake Time: 45 minutes

The "Ultimate" Peanut Butter Whoopie Pie

Pies

- ½ **Butter Flavor CRISCO® Stick or ½ cup Butter Flavor CRISCO® all-vegetable shortening plus additional for greasing**
- 1 **cup milk**
- 1 **tablespoon white vinegar**
- 1 **cup granulated sugar**
- 1 **cup firmly packed brown sugar**
- ¾ **cup JIF® Crunchy Peanut Butter**
- 1 **cup boiling water**
- 1 **teaspoon vanilla**
- 4 **cups all-purpose flour**
- ½ **cup unsweetened cocoa powder**
- 2 **teaspoons baking soda**
- ½ **teaspoon baking powder**
- ½ **teaspoon salt**

Filling

- ½ **cup milk**
- 3 **tablespoons all-purpose flour**
- 2 **cups confectioners' sugar**
- ½ **Butter Flavor CRISCO® Stick or ½ cup Butter Flavor CRISCO® all-vegetable shortening**
- ½ **cup JIF® Creamy Peanut Butter**
- 1 **teaspoon vanilla**

1. Heat oven to 425°F. Grease baking sheet with shortening. Place sheets of foil on countertop for cooling pies.

2. For pies, combine 1 cup milk and vinegar in small microwavable bowl. Microwave at HIGH to warm slightly (or on rangetop in small saucepan on medium heat). Mixture will appear separated and curdled.

3. Combine granulated sugar, brown sugar and crunchy peanut butter in large bowl. Beat at medium speed with electric mixer until crumbly.

4. Combine ½ cup shortening and boiling water. Stir to melt shortening. Add to peanut butter mixture along with milk mixture and vanilla. Beat at low speed. Mixture will be very fluid and somewhat separated.

5. Combine 4 cups flour, cocoa, baking soda, baking powder and salt. Stir well. Add all at once to peanut butter mixture. Beat at low speed until mixture is blended and resembles thick cake batter. Let stand 20 minutes. Drop by rounded measuring tablespoonfuls 2 inches apart onto prepared baking sheet.

6. Bake in upper half of oven for 8 to 10 minutes or until set. *Do not overbake.* Cool 2 minutes on baking sheet. Remove pies to foil to cool completely.

7. For filling, combine ½ cup milk and 3 tablespoons flour in small saucepan. Cook and stir on medium heat until thickened. Cool completely. Add confectioners' sugar, ½ cup shortening, creamy peanut butter and vanilla. Beat at low speed until blended. Beat at high until smooth. Refrigerate until ready to use. Spread filling on bottoms of half of the pies. Top with remaining halves. Press together gently.

Makes 2½ dozen Whoopie Pies

Cider Apple Pie in Cheddar Crust

Crust

   2 cups sifted all-purpose flour

   1 cup shredded Cheddar cheese

   ½ teaspoon salt

   ⅔ CRISCO® Stick or ⅔ cup CRISCO® all-vegetable shortening

   5 to 6 tablespoons ice water

Filling

   6 cups sliced peeled apples (about 2 pounds or 6 medium)

   1 cup apple cider

   ⅔ cup sugar

   2 tablespoons cornstarch

   2 tablespoons water

   ½ teaspoon cinnamon

   1 tablespoon butter or margarine

Glaze

   1 egg yolk

   1 tablespoon water

1. Heat oven to 400°F.

2. For crust, place flour, cheese and salt in food processor bowl. Add shortening. Process 15 seconds. Sprinkle water through food chute, 1 tablespoon at a time, until dough just forms (process time not to exceed 20 seconds). Shape into ball. Divide dough in half. Press between hands to form two 5- to 6-inch "pancakes." Roll and press bottom crust into 9-inch pie plate.

3. For filling, combine apples, apple cider and sugar in large saucepan. Cook and stir on medium-high heat until mixture comes to a boil. Reduce heat to low. Simmer 5 minutes. Combine cornstarch, water and cinnamon. Stir into apples. Cook and stir until mixture comes to a boil. Remove from heat. Stir in butter. Spoon into unbaked pie crust. Moisten pastry edge with water.

4. Roll top crust. Lift onto filled pie. Trim ½ inch beyond edge of pie plate. Fold top edge under bottom crust. Flute. Cut slits or design in top crust to allow steam to escape.

5. For glaze, beat egg yolk with fork. Stir in water. Brush over top.

6. Bake at 400°F for 35 to 40 minutes or until filling in center is bubbly and crust is golden brown. Cover edge with foil, if necessary, to prevent overbrowning. *Do not overbake.* Cool to room temperature before serving.   *Makes 1 (9-inch) pie*

Note: Golden Delicious, Granny Smith and Jonathan apples are all suitable for pie baking.

Chocolate Brownie Pie

   2 eggs

   1 cup sugar

   ½ cup (1 stick) butter or margarine, melted

   ½ cup all-purpose flour

   ⅓ cup HERSHEY'S Cocoa

   ¼ teaspoon salt

   ½ cup HERSHEY'S Semi-Sweet Chocolate Chips

   ½ cup chopped nuts

   1 teaspoon vanilla extract

   Vanilla ice cream

   HERSHEY'S Chocolate Shoppe Topping

1. Heat oven to 350°F. Grease 9-inch pie plate.

2. Beat eggs in small bowl; blend in sugar and butter. Stir together flour, cocoa and salt. Add to egg mixture; beat until blended. Stir in chocolate chips, nuts and vanilla. Spread batter into prepared pie plate.

3. Bake 30 to 35 minutes or until set. (Pie will not test done in center.) Cool completely on wire rack. Serve with ice cream and topping.

Makes 6 to 8 servings

Cider Apple Pie in Cheddar Crust

Chocolate Truffle Tart

Crust
- ⅔ cup all-purpose flour
- ½ cup powdered sugar
- ½ cup ground walnuts
- 6 tablespoons butter or margarine, softened
- ⅓ cup NESTLÉ® TOLL HOUSE® Baking Cocoa

Filling
- 1¼ cups heavy whipping cream
- ¼ cup granulated sugar
- 2 cups (12-ounce package) NESTLÉ® TOLL HOUSE® Semi-Sweet Chocolate Morsels
- 2 tablespoons seedless raspberry jam
- Sweetened whipped cream (optional)
- Fresh raspberries (optional)

For Crust
PREHEAT oven to 350°F.

BEAT flour, sugar, nuts, butter and cocoa in large mixer bowl until soft dough forms. Press dough onto bottom and side of ungreased 9 or 9½-inch fluted tart pan with removable bottom.

BAKE for 12 to 14 minutes or until puffed. Cool completely in pan on wire rack.

For Filling
BRING cream and sugar in medium saucepan just to a boil, stirring occasionally. Remove from heat. Stir in morsels and jam; let stand for 5 minutes. Whisk until smooth. Transfer to small mixer bowl. Cover; refrigerate for 45 to 60 minutes or until mixture is cool and slightly thickened.

BEAT for 20 to 30 seconds or just until color lightens slightly. Spoon into crust. Refrigerate until firm. Remove side of pan; garnish with whipped cream and raspberries.

Makes 8 servings

Note: May be made in 9-inch pie plate.

Country Pecan Pie

- Pie pastry for single 9-inch pie crust
- 1¼ cups dark corn syrup
- 4 eggs
- ½ cup packed light brown sugar
- ¼ cup (½ stick) butter or margarine, melted
- 2 teaspoons all-purpose flour
- 1½ teaspoons vanilla
- 1½ cups pecan halves

1. Preheat oven to 350°F. Roll pastry on lightly floured surface to form 13-inch circle. Fit into 9-inch pie plate. Trim edges; flute. Set aside.

2. Combine corn syrup, eggs, brown sugar and melted butter in large bowl; beat with electric mixer on medium speed until well blended. Stir in flour and vanilla until blended. Pour into unbaked pie crust. Arrange pecans on top.

3. Bake 40 to 45 minutes until center of filling is puffed and golden brown. Cool completely on wire rack. Garnish as desired.

Makes one 9-inch pie

The Best Cherry Pie

Reduced-Fat Pie Pastry (recipe follows)

2 bags (12 ounces each) frozen no-sugar-added cherries, thawed and well drained

¾ cup plus 2 teaspoons sugar, divided

1 tablespoon plus 1½ teaspoons cornstarch

1 tablespoon plus 1½ teaspoons quick-cooking tapioca

1 teaspoon fat-free (skim) milk

1. Preheat oven to 425°F.

2. Roll ⅔ of pie pastry on lightly floured surface to 9½-inch circle. Gently press pastry into 8-inch pie pan.

3. Combine cherries, ¾ cup sugar, cornstarch and tapioca in large bowl. Spoon cherry mixture into pastry. Roll remaining pastry into circle large enough to fit top of pie; trim off any excess pastry. Cover pie with crust. Press edges of top and bottom crust together; trim and flute. Cut steam vents in top of pie; brush with milk and sprinkle with remaining 2 teaspoons sugar.

4. Bake 10 minutes. Reduce heat to 375°F; bake 45 to 50 minutes or until pie is bubbly and crust is golden. (Cover edge of crust with foil, if necessary, to prevent burning.) Cool on wire rack; serve warm.

Makes 8 servings

Reduced-Fat Pie Pastry

2 cups all-purpose flour

2 tablespoons sugar

½ teaspoon baking powder

¼ teaspoon salt

7 tablespoons cold shortening

6 to 8 tablespoons ice water

1. Combine flour, sugar, baking powder and salt in medium bowl. Cut in shortening with pastry blender or 2 knives until mixture resembles coarse crumbs. Mix in water, 1 tablespoon at a time, until stiff dough is formed.

2. Cover dough with plastic wrap; refrigerate 30 minutes.

Upside-Down Hot Fudge Sundae Pie

⅔ cup butter or margarine

⅓ cup HERSHEY'S Cocoa

2 eggs

¼ cup milk

1 teaspoon vanilla extract

1 cup packed light brown sugar

½ cup granulated sugar

1 tablespoon all-purpose flour

⅛ teaspoon salt

1 unbaked 9-inch pie crust

2 bananas, peeled and thinly sliced
  Ice cream, any flavor
  Whipped topping

1. Heat oven to 350°F.

2. Melt butter in medium saucepan over low heat. Add cocoa; stir until smooth. Remove from heat. Stir together eggs, milk and vanilla in small bowl. Add egg mixture to cocoa mixture; stir with whisk until smooth and slightly thickened. Add brown sugar, granulated sugar, flour and salt; stir with whisk until smooth. Pour mixture into unbaked crust.

3. Bake 30 to 35 minutes until edge is set. (Center will be soft.) Cool about 2 hours. Just before serving, top each serving with banana slices, ice cream and whipped topping. *Makes 8 servings*

Fabulous Fruit Tart

Pastry for single-crust 9-inch pie

1 package (8 ounces) reduced-fat cream cheese, softened

⅓ cup no-sugar-added raspberry fruit spread

½ cup sliced peaches or nectarines*

½ cup kiwifruit slices*

⅓ cup sliced strawberries*

⅓ cup raspberries*

3 tablespoons no-sugar-added apricot pourable fruit**

2 teaspoons raspberry-flavored liqueur (optional)

Sliced bananas, plums or blueberries may be substituted.

**2 tablespoons no-sugar-added apricot fruit spread combined with 1 tablespoon warm water may be substituted.*

Preheat oven to 350°F. Roll out pastry to 12-inch circle; place in 10-inch tart pan with removable bottom or 10-inch quiche dish. Prick bottom and sides of pastry with fork. Bake 18 to 20 minutes or until golden brown. Cool completely on wire rack.

Combine cream cheese and fruit spread; mix well. Spread onto bottom of cooled pastry. Chill at least 1 hour. Just before serving, arrange fruit over cream cheese layer. Combine pourable fruit and liqueur, if desired; brush evenly over fruit.

Makes 8 servings

The Best Cherry Pie

Minnesota's Fresh Blueberry Cream Cheese Pie

Crust

Classic CRISCO® 9-inch Double Crust (recipe page 132)

Milk or cream

Sugar

Filling

¾ cup plus 2 tablespoons sugar

2 tablespoons cornstarch

⅛ teaspoon salt

1 tablespoon lemon juice

3 cups fresh blueberries, divided

2 tablespoons butter or margarine

Cheese Layer

1 package (3 ounces) cream cheese, softened

2 tablespoons sugar

¼ cup dairy sour cream

½ teaspoon grated lemon peel

Decorations

Baked flower cutouts

7 blueberries

1. Heat oven to 425°F.

2. For crust, prepare as directed. Press two thirds of dough between hands to form 5- to 6-inch "pancake." Form remaining dough into smaller "pancake." Roll and press larger "pancake" into 9-inch pie plate. Bake and cool completely.

3. Roll remaining dough to ⅛-inch thickness. Cut out seven 2-inch flowers using a cookie cutter. Cut ¼-inch hole in center of each. Place on ungreased baking sheet. Brush with milk. Sprinkle with sugar.

4. Bake at 425°F for 7 to 9 minutes or until lightly browned. *Do not overbake.* Cool completely.

5. For filling, combine ¾ cup plus 2 tablespoons sugar, cornstarch and salt in medium saucepan. Add lemon juice and 1½ cups blueberries. Cook and stir on medium heat, until mixture comes to a boil. Simmer, stirring often, until thickened. Remove from heat. Stir in butter. Cool to room temperature. Fold in remaining 1½ cups blueberries.

6. For cheese layer, combine cream cheese, 2 tablespoons sugar, sour cream and lemon peel in small bowl. Beat at medium speed of electric mixer until smooth. Spread on bottom of baked pie crust. Spoon filling over cheese layer.

7. For decorations, place one flower cutout in center of pie and remaining 6 cutouts around edge of filling. Place 1 blueberry in center of each flower. Refrigerate.

Makes 1 (9-inch) pie

Lemon Meringue Pie

1 cup graham cracker crumbs

¼ cup powdered sugar

2 tablespoons margarine, melted

1 tablespoon water

1½ cups granulated sugar, divided

⅓ cup cornstarch

1½ cups hot water

¼ cup cholesterol-free egg substitute

½ cup fresh lemon juice

1½ teaspoons grated lemon peel

3 egg whites

½ teaspoon vanilla

¼ teaspoon cream of tartar

1. Preheat oven to 375°F. Combine graham cracker crumbs and powdered sugar in small bowl. Stir in margarine and water; mix until crumbs are moistened. Press crumb mixture onto bottom and up side of 9-inch pie plate. Bake 6 to 9 minutes or until edges are golden brown. Cool on wire rack. *Reduce oven temperature to 350°F.*

2. Combine ½ cup granulated sugar and cornstarch in medium saucepan over low heat. Gradually stir in hot water until smooth. Add egg substitute. Bring to a boil, stirring constantly with wire whisk. Boil 1 minute. Remove from heat; stir in lemon juice and lemon peel. Pour hot filling into cooled crust.

3. Beat egg whites, vanilla and cream of tartar in large bowl until soft peaks form. Gradually add remaining 1 cup granulated sugar, beating until stiff peaks form. Spread meringue over filling, sealing carefully to edge of crust.

4. Bake 12 to 15 minutes or until meringue is golden brown. Cool to room temperature before serving. *Makes 8 servings*

Minnesota's Fresh Blueberry Cream Cheese Pie

Strawberry Rhubarb Pie

Pastry for double-crust 9-inch pie

4 cups sliced (1-inch pieces) fresh rhubarb

3 cups (1 pint) fresh strawberries, sliced

1½ cups sugar

½ cup cornstarch

2 tablespoons quick-cooking tapioca

1 tablespoon grated lemon peel

¼ teaspoon ground allspice

1 egg, lightly beaten

1. Preheat oven to 425°F. Roll out half the pastry; place in 9-inch pie plate. Trim pastry; flute edges, sealing to edge of pie plate. Set aside.

2. Place fruit in large bowl. In medium bowl, combine sugar, cornstarch, tapioca, lemon peel and allspice; mix well. Sprinkle sugar mixture over fruit; toss to coat well. Fill pie shell evenly with fruit. (Do not mound in center.)

3. Roll out remaining pastry to 10-inch circle. Cut into ½-inch-wide strips. Form into lattice design over fruit. Brush egg over pastry. Bake 50 minutes or until filling is bubbly and thick. Cool on wire rack. Serve warm or at room temperature.

Makes 8 servings

Decadent Pie

¾ cup packed brown sugar

¾ cup light *or* dark corn syrup

4 squares BAKER'S® Semi-Sweet Baking Chocolate

6 tablespoons butter *or* margarine

3 eggs

1⅓ cups BAKER'S® ANGEL FLAKE® Coconut

1 cup chopped pecans

1 unbaked deep dish pie crust (9 inch)

1 tub (8 ounces) COOL WHIP® Whipped Topping, thawed

2 tablespoons bourbon whiskey (optional)

HEAT oven to 350°F.

MICROWAVE brown sugar and corn syrup in large microwavable bowl on HIGH 3 minutes or until boiling. Stir in chocolate and butter until chocolate is completely melted. Cool slightly.

STIR in eggs, one at a time, beating well after each addition. Stir in coconut and pecans. Pour into crust.

BAKE 1 hour or until pie is set. Cool on wire rack. Mix whipped topping and bourbon. Serve with pie.

Makes 8 servings

Top of Stove Directions: Cook and stir brown sugar and corn syrup in heavy 3-quart saucepan on medium heat until boiling. Remove from heat. Add chocolate and butter; stir until chocolate is completely melted. Cool slightly. Continue as directed above.

Prep Time: 15 minutes
Bake Time: 1 hour

Chocolate Almond Pear Torte

⅔ cup flour

2 tablespoons sugar

⅓ cup butter or margarine

½ cup toasted finely chopped blanched almonds

4 squares BAKER'S® Semi-Sweet Baking Chocolate

½ cup (1 stick) butter or margarine

½ cup sugar

⅓ cup heavy (whipping) cream

2 eggs

½ teaspoon vanilla

1 can (16 ounces) pear halves, drained

½ cup toasted coarsely chopped blanched almonds

1 square BAKER'S® Semi-Sweet Baking Chocolate, melted

HEAT oven to 375°F.

MIX flour and 2 tablespoons sugar in medium bowl; cut in ⅓ cup butter until mixture resembles coarse crumbs. Stir in finely chopped almonds. Press firmly onto bottom of 9-inch springform pan or pie plate. Bake for 10 minutes.

MEANWHILE microwave 4 squares chocolate and ½ cup butter in large microwavable bowl on HIGH 2 minutes or until butter is melted. Stir until chocolate is completely melted.

STIR ½ cup sugar and cream into chocolate mixture until well blended. Mix in eggs and vanilla. Pour over crust.

SLICE pears and arrange, cut sides down, over filling. Sprinkle with coarsely chopped almonds. Bake for 35 to 40 minutes or until toothpick inserted into center comes out almost clean. (Center may be slightly soft.)

Cool completely on wire rack. Refrigerate until ready to serve. For garnish, drizzle with 1 square melted chocolate.

Makes 8 servings

High Altitude Directions: Press crust into bottom of 10-inch pie plate. Bake at 375°F for 8 minutes. For filling, add 2 tablespoons flour with vanilla. Bake at 375°F for 15 minutes. *Reduce oven temperature to 350°F and bake about 25 minutes of until toothpick comes out almost clean.*

Prep Time: 30 minutes
Bake Time: 50 minutes

Oven-Tested Tips

Toasting nuts before using them intensifies their flavor and crunch. Simply spread them on a baking sheet and place in a preheated 350°F oven for 10 to 15 minutes. Or, toast nuts in an ungreased skillet over medium heat until golden brown, stirring frequently. Always cool nuts to room temperature before combining them with other ingredients.

Chocolate Almond Pear Torte

Fresh Nectarine Pie with Strawberry Topping

Pie Crust (recipe follows)
1½ pounds nectarines, pitted and cut into ½-inch-thick slices
½ cup sugar, divided
1 pint strawberries, hulled
1 tablespoon lemon juice
1 tablespoon cornstarch

Preheat oven to 425°F. Prepare Pie Crust. Reserve 6 to 8 nectarine slices for garnish. Chop remaining nectarines; place on top of pie crust. Sprinkle evenly with 2 tablespoons sugar. Bake 30 minutes or until crust is browned and fruit is easily pierced with sharp knife. Let cool, uncovered, on wire rack 30 minutes or until room temperature.

Meanwhile, place strawberries in food processor; process until strawberries are puréed, scraping down side of bowl once or twice. Press purée through strainer, discarding seeds and pulp. Pour liquid into 1-cup measure. Add lemon juice and enough water to equal 1 cup liquid.

Combine remaining 6 tablespoons sugar with cornstarch in small saucepan. Gradually blend in strawberry mixture until sugar and cornstarch are dissolved. Bring to boil over medium heat. Cook and stir 5 minutes or until mixture boils and thickens. Remove from heat; let cool 15 minutes. Spoon mixture over pie, spreading to cover nectarines. Let cool completely. Garnish with reserved nectarine pieces.

Refrigerate at least 2 hours or up to 8 hours before serving. Cover with plastic wrap after 1 hour in refrigerator.   *Makes 8 servings*

Pie Crust

1¼ cups all-purpose flour
¼ teaspoon baking powder
   Dash salt
¼ cup canola or vegetable oil
3 tablespoons skim milk, divided

Combine flour, baking powder and salt in medium bowl. Add oil and 2 tablespoons milk; mix well. Add enough remaining milk to hold mixture together. Shape dough into a ball.

Flatten dough to 1-inch thickness on 12-inch square of waxed paper; cover with second square of waxed paper. Roll out gently to form 12-inch round crust. Mend any tears or ragged edges by pressing together with fingers. *Do not moisten.* Remove 1 layer of waxed paper from crust. Place dough, paper side up, in 9-inch pie pan. Carefully peel off remaining paper. Press pastry gently into pan and flute edge.

Oven-Tested Tips

For tender, flaky pie crusts, follow these two basic rules: 1) keep the ingredients cold and 2) handle the dough as little as possible. Tough crusts are the result of overdeveloping gluten, a protein present in flour. Following these rules helps prevent the development of gluten.

Raspberry Chocolate Mousse Pie

40 chocolate wafer cookies, finely crushed

½ cup butter, melted

½ cup water

7 tablespoons sugar

5 egg yolks

6 squares (1 ounce each) semisweet chocolate, melted and cooled slightly

3 tablespoons raspberry-flavored liqueur

3½ cups frozen nondairy whipped topping, thawed

Sweetened whipped cream, fresh raspberries and mint leaves (optional)

1. Combine cookie crumbs and butter in medium bowl; mix well. Press onto bottom and 1 inch up side of 9-inch springform pan.

2. Combine water and sugar in medium saucepan. Bring to a boil over medium-high heat. Boil 1 minute.

3. Place egg yolks in large bowl. Gradually whisk in hot sugar mixture. Return mixture to medium saucepan; whisk over low heat 1 to 2 minutes or until mixture is thick and creamy. Remove from heat; pour mixture back into large bowl.

4. Whisk in melted chocolate and liqueur. Beat mixture until cool. Fold in whipped topping. Pour mixture into prepared crust. Freeze until firm. Allow pie to stand at room temperature 20 minutes before serving. Remove side of pan. Garnish with sweetened whipped cream, fresh raspberries and mint leaves, if desired.

Makes 10 servings

Raspberry Chocolate Mousse Pie

Celia's Flat Fruit Pie

2 packages (8 ounces each) mixed dried fruit (pitted prunes, pears, apples, apricots and peaches)

3 cups water

½ cup sugar

½ teaspoon ground cinnamon

¼ teaspoon ground cloves

1 teaspoon lemon juice

Flaky Pastry (recipe follows)

1. Combine fruit, water, sugar, cinnamon and cloves in 3-quart pan. Cook, stirring occasionally, over medium heat until sugar is dissolved. Cover; reduce heat and simmer 45 minutes or until fruit is tender.

2. Pour fruit and liquid into blender or food processor container fitted with metal blade; process to make coarse purée. (Purée should measure 3 cups. If purée measures more, return to pan and cook, stirring frequently, to reduce to 3 cups.) Stir in lemon juice. Let cool. While fruit is cooling, prepare Flaky Pastry.

3. Preheat oven to 400°F. Roll one pastry ball on lightly floured board to 13-inch circle about ⅛ inch thick. Fold pastry into quarters. Place in 12-inch pizza pan; unfold. Trim edge of pastry to leave ½-inch overhang. Spread fruit purée in even layer over pastry.

4. Roll out second ball to 13-inch circle; place over filling. Cut slits or design in center. Fold edge of top crust under edge of bottom crust; flute edge. Bake 35 to 40 minutes or until pastry is golden brown. Let cool on rack 1 hour before cutting into thin wedges. *Makes 12 servings*

Flaky Pastry

3⅓ cups all-purpose flour

¾ teaspoon salt

1 cup shortening or lard

6 to 8 tablespoons cold water

Combine flour and salt in medium bowl. With fingers, pastry blender or 2 knives, rub or cut shortening into flour mixture until it resembles fine crumbs. Gradually add water; stir with fork until mixture forms dough. Shape into 2 balls. Wrap in plastic wrap; refrigerate 30 minutes.

Tropical Fruit Coconut Tart

1 cup cornflakes, crushed

1 can (3½ ounces) sweetened flaked coconut

2 egg whites

1 can (15¼ ounces) pineapple tidbits in juice

2 teaspoons cornstarch

2 packets sugar substitute *or* equivalent of 4 teaspoons sugar

1 teaspoon coconut extract (optional)

1 mango, peeled and thinly sliced

1 banana, thinly sliced

1. Preheat oven to 425°F. Coat 9-inch springform pan with nonstick cooking spray; set aside.

2. Combine cereal, coconut and egg whites in medium bowl; toss gently to blend. Place coconut mixture in prepared pan; press firmly to coat bottom and ½ inch up side of pan.

3. Bake 8 minutes or until edge begins to brown. Cool completely on wire rack.

4. Drain pineapple, reserving pineapple juice. Combine pineapple juice and cornstarch in small saucepan; stir until cornstarch is dissolved. Bring to a boil over high heat. Continue boiling 1 minute, stirring constantly. Remove from heat; cool completely. Stir in sugar substitute and coconut extract, if desired.

5. Combine pineapple, mango slices and banana slices in medium bowl. Spoon into crust; drizzle with pineapple sauce. Cover with plastic wrap and refrigerate 2 hours.

Makes 8 servings

Note: The crust may be made 24 hours in advance, if desired.

Celia's Flat Fruit Pie

Wisconsin Ricotta Tart with Kiwi and Raspberry Sauce

⅓ cup all-purpose flour

⅓ cup packed brown sugar

3 tablespoons butter

1 cup flaked coconut

½ cup chopped pecans or macadamia nuts

2 cups (16 ounces) Wisconsin Ricotta cheese

½ cup powdered sugar

1 teaspoon grated lime peel

1 teaspoon vanilla

1 package (10 ounces) frozen raspberries, thawed

1 kiwifruit

Preheat oven to 350°F. Combine flour and brown sugar; cut in butter until mixture resembles coarse crumbs. Stir in coconut and nuts. Press into 10-inch tart pan or pie plate. Bake crust 15 minutes. Remove from oven and cool.

Combine cheese, powdered sugar, lime peel and vanilla in food processor or blender; process until smooth. Spoon mixture into prepared crust. Refrigerate 1 hour. Before serving, place raspberries in food processor or blender; process until sauce forms. Cut kiwi into slices and arrange in circle on top of tart.* Drizzle tart with ½ of the raspberry sauce. Serve with remaining sauce.

Makes 8 to 10 servings

*Recipe can be prepared to this point and refrigerated until ready to serve.

Favorite recipe from **Wisconsin Milk Marketing Board**

Wisconsin Ricotta Tart with Kiwi and Raspberry Sauce

Peanut Butter Crumble Topped Apple Pie

1 container (8 ounces) dairy sour cream

¾ cup sugar, divided

2 eggs

2 tablespoons plus ¾ cup all-purpose flour, divided

2 teaspoons vanilla extract

¼ teaspoon salt

4 cups peeled, thinly sliced apples (about 5 apples)

1 unbaked 9-inch pie crust

1 cup quick-cooking or regular rolled oats

1 teaspoon ground cinnamon

1 cup REESE'S® Creamy Peanut Butter

1 tablespoon butter or margarine, softened

1. Heat oven to 350°F.

2. Blend sour cream, ½ cup sugar, eggs, 2 tablespoons flour, vanilla and salt in large bowl with whisk. Add apples; stir until well coated. Spoon into unbaked crust.

3. Stir together oats, remaining ¾ cup flour, remaining ¼ cup sugar and cinnamon. In small microwave-safe bowl, place peanut butter and butter. Microwave at HIGH (100%) 30 seconds or until butter is melted. Stir mixture until smooth. Add to oat mixture; blend until crumbs are formed. Sprinkle crumb mixture over apples.

4. Bake 55 to 60 minutes or until apples are tender and topping is golden brown. Cool completely on wire rack. Cover; refrigerate leftover pie.   *Makes 6 to 8 servings*

Pineapple Sweet Potato Pie

1 (9-inch) pastry shell, unbaked

2 cups mashed cooked sweet potatoes

⅔ cup firmly packed brown sugar

¼ cup half-and-half

1 egg, beaten

2 tablespoons butter or margarine, melted

1 teaspoon vanilla extract, divided

½ teaspoon ground cinnamon

¼ teaspoon ground nutmeg

¼ teaspoon salt

1 can (15¼ ounces) DEL MONTE® Sliced Pineapple In Its Own Juice, undrained

1 teaspoon cornstarch

1 teaspoon minced candied ginger

1. Prepare pastry shell; set aside.

2. Combine sweet potatoes, brown sugar, half-and-half, egg, butter, ½ teaspoon vanilla, cinnamon, nutmeg and salt; mix well. Pour into pastry shell.

3. Bake at 425°F, 25 to 30 minutes or until set in center; cool.

4. Drain pineapple, reserving ½ cup juice. Pour reserved juice into small saucepan. Add cornstarch; stir until dissolved. Cook, stirring constantly, until thickened and translucent. Stir in ginger and remaining ½ teaspoon vanilla.

5. Cut pineapple slices in half; arrange pineapple over pie. Spoon juice mixture over pineapple. Garnish, if desired.
Makes 8 servings

Prep and Cook Time: 1 hour

Pennsylvania Shoo-Fly Pie

Crust

Classic CRISCO® Single Crust
(recipe follows)

Crumb Mixture

2 cups all-purpose flour

½ cup firmly packed brown sugar

⅓ cup butter or margarine, softened

Liquid Mixture

1 cup boiling water

1 teaspoon baking soda

¾ cup plus 2 tablespoons dark
molasses

2 tablespoons light molasses

1. **For crust,** prepare as directed. Do not bake. Heat oven to 375°F.

2. **For crumb mixture,** combine flour, brown sugar and butter in bowl. Mix until fine crumbs form. Reserve ½ cup for topping.

3. **For liquid mixture,** combine water and baking soda in large bowl. Stir until foamy. Add dark and light molasses. Stir well until foamy. Pour into unbaked pie crust. Add crumb mixture. Stir slightly until mixed. Sprinkle reserved ½ cup crumbs on top. Bake at 375°F for 45 to 55 minutes or until set. *Do not overbake.* Cool until warm or to room temperature before serving.

Makes 1 (10-inch) pie

Classic Crisco® Crust

8-, 9- or 10-inch Single Crust

1⅓ cups all-purpose flour

½ teaspoon salt

½ CRISCO® Stick or ½ cup
CRISCO® Shortening

3 tablespoons cold water

8- or 9-inch Double Crust

2 cups all-purpose flour

1 teaspoon salt

¾ CRISCO® Stick or ¾ cup
CRISCO® Shortening

5 tablespoons cold water

10-inch Double Crust

2⅔ cups all-purpose flour

1 teaspoon salt

1 CRISCO® Stick or 1 cup CRISCO®
Shortening

7 to 8 tablespoons cold water

1. Spoon flour into measuring cup and level. Combine flour and salt in medium bowl.

2. Cut in shortening using pastry blender (or 2 knives) until all flour is blended to form pea-size chunks.

3. Sprinkle with water, 1 tablespoon at a time. Toss lightly with fork until dough forms a ball.

For Single Crust Pies

1. Press dough between hands to form 5- to 6-inch "pancake." Flour rolling surface and rolling pin lightly. Roll dough into circle.

2. Trim 1 inch larger than upside-down pie plate. Loosen dough carefully.

3. Fold dough into quarters. Unfold and press into pie plate. Fold edge under. Flute.

For Baked Pie Crusts

1. For recipes using baked pie crust, heat oven to 425°F. Prick bottom and side thoroughly with fork (50 times) to prevent shrinkage.

2. Bake at 425°F for 10 to 15 minutes or until lightly browned.

For Unbaked Pie Crusts

1. For recipes using unbaked pie crust, follow baking directions given in each recipe.

For Double Crust Pies

1. Divide dough in half. Roll each half separately. Transfer bottom crust to pie plate. Trim edge even with pie plate.

2. Add desired filling to unbaked pie crust. Moisten pastry edge with water. Lift top crust onto filled pie. Trim ½ inch beyond edge of pie plate. Fold top edge under bottom crust. Flute. Cut slits in top crust to allow steam to escape. Bake according to specific recipe directions.

Pennsylvania Shoo-Fly Pie

Peach Delight Pie

Filling

2½ cups sliced peeled peaches (about
    1¼ pounds or 2 to 3 large)
¾ cup granulated sugar
¼ cup quick-cooking tapioca
1 teaspoon lemon juice
1 teaspoon peach-flavored brandy

Crumb Mixture

¼ cup all-purpose flour
¼ cup packed brown sugar
¼ cup chopped almonds
3 tablespoons butter or margarine,
    melted

Crust

1 9-inch Classic CRISCO® Double
    Crust (recipe page 132)

Glaze

1 egg white, lightly beaten
Granulated sugar

1. **For filling,** combine peaches, ¾ cup
granulated sugar, tapioca, lemon juice and
brandy in medium bowl. Stir well. Let stand
while making crumb mixture and crust.

2. **For crumb mixture,** combine flour,
brown sugar, almonds and butter. Mix until
crumbly. Heat oven to 425°F.

3. **For crust,** prepare as directed. Roll and
press bottom crust into 9-inch pie plate. Do
not bake. Sprinkle half of crumb mixture
over unbaked pie crust. Add filling. Top
with remaining crumb mixture.

4. Cut out desired shapes from top crust
with cookie cutter. Place on filling around
edge of pie.

5. **For glaze,** brush cutouts with egg white.
Sprinkle with granulated sugar. Cover edge
of pie with foil to prevent overbrowning.

6. Bake at 425°F for 10 minutes. *Reduce
oven temperature to 350°F. Bake 25 minutes.
Do not overbake.* Remove foil. Bake
5 minutes. Serve warm or at room
temperature.   *Makes 1 (9-inch) pie*

Easy Raspberry Chiffon Pie

Pastry for single-crust 9-inch pie
2 cups heavy cream
6 ounces cream cheese, softened
2 teaspoons vanilla
1 jar (10 ounces) no-sugar-added
    raspberry fruit spread (about
    1 cup)
Fresh raspberries (optional)
Fresh mint leaves (optional)

1. Preheat oven to 375°F. Roll out pastry to
11-inch circle; place in 9-inch pie plate.
Trim and flute edges; prick bottom and sides
of pastry with fork. Bake 15 minutes or until
golden brown. Cool on wire rack.

2. Beat cream in small bowl at high speed
with electric mixer until stiff peaks form; set
aside. Combine cream cheese and vanilla in
medium bowl; beat until light and fluffy.
Blend in fruit spread, scraping sides of bowl
frequently.

3. Reserve ½ cup of whipped cream for
garnish; fold remaining whipped cream into
cream cheese mixture until no white streaks
remain. Spread evenly into cooled pie shell.

4. Chill at least 2 hours or up to 24 hours.
Just before serving, pipe or spoon reserved
whipped cream around edge of pie. Garnish
with raspberries and mint leaves, if desired.
                          Makes 8 servings

Peach Delight Pie

Bread Machine Marvels

If you don't already have a bread machine, this chapter may convince you to buy one. The recipes here will show you how to turn out foolproof Multigrain Bread, elegant Almond Amaretto Loaf and much more without proofing, kneading, or even turning on the oven. When you get tired of loafing around, make some sweet treats like Triple Chocolate Sticky Buns!

Crusty Rye Bread

    1 cup water
    1 tablespoon butter or margarine, softened
    1 teaspoon salt
2½ cups all-purpose flour
    ½ cup rye flour
    ¼ cup packed light brown sugar
1½ teaspoons grated orange peel
    1 teaspoon caraway seeds
    2 teaspoons active dry yeast

1. Measuring carefully, place all ingredients in bread machine pan in order specified by owner's manual.

2. Program basic or white cycle and desired crust setting; press start. Remove baked bread from pan; cool on wire rack.   *Makes 1 (1½-pound) loaf*

Oven-Tested Tips

It is extremely important to measure ingredients accurately when using a bread machine. As little as 1 tablespoon of liquid can make the difference between success and failure. Be sure to measure liquids at eye level and with the measuring cup on a flat surface.

Chili Cheese Bread

1½-Pound Loaf

  2 tablespoons butter, softened

  ½ cup finely chopped onion

  1 clove garlic, minced

  ¾ cup milk

  1 egg

  1 teaspoon salt

2¾ cups bread flour

  1 tablespoon sugar

  2 to 3 teaspoons chili powder

  1 teaspoon dried basil leaves

1¼ teaspoons active dry yeast

1¼ cups (5 ounces) shredded sharp
    Cheddar cheese

2-Pound Loaf

  2 tablespoons butter, softened

  ½ cup finely chopped onion

  1 clove garlic, minced

  1 cup milk

  1 egg

1¼ teaspoons salt

3½ cups bread flour

  4 teaspoons sugar

  3 to 4 teaspoons chili powder

1¼ teaspoons dried basil leaves

1½ teaspoons active dry yeast

1½ cups (6 ounces) shredded sharp
    Cheddar cheese

1. Melt butter in medium skillet over medium heat. Add onion and garlic; cook and stir 5 minutes or until onion is tender.

2. Measuring carefully, place all ingredients except cheese in bread machine pan in order specified by owner's manual.

3. Program basic cycle and desired crust setting; press start. (*Do not use delay cycle.*) Add cheese when bread machine signals or at end of first kneading cycle. Immediately remove baked bread from pan; cool on rack.

Makes 1 loaf

Oatmeal Bread

2¼ teaspoons quick-rise active dry
    yeast (one 1¼ ounce package)

  3 cups bread flour

  1 cup QUAKER® Oats (quick or old
    fashioned, uncooked)

  2 tablespoons sugar

  1 teaspoon salt

1¼ to 1⅓ cups milk or water

  2 tablespoons butter or margarine,
    melted or 1 tablespoon vegetable
    oil

Bring all ingredients to room temperature by letting them stand on the counter for about 30 minutes.* Place yeast in bread machine according to directions in manual. Combine flour, oats, sugar and salt in a bowl; mix well. In a separate bowl combine milk and butter; mix well. Place into bread machine according to manual. When baking, use white bread and light crust setting.

Makes one 1½-pound loaf

This can be done quickly by microwaving the ingredients for 15 to 20 seconds.

Maple Fruit Variation: Combine ⅓ cup pancake syrup with butter and only 1 cup milk. Proceed as directed above. Add ½ cup dried fruit to bread dough partially through kneading cycle according to bread machine manual.

Whole Wheat Variation: Combine 1½ cups bread flour with 1½ cups whole wheat flour. Proceed as directed above.

Chili Cheese Bread

Banana-Chocolate Chip Bread

1-Pound Loaf

⅓ cup milk

⅓ cup mashed very ripe banana

1 large egg

1 tablespoon butter or margarine

¾ teaspoon salt

2 cups bread flour

¼ cup semisweet chocolate pieces

1½ teaspoons FLEISCHMANN'S® Bread Machine Yeast

1½-Pound Loaf

½ cup milk

½ cup mashed very ripe banana

1 large egg

1 tablespoon butter or margarine

1 teaspoon salt

3 cups bread flour

⅓ cup semisweet chocolate pieces

2 teaspoons FLEISCHMANN'S® Bread Machine Yeast

Use the 1-pound recipe if your machine pan holds 10 cups or less of water. Add ingredients to bread machine pan in the order suggested by manufacturer, adding mashed banana with milk, and semisweet chocolate pieces with flour. Recommended cycle: Basic/white bread cycle; medium/ normal or light crust color setting. (*Do not use delay cycle.*)   *Makes 1 loaf*

Note: How this bread turns out depends on your machine. Some machines will make a smooth chocolate-colored bread. Others will leave bits of chocolate chips, and still others will give a marbled loaf.

Pizza Breadsticks

1 cup water

1 tablespoon olive oil

1 teaspoon salt

3 cups all-purpose flour

½ cup (2 ounces) shredded mozzarella cheese

¼ cup (1 ounce) shredded Parmesan cheese

¼ cup chopped red bell pepper

1 green onion with top, sliced

1 clove garlic, minced

½ teaspoon dried basil leaves

½ teaspoon dried oregano leaves

¼ teaspoon red pepper flakes (optional)

1½ teaspoons active dry yeast

1. Measuring carefully, place all ingredients in bread machine pan in order specified by owner's manual. Program dough cycle setting; press start. Grease large baking sheets; set aside.

2. When cycle is complete, remove dough to lightly floured surface. If necessary, knead in additional all-purpose flour to make dough easy to handle. Roll dough into 14×8-inch rectangle. Let dough rest 5 minutes. Cut dough crosswise into 28 (8×½-inch) strips. Twist each strip 3 to 4 times; place 2 inches apart on prepared baking sheets, pressing both ends to baking sheet. Cover with clean towels; let rise in warm, draft-free place 30 minutes or until doubled in size.

3. Preheat oven to 425°F. Bake 15 to 20 minutes or until golden brown. Remove from baking sheets; cool on wire racks.

Makes 28 breadsticks

Banana-Chocolate Chip Bread

Black Pepper-Onion Bread

1-Pound Loaf

⅔ cup water

1 tablespoon butter or margarine

¾ teaspoon salt

2 cups bread flour

2 tablespoons nonfat dry milk powder

2 teaspoons sugar

1 teaspoon SPICE ISLANDS® Minced Onions

½ teaspoon SPICE ISLANDS® Medium Grind Java Black Pepper*

⅛ teaspoon SPICE ISLANDS® Garlic Powder

1½ teaspoons FLEISCHMANN'S® Bread Machine Yeast

1½-Pound Loaf

1 cup water

1 tablespoon butter or margarine

1 teaspoon salt

3 cups bread flour

3 tablespoons nonfat dry milk powder

1 tablespoon sugar

1½ teaspoons SPICE ISLANDS® Minced Onions

¾ teaspoon SPICE ISLANDS® Medium Grind Java Black Pepper*

¼ teaspoon SPICE ISLANDS® Garlic Powder

2 teaspoons FLEISCHMANN'S® Bread Machine Yeast

If using a finer grind of pepper, reduce the amount to ¼ teaspoon for either loaf size.

Use the 1-pound recipe if your machine pan holds 10 cups or less of water. Add ingredients to bread machine pan in the order suggested by manufacturer. Recommended cycle: Basic/white bread cycle; medium/normal crust color setting. Timed-bake feature can be used.

Makes 1 loaf (8 or 12 slices)

Golden Cherry Granola Bread

2½ teaspoons active dry yeast

2 cups bread flour

1¼ cups whole wheat flour

3 tablespoons nonfat dry milk powder

1½ teaspoons salt

1¼ cups water

2 tablespoons honey

2 tablespoons vegetable oil

⅔ cup granola

½ cup dried tart cherries

1. Measure carefully, placing all ingredients except granola and cherries in bread machine pan in order specified by owner's manual.

2. Program desired cycle; press start. Add granola and cherries at the beep or at end of first kneading cycle. Remove baked bread from pan; cool on wire rack.

Makes 1 loaf, about 16 slices

Favorite recipe from **Cherry Marketing Institute**

Cinnamon-Pecan Pull-Apart Bread

1½ cups water
¾ cup butter, divided
1 teaspoon salt
3¾ cups all-purpose flour
1¼ cups sugar, divided
2 teaspoons active dry yeast
¾ cup finely chopped pecans
1½ teaspoons ground cinnamon
½ cup raisins

1. Measuring carefully, place water, ¼ cup butter, salt, flour, ¼ cup sugar and yeast in bread machine pan in order specified by owner's manual. Program dough cycle setting; press start.

2. Melt remaining ½ cup butter. Combine remaining 1 cup sugar, pecans and cinnamon in small bowl. Divide dough in half; shape each half into twenty balls. Dip balls first in butter, then in sugar mixture. Arrange 20 balls in bottom of greased 12-cup tube pan; sprinkle with raisins. Top with remaining 20 balls. Cover and let rise in warm place 45 minutes or until doubled.

3. Preheat oven to 350°F. Bake 35 to 40 minutes or until evenly browned. Invert onto heatproof serving plate; let stand 1 minute before removing pan. Serve warm.
Makes 8 to 12 servings

Cinnamon-Pecan Pull-Apart Bread

Pumpernickel Bread

1½ cups water

3 eggs

3 tablespoons canola oil

3 tablespoons molasses

1 teaspoon vinegar

2 cups brown rice flour

½ cup tapioca flour

½ cup potato starch flour

½ cup dry milk powder

3 tablespoons sugar

1 tablespoon xanthan gum*

1 tablespoon caraway seeds

1 tablespoon cocoa powder

2¼ teaspoons RED STAR® Active Dry Yeast

1½ teaspoons salt

1 teaspoon grated orange peel

Xanthan gum is available in health food stores.

Combine water, eggs, oil, molasses and vinegar; pour into baking pan. Combine flours, milk powder, sugar, xanthan gum, caraway seeds, cocoa, yeast, salt and orange peel. Blend thoroughly in bowl with wire whisk or shake together in large resealing plastic food storage bag. (Gluten-free flours are very fine and need to be well blended before liquid is added.)

Select Normal or Basic cycle; start machine. For bread machines with Bake Only cycle, select Dough cycle for mixing and rising. Press Stop when cycle is complete; then select Bake Only to complete.

After mixing action begins, help any unmixed ingredients into dough with rubber spatula, keeping to edges of batter to prevent interference with kneading blade.

When Bake cycle is complete, remove pan and allow bread to cool about 10 minutes. Remove bread from pan and cool upright on rack before slicing.   *Makes 1 loaf*

Thyme-Cheese Bubble Loaf

1 cup water

2 tablespoons vegetable oil

1 teaspoon salt

3 cups all-purpose flour

1 cup (4 ounces) shredded Monterey Jack cheese

1 teaspoon sugar

1½ teaspoons active dry yeast

¼ cup chopped fresh parsley

1 tablespoon finely chopped fresh thyme *or* ¾ teaspoon dried thyme leaves, crushed

¼ cup butter, melted

1. Measuring carefully, place all ingredients except parsley, thyme and melted butter in bread machine pan in order specified by owner's manual. Program dough cycle setting; press start. Combine parsley and thyme in shallow bowl; set aside. Lightly grease 8½×4½-inch loaf pan or 1½-quart casserole dish; set aside.

2. When cycle is complete, remove dough to lightly floured surface. If necessary, knead in additional all-purpose flour to make dough easy to handle. Divide dough into 48 equal pieces. Shape each piece into smooth ball. Dip each ball into melted butter and then in herb mixture; place, in two evenly spaced layers, in prepared pan. Cover with clean towel; let rise in warm, draft-free place 45 minutes or until doubled in size.

3. Preheat oven to 375°F. Bake 25 to 35 minutes or until golden brown. Remove from pan; cool on wire rack.

Makes 1 (1½-pound) loaf

Honey Wheat Bread

½ cup water

1 egg

2 tablespoons butter or margarine, softened

3 tablespoons honey

1 teaspoon salt

2 cups all-purpose flour

¾ cup whole wheat flour

¼ cup nonfat dry milk powder

2 teaspoons active dry yeast

1. Measuring carefully, place all ingredients in bread machine pan in order specified by owner's manual.

2. Program basic or white cycle and desired crust setting; press start. (*Do not use delay cycles.*) Remove baked bread from pan; cool on wire rack. *Makes 1 (1-pound) loaf*

Honey Wheat Bread

English Muffin Bread

1-Pound Loaf

1 cup water (70° to 80°F)

2 tablespoons sugar

3 tablespoons nonfat dry milk powder

1 teaspoon salt

¼ teaspoon baking soda

2½ cups bread flour

1 tablespoon gluten* (optional)

1¾ teaspoons FLEISCHMANN'S® Bread Machine Yeast

1½-Pound Loaf

1½ cups water (70° to 80°F)

3 tablespoons sugar

¼ cup nonfat dry milk powder

1½ teaspoons salt

¼ teaspoon baking soda

3½ cups bread flour

1 tablespoon gluten* (optional)

2¼ teaspoons FLEISCHMANN'S® Bread Machine Yeast

Gluten, a protein product from flour, improves loaf height, texture and structure; it can be found in health food stores and some supermarkets.

Add ingredients to bread machine pan in the order suggested by manufacturer. Recommended cycle: Basic/white bread cycle; medium/normal crust color setting. Do not use delayed-bake feature. Remove bread from pan; cool on wire rack. Slice and toast to serve. Store bread in airtight container or plastic storage bag at room temperature for up to 3 days. Or, slice, wrap airtight and freeze for up to one month; toast frozen slices without thawing, as needed.   *Makes 1 loaf (8 or 12 slices)*

Note: Do not make loaves larger than recommended by bread machine manufacturer. Use the 1-pound recipe if your bread machine pan holds 10 cups or less of water.

Adjusting Dough Consistency: Check dough after 5 minutes of mixing; it should form a soft, smooth ball around the blade. If dough is too stiff or dry, add additional liquid, 1 teaspoon at a time, until dough is of the right consistency. If dough is too soft or sticky, add additional bread flour, 1 teaspoon at a time.

Cinnamon-Pecan English Muffin Bread: Add ⅓ cup toasted chopped pecans and ¾ teaspoon SPICE ISLANDS® Ground Cinnamon along with flour; proceed as directed with recipe. Slice and toast. Drizzle with honey, if desired.

State Fair Cracked Wheat Bread

1⅓ cups water

2 tablespoons butter or margarine

1 teaspoon salt

¼ cup cracked wheat

3 cups bread flour

½ cup whole wheat flour

3 tablespoons nonfat dry milk powder

2 tablespoons firmly packed brown sugar

2 teaspoons FLEISCHMANN'S® Bread Machine Yeast

Add ingredients to bread machine pan in the order suggested by manufacturer. (If dough is too dry or stiff or too soft or slack, adjust dough consistency). Recommended cycle: Basic/white bread cycle; medium/normal crust color setting.

Makes 1 (2-pound) loaf

State Fair Cracked Wheat Bread

COUR
1. Basic Re
2. Basic Med
3. Basic Dark C
4. Whole Wheat (1
5. Whole Wheat (2 lb
6. Whole Wheat (Rapid
7. French
8. Fruit & Nut
9. Dough

Dried Tomato and Rosemary Bread

1½-Pound Loaf

- 1 cup water
- 3 tablespoons snipped unsalted dried tomatoes (do not use oil packed)
- 1 tablespoon olive or vegetable oil
- 1 teaspoon salt
- 3 cups bread flour
- ¼ cup nonfat dry milk powder
- 1 tablespoon sugar
- 1 teaspoon dried rosemary, crushed
- ¾ teaspoon paprika
- 2 teaspoons FLEISCHMANN'S® Bread Machine Yeast

2-Pound Loaf

- 1⅓ cups water
- ¼ cup snipped unsalted dried tomatoes (do not use oil packed)
- 2 tablespoons olive or vegetable oil
- 1½ teaspoons salt
- 4 cups bread flour
- ¼ cup plus 2 tablespoons nonfat dry milk powder
- 1 tablespoon plus 1 teaspoon sugar
- 1 teaspoon dried rosemary, crushed
- 1 teaspoon paprika
- 2 teaspoons FLEISCHMANN'S® Bread Machine Yeast

Add ingredients to bread machine pan in the order suggested by manufacturer, adding dried tomatoes with water. Recommended cycle: Basic/white bread cycle; medium/normal color setting.

Makes 1 loaf (8 or 12 slices)

Serving Suggestion: Make pizza appetizers using small slices of this savory bread. Spread with an herb butter (recipes follow) and top with tomato slices, shredded cheese and sliced green onions.

Flavored Butters: Flavored butters will make your fresh-baked breads even more special. For savory breads, try an herb-flavored butter, using the same herb as in the bread or a complementary herb for more zip. Just stir ¾ teaspoon SPICE ISLANDS® herb, crushed, into ½ cup softened butter. For sweeter breads, try a fruit- or honey-flavored butter. To make a citrus butter, stir 2 teaspoons sugar, ¼ teaspoon finely shredded orange or lemon peel and 1 teaspoon orange or lemon juice into ½ cup softened butter. To make honey butter, stir 2 teaspoons honey into ⅓ cup softened butter.

Optional Appetizer Topping

- ¾ teaspoon rosemary, crushed
- ½ cup butter, softened
- 1 medium fresh tomato, sliced
- 1 cup shredded Cheddar cheese
- ¼ cup green onions, sliced

Slice bread into ½-inch thick slices. Stir rosemary into softened butter; spread on one side of each bread slice. Top with tomato slices, cheese and green onions.

Oven-Tested Tips

Never use a knife or metal spatula to remove a loaf that is sticking to a bread machine pan. It could scratch the pan's nonstick coating. Instead rap the corner of the bread pan on a wooden cutting board or padded surface several times to help release the loaf. You can also try tapping lightly on the sides of the pan with a wooden mallet.

Whole Wheat Loaves

1½-Pound Loaf

1 cup water

2 tablespoons honey

1 tablespoon butter, softened

1 teaspoon salt

2 cups all-purpose flour

¾ cup whole wheat flour

⅓ cup nonfat dry milk powder

⅓ cup wheat germ

1½ teaspoons active dry yeast

2-Pound Loaf

1¼ cups water

3 tablespoons honey

2 tablespoons butter, softened

1½ teaspoons salt

2½ cups all-purpose flour

1 cup whole wheat flour

½ cup nonfat dry milk powder

½ cup wheat germ

2 teaspoons active dry yeast

1. Measuring carefully, place all ingredients in bread machine pan in order specified by owner's manual.

2. Program basic cycle and desired crust setting; press start. Immediately remove baked bread from pan; cool on wire rack.

Makes 1 loaf

Variation: Follow instructions through Step 1. Program dough cycle setting instead of basic cycle; press start. For 1½-pound loaf, grease 8½×4½-inch loaf pan; set aside. For 2-pound loaf, grease 12×4½-inch loaf pan; set aside. When cycle is complete, remove dough to lightly floured surface. If necessary, knead in additional all-purpose flour to make dough easy to handle. Shape dough into smooth loaf and place in prepared pan. Cover dough with clean towel; let rise in warm, draft-free place 45 minutes or until doubled in size. Preheat oven to 375°F. Bake 25 to 35 minutes or until loaf is golden brown and sounds hollow when tapped. Remove from pan; cool on wire rack.

Oatmeal-Raisin Bread

1½-Pound Loaf

1¼ cups water

2 tablespoons honey

1 tablespoon butter or margarine

1½ teaspoons salt

3 cups bread flour

¼ cup nonfat dry milk powder

1½ teaspoons rapid-rise active dry yeast

½ cup uncooked old-fashioned oats

½ cup raisins

2-Pound Loaf

1½ cups water

3 tablespoons honey

2 tablespoons butter or margarine

2 teaspoons salt

4 cups bread flour

⅓ cup nonfat dry milk powder

2 teaspoons rapid-rise active dry yeast

¾ cup uncooked old-fashioned oats

¾ cup raisins

1. Measuring carefully, place all ingredients except oats and raisins in bread machine pan in order specified by owner's manual.

2. Program basic cycle and desired crust setting; press start. Add oats and raisins when bread machine signals, or at end of first kneading cycle. Remove baked bread from pan; cool on wire rack.

Makes 1 loaf

Multigrain Bread

1½-Pound Loaf

 1¼ cups boiling water

  ¼ cup multigrain cereal

 2 tablespoons quick oats

 2 tablespoons honey

 1 tablespoon butter or margarine, softened

 1 teaspoon salt

 2½ cups bread flour

 1½ teaspoons rapid-rise active dry yeast

2-Pound Loaf

 1½ cups boiling water

  ⅓ cup multigrain cereal

  ¼ cup quick oats

 3 tablespoons honey

 1½ tablespoons butter or margarine, softened

 1½ teaspoons salt

 3¼ cups bread flour

 2 teaspoons rapid-rise active dry yeast

1. Measuring carefully, place water in bread machine pan. Add cereal and oats. Let stand 30 minutes or until cool. Add remaining ingredients in order specified by owner's manual.

2. Program basic cycle and desired crust setting; press start. Remove baked bread from pan; cool on wire rack.

Makes 1 loaf

Serving Suggestion: Serve with an orange-flavored butter. To make, combine ½ cup softened butter and 1 tablespoon freshly grated orange peel in a small bowl.

Shortcut "Sourdough" Corn Bread

1-Pound Loaf

  ½ cup plain low-fat yogurt

  ¼ cup milk

 1 tablespoon butter or margarine

  ¾ teaspoon salt

 1¾ cups bread flour

  ⅓ cup cornmeal

 2 teaspoons sugar

 1½ teaspoons FLEISCHMANN'S® Bread Machine Yeast

1½-Pound Loaf

  ⅔ cup plain low-fat yogurt

  ⅓ cup milk

 1 tablespoon butter or margarine

 1 teaspoon salt

 2¾ cups bread flour

  ½ cup cornmeal

 1 tablespoon sugar

 2 teaspoons FLEISCHMANN'S® Bread Machine Yeast

Add ingredients to bread machine pan in the order suggested by manufacturer, adding yogurt with milk. (Yogurts vary in moisture content. If dough is too dry or stiff, or too soft or slack, adjust dough consistency—see Adjusting Dough Consistency tip below.) Recommended cycle: Basic/white bread cycle; medium/normal crust color setting.

Makes 1 loaf (8 or 12 slices)

Adjusting Dough Consistency: Check dough after 5 minutes of mixing; it should form a soft, smooth ball around the blade. If dough is too stiff or dry, add additional liquid, 1 teaspoon at a time, until dough is of the right consistency. If dough is too soft or sticky, add additional bread flour, 1 teaspoon at a time.

Almond Amaretto Loaf

Almond Amaretto Loaf

1 cup milk

1 large egg

2 tablespoons butter or margarine

¼ cup amaretto liqueur

1 teaspoon lemon juice

¾ teaspoon salt

3 cups bread flour

½ cup chopped almonds, toasted

¼ cup sugar

2 teaspoons FLEISCHMANN'S®
  Bread Machine Yeast

  Amaretto Glaze (recipe follows)

¼ cup sliced almonds, toasted

Add all ingredients except glaze and sliced almonds to bread machine pan in the order suggested by manufacturer, adding chopped almonds with flour. (If dough is too dry or stiff, or too soft or slack, adjust dough consistency). Recommended cycle: Basic/white bread cycle; light or medium/ normal crust color setting. (*Do not use delay cycle.*)

Remove bread from pan; cool on wire rack. Drizzle with Amaretto Glaze and sprinkle with sliced almonds.

Makes 1 (1½-pound) loaf

Amaretto Glaze: Combine 1 cup powdered sugar, sifted, 2 tablespoons amaretto liqueur and enough milk (1 to 2 teaspoons) to make glaze of drizzling consistency.

Carrot-Raisin-Nut Bread

1½-Pound Loaf

    1 cup water
    1 cup shredded carrots
    2 tablespoons honey
    2 tablespoons butter or margarine
    1½ teaspoons salt
    3 cups bread flour
    ¼ cup whole wheat flour
    1½ teaspoons rapid-rise active dry
        yeast
    ⅓ cup chopped walnuts
    ⅓ cup raisins

2-Pound Loaf

    1¼ cups water
    1½ cups shredded carrots
    3 tablespoons honey
    3 tablespoons butter or margarine
    2 teaspoons salt
    4 cups bread flour
    ⅓ cup whole wheat flour
    2 teaspoons rapid-rise active dry
        yeast
    ½ cup chopped walnuts
    ½ cup raisins

1. Measuring carefully, place all ingredients except walnuts and raisins in bread machine pan in order specified by owner's manual.

2. Program basic cycle and desired crust setting; press start. Add walnuts and raisins when bread machine signals, or at end of first kneading cycle. Remove baked bread from pan; cool on wire rack.

Makes 1 loaf

Oven-Tested Tips

To keep ingredients like raisins and nuts evenly distributed in the batter, don't add them all clumped together. Dusting them first with a little flour or cinnamon will help keep them separated. If your machine doesn't have a raisin/nut cycle, try freezing the raisins, dried fruit and nuts before adding them at the start of the regular cycle. (To freeze, spread them out on a cookie sheet and place in the freezer.) They won't break down as easily

Carrot-Raisin-Nut Bread

Potato Bread

1½-Pound Loaf

1⅓ cups water

1½ tablespoons butter or margarine, softened

1½ teaspoons salt

3 cups bread flour

½ cup mashed potato flakes

2 tablespoons sugar

2 tablespoons nonfat dry milk powder

1½ teaspoons rapid-rise active dry yeast

2-Pound Loaf

1¾ cups water

2 tablespoons butter or margarine, softened

2 teaspoons salt

4 cups bread flour

¾ cup mashed potato flakes

3 tablespoons sugar

3 tablespoons nonfat dry milk powder

2 teaspoons rapid-rise active dry yeast

1. Measuring carefully, place all ingredients in bread machine pan in order specified by owner's manual.

2. Program basic cycle and desired crust setting; press start. Remove baked bread from pan; cool on wire rack.

Makes 1 loaf

Serving Suggestion: Serve with a homemade herb butter. To make, combine ½ cup softened butter and 1 tablespoon of your favorite chopped fresh herbs in a small bowl.

Wild Rice-Spinach-Feta Bread

¾ cup water

2 tablespoons honey

2 ounces frozen chopped spinach, thawed and squeezed dry

2½ cups bread flour

½ cup whole wheat flour

¾ teaspoon salt

1 tablespoon dried Italian seasoning

1 cup cooked wild rice

2 ounces crumbled feta cheese

2 teaspoons active dry yeast (not rapid-rise)

1. Measure carefully, placing ingredients in bread machine pan in order specified by owner's manual. Program dough cycle; press start.

2. Turn out dough onto lightly floured surface; shape into 2 to 3 baguettes. Place on greased baking sheet; cover and let rise in warm place 45 minutes or until doubled.

3. Bake in preheated 375°F oven 20 to 25 minutes or until browned and loaves sound hollow when lightly tapped.

Makes 2 to 3 baguettes

Favorite recipe from **Minnesota Cultivated Wild Rice Council**

Oven-Tested Tips

Never use the delayed start feature on your bread machine if the recipe includes perishable ingredients, like milk, eggs or cheese. It's also important to keep the yeast separated from wet ingredients, so it won't activate too soon.

Potato Bread

Triple Chocolate Sticky Buns

Dough

- ¼ cup water
- ½ cup sour cream
- 1 egg
- 3 tablespoons butter, softened
- 1 teaspoon salt
- 2¾ cups bread flour
- ⅓ cup unsweetened cocoa powder
- ¼ cup sugar
- 2 teaspoons active dry yeast

Topping

- ⅓ cup packed brown sugar
- ¼ cup butter
- 2 tablespoons light corn syrup
- 1 tablespoon unsweetened cocoa powder

Filling

- ⅓ cup packed brown sugar
- 3 tablespoons butter, softened
- ½ teaspoon ground cinnamon
- ½ to ¾ cup coarsely chopped walnuts, toasted*
- ½ cup semisweet chocolate chips

To toast walnuts, spread in single layer on baking sheet. Bake in preheated 350°F oven 8 to 10 minutes or until golden brown, stirring frequently.

1. Measuring carefully, place all dough ingredients in bread machine pan in order specified by owner's manual. Program dough cycle; press start. *(Do not use delay cycle.)* Lightly grease 9-inch round cake pan; set aside.

2. While dough is rising prepare topping by combining brown sugar, butter, corn syrup and cocoa powder in small saucepan. Cook over medium heat, stirring constantly, until sugar is dissolved and mixture bubbles around edge. Pour into prepared pan; set aside.

3. For filling, combine brown sugar, butter and cinnamon in small bowl; set aside.

4. When cycle is complete, punch down dough and remove to lightly floured surface. If necessary, knead in additional bread flour to make dough easy to handle. Roll into 12×8-inch rectangle. Spread with filling mixture. Sprinkle with walnuts and chocolate chips. Starting at long side, roll up tightly, jelly-roll fashion. Pinch seam to seal. Cut crosswise into 12 slices. Arrange over topping in pan. Cover with greased waxed paper. Let rise in warm place 45 to 60 minutes or until doubled in size.

5. Place piece of foil on oven rack to catch drippings. Preheat oven to 375°F. Bake about 25 minutes or just until buns in center of pan are firm to the touch. *Do not overbake.* Immediately invert onto serving plate. Serve warm or at room temperature.

Makes 12 rolls

Oven-Tested Tips

When shaping dough into rolls, buns or braids, you may need to let it rest. If the dough seems to spring back to its original size every time you try to stretch it, just place it on a lightly floured surface, cover it and give it 10 to 15 minutes of rest. This allows the elastic gluten strands in the dough to relax and makes it much easier to handle.

Triple Chocolate Sticky Bun

Roasted Pepper-Olive Loaf

1-Pound Loaf

- ½ cup water
- 2 tablespoons drained diced roasted red bell peppers or pimientos
- 1 tablespoon sliced pitted ripe olives, drained
- 1 tablespoon butter or margarine
- ¾ teaspoon salt
- 2 cups bread flour
- 2 tablespoons nonfat dry milk powder
- 2 teaspoons sugar
- 1½ teaspoons FLEISCHMANN'S® Bread Machine Yeast

1½-Pound Loaf

- ¾ cup water
- 3 tablespoons drained diced roasted red bell peppers or pimientos
- 2 tablespoons sliced pitted ripe olives, drained
- 1 tablespoon butter or margarine
- 1 teaspoon salt
- 3 cups bread flour
- 3 tablespoons nonfat dry milk powder
- 1 tablespoon sugar
- 2 teaspoons FLEISCHMANN'S® Bread Machine Yeast

Use the 1-pound recipe if your machine pan holds 10 cups or less of water. Add ingredients to bread machine pan in the order suggested by manufacturer, adding roasted red bell peppers and olives with water. Recommended cycle: Basic/white bread cycle; medium/normal crust color setting. Timed-bake feature can be used.

Makes 1 loaf (8 or 12 slices)

Serving Suggestion: For elegant, yet easy hors d'oeuvres, cut slices of this colorful bread into triangles. Serve the triangles topped with your favorite Cheddar, Swiss or cream cheese spread.

Maple-Walnut Bread

1½-Pound Loaf

- 1¼ cups water
- ¼ cup maple or pancake syrup
- ¼ teaspoon maple extract
- 1 tablespoon butter
- 1½ teaspoons salt
- 3 cups bread flour
- ¼ cup whole wheat flour
- ½ teaspoon ground cinnamon
- ½ cup coarsely chopped walnuts
- 1½ teaspoons rapid-rise active dry yeast

2-Pound Loaf

- 1½ cups water
- ⅓ cup maple or pancake syrup
- ½ teaspoon maple extract
- 2 tablespoons butter
- 2 teaspoons salt
- 4 cups bread flour
- ⅓ cup whole wheat flour
- ¾ teaspoon ground cinnamon
- ¾ cup coarsely chopped walnuts
- 2 teaspoons rapid-rise active dry yeast

1. Measuring carefully, place all ingredients in bread machine pan in order specified by owner's manual.

2. Program basic or white cycle and desired crust setting; press start. Remove baked bread from pan; cool on wire rack.

Makes 1 loaf (12 or 16 servings)

Ginger-Peach Blossoms

1 can (16 ounces) sliced peaches in light syrup, divided

Dough

¼ cup juice reserved from peaches

3 tablespoons milk

1 egg

3 tablespoons butter, softened

1 teaspoon salt

2¾ cups all-purpose flour

¼ cup granulated sugar

¼ cup packed brown sugar

1½ teaspoons ground ginger

1 teaspoon ground cinnamon

⅛ teaspoon ground cloves

⅛ teaspoon ground nutmeg

2 teaspoons active dry yeast

Topping

2 tablespoons granulated sugar, divided

⅛ teaspoon ground ginger

⅛ teaspoon ground cinnamon

1 egg, lightly beaten

1. Drain peaches, reserving ¼ cup juice. Coarsely chop peaches. Measuring carefully, place all dough ingredients and ½ cup chopped peaches in bread machine pan in order specified by owner's manual. Program dough cycle setting; press start. (*Do not use delay cycle.*) For topping, combine remaining peaches, 1 tablespoon granulated sugar, ginger and cinnamon in small bowl; set aside. Lightly grease 2 baking sheets; set aside.

2. When cycle is complete, punch down dough and remove to lightly floured surface. If necessary, knead in additional flour to make dough easy to handle. Divide dough into 12 equal pieces. Shape each piece into smooth ball. Place 2 inches apart on prepared baking sheets. Cover with clean towel; let rise in warm, draft-free place 45 to 60 minutes or until doubled in size.

3. Preheat oven to 350°F. Make indentation in center of each roll. Spoon heaping teaspoon peach mixture into each indentation. Using kitchen shears, make 5 deep vertical cuts around perimeter of each roll to form flower petals. Brush beaten egg over petals; sprinkle with remaining 1 tablespoon granulated sugar.

4. Bake 15 to 20 minutes or until golden brown. Remove from baking sheets; cool slightly on wire racks. Serve warm or at room temperature. *Makes 12 rolls*

Oven-Tested Tips

Learn to check the dough in your bread machine for the proper consistency during the kneading cycle. If your machine doesn't have a window, it's usually alright to lift the lid and peek. (Just don't do it during the rising or baking cycles.) The dough should form a soft, pliable mass around the blades. If it's in chunks, the dough is too dry. Add additional liquid, a teaspoon at a time. Dough that's too moist can be corrected by adding flour, a tablespoon at a time. Take note of the adjustments you make, so you can use them the next time you make the recipe.

Dilled Buttermilk Bread

1½-Pound Loaf
- ½ cup water
- 1 egg, lightly beaten
- ½ cup buttermilk*
- 1 tablespoon butter
- 1 teaspoon salt
- 3 cups bread flour
- 1 tablespoon sugar
- 1½ teaspoons dried dill weed
- 1½ teaspoons rapid-rise active dry yeast

2-Pound loaf
- ¾ cup water
- 1 egg, lightly beaten
- ¾ cup buttermilk*
- 1½ tablespoons butter
- 1½ teaspoons salt
- 4 cups bread flour
- 2 tablespoons sugar
- 2 teaspoons dried dill weed
- 2 teaspoons rapid-rise active dry yeast

You may substitute soured fresh milk. To sour milk, place 1 tablespoon lemon juice plus enough milk to equal 1 cup in 2-cup measure. Stir; let stand 5 minutes before using.

1. Measuring carefully, place all ingredients in bread machine pan in order specified by owner's manual.

2. Program basic cycle and desired crust setting; press start. (*Do not use delay cycle.*) Remove baked bread from pan; cool on wire rack.   *Makes 1 loaf*

Serving Suggestion: Serve with a flavored butter. To make, combine ½ cup softened butter, 1 tablespoon chopped fresh parsley and 1 tablespoon chopped red bell pepper in a small bowl.

Dried Cherry-Almond Bread

1-Pound Loaf
- ¾ cup milk
- 1 tablespoon butter or margarine
- 1 large egg
- ¾ teaspoon salt
- 2 cups bread flour
- ⅓ cup dried tart red cherries or dried cranberries
- ¼ cup slivered almonds, toasted*
- 1 tablespoon sugar
- 1½ teaspoons FLEISCHMANN'S® Bread Machine Yeast

1½-Pound Loaf
- 1 cup plus 2 tablespoons milk
- 1 tablespoon butter or margarine
- 1 large egg
- 1 teaspoon salt
- 3 cups bread flour
- ½ cup dried tart red cherries or dried cranberries
- ⅓ cup slivered almonds, toasted*
- 4 teaspoons sugar
- 2 teaspoons FLEISCHMANN'S® Bread Machine Yeast

Toasting nuts brings out their full flavor and helps keep them crisp. To toast, spread chopped nuts in a shallow baking pan in a single layer. Bake at 350°F for 5 to 15 minutes or until lightly toasted, stirring several times and checking often. Be sure to cool the nuts before adding to the bread machine.

Use the 1-pound recipe if your machine pan holds 10 cups or less of water. Add ingredients to bread machine pan in the order suggested by manufacturer, adding dried tart red cherries and almonds with flour. Recommended cycle: Basic/white bread cycle; light or medium/normal crust color setting. (*Do not use delay cycle.*)
          Makes 1 loaf (8 or 12 slices)

Dilled Buttermilk Bread

Take the Cake

Nothing is more celebratory, or more appreciated by family and friends, than a homemade cake. They're all here—chocolate cakes, pound cakes, cake rolls, whipped cream cakes, tortes and tube cakes—so don't wait for a birthday to get out those pans. With these recipes, turning simple ingredients into a memorable dessert is a cakewalk.

Chocolate Squares with Nutty Caramel Sauce

1 cup sugar

¾ cup all-purpose flour

½ cup HERSHEY'S Dutch Processed Cocoa or HERSHEY'S Cocoa

½ teaspoon baking powder

½ teaspoon salt

¾ cup vegetable oil

¼ cup milk

3 eggs

½ teaspoon vanilla extract

1 bag (14 ounces) caramel candies

½ cup water

1 cup pecan pieces

Sweetened whipped cream (optional)

1. Heat oven to 350°F. Grease bottom only of 8-inch square baking pan.

2. Stir together sugar, flour, cocoa, baking powder and salt in medium bowl. Add oil, milk, eggs and vanilla; beat until smooth. Pour batter into prepared pan.

3. Bake 35 to 40 minutes or until wooden pick inserted in center comes out clean. Cool completely in pan on wire rack.

4. Remove wrappers from caramels. Combine caramels and water in small saucepan. Cook over low heat, stirring occasionally, until smooth and well blended. Stir in pecans; cool until thickened slightly. Cut cake into squares; serve with warm caramel nut sauce and sweetened whipped cream, if desired.

Makes 9 servings

Chocolate Raspberry Avalanche Cake

2 cups all-purpose flour

2 cups granulated sugar

6 tablespoons unsweetened cocoa

1½ teaspoons baking soda

1 teaspoon salt

1 cup hot coffee

¾ Butter Flavor CRISCO® Stick or ¾ cup Butter Flavor CRISCO® all-vegetable shortening plus additional for greasing

½ cup milk

3 eggs

¼ cup raspberry-flavored liqueur
Confectioners' sugar

1 cup fresh raspberries

1. Heat oven to 350°F. Grease 10-inch (12-cup) Bundt pan with shortening. Flour lightly. Place wire rack on counter for cooling cake.

2. Combine flour, granulated sugar, cocoa, baking soda and salt in large bowl. Add coffee and ¾ cup shortening. Beat at low speed of electric mixer until dry ingredients are moistened. Add milk. Beat at medium speed 1½ minutes. Add eggs, 1 at a time, beating well after each addition. Pour into prepared pan.

3. Bake at 350°F for 40 to 45 minutes, or until toothpick inserted in center comes out clean. *Do not overbake.* Cool 10 minutes before removing from pan. Place cake, fluted side up, on wire rack. Cool 10 minutes. Brush top and side with liqueur. Cool completely. Dust top with confectioners' sugar.

4. Place cake on serving plate. Fill center with raspberries.

Makes 1 (10-inch) cake (12 to 16 servings)

Crunchy-Topped Cocoa Cake

1½ cups all-purpose flour

1 cup sugar

¼ cup HERSHEY'S Cocoa

1 teaspoon baking soda

½ teaspoon salt

1 cup water

¼ cup plus 2 tablespoons vegetable oil

1 tablespoon white vinegar

1 teaspoon vanilla extract
Broiled Topping (recipe follows)

1. Heat oven to 350°F. Grease and flour 8-inch square baking pan.

2. Stir together flour, sugar, cocoa, baking soda and salt in large bowl. Add water, oil, vinegar and vanilla; beat with spoon or whisk just until batter is smooth and well blended. Pour batter into prepared pan.

3. Bake 35 to 40 minutes or until wooden pick inserted in center comes out clean. Meanwhile, prepare Broiled Topping; spread on warm cake. Set oven to broil; place pan about 4 inches from heat. Broil 3 minutes or until top is bubbly and golden brown. Cool in pan on wire rack. *Makes 9 servings*

Broiled Topping

¼ cup butter or margarine

½ cup packed light brown sugar

½ cup coarsely chopped nuts

½ cup Mounds® Sweetened Coconut Flakes

3 tablespoons light cream or evaporated milk

Stir together all ingredients in small bowl until well-blended.

Chocolate Raspberry Avalanche Cake

Mom's Favorite White Cake

2¼ cups cake flour

1 tablespoon baking powder

½ teaspoon salt

½ cup butter, softened

1½ cups sugar

4 egg whites

2 teaspoons vanilla

1 cup milk

Strawberry Frosting (recipe follows)

Fruit Filling (recipe follows)

Fresh strawberries (optional)

Preheat oven to 350°F. Line bottoms of two 9-inch round cake pans with waxed paper; lightly grease paper. Combine flour, baking powder and salt in medium bowl; set aside.

Beat butter and sugar in large bowl with electric mixer at medium speed until light and fluffy. Add egg whites, two at a time, beating well after each addition. Add vanilla; beat until blended. With electric mixer at low speed, add flour mixture alternately with milk, beating well after each addition. Pour batter evenly into prepared pans.

Bake 25 minutes or until wooden toothpick inserted into centers comes out clean. Cool layers in pans on wire rack 10 minutes. Loosen edges and invert layers onto rack to cool completely.

Prepare Strawberry Frosting and Fruit Filling. To fill and frost cake, place one layer on cake plate; spread top with Fruit Filling. Place second layer over filling. Frost top and sides with Strawberry Frosting. Place strawberries on top of cake, if desired. Refrigerate; allow cake to stand at room temperature 15 minutes before serving.

Makes 12 servings

Strawberry Frosting

2 envelopes (1.3 ounces each) whipped topping mix

⅔ cup milk

1 cup (6 ounces) white chocolate chips, melted

¼ cup strawberry jam

Beat whipped topping mix and milk in medium deep bowl with electric mixer on low speed until blended. Beat on high speed 4 minutes until topping thickens and forms peaks. With mixer on low speed, beat melted chocolate into topping. Add jam; beat until blended. Chill 15 minutes or until spreading consistency.

Fruit Filling

1 cup Strawberry Frosting (recipe above)

1 can (8 ounces) crushed pineapple, drained

1 cup sliced strawberries

Combine Strawberry Frosting, pineapple and strawberries in medium bowl; mix well.

Oven-Tested Tips

Always cool a cake completely before frosting it. Use a soft pastry brush to remove all loose cake crumbs. If possible, make the cake the day before you plan to frost it; this makes it easier to work with. If you wish to decorate the cake the day it is made, place it in the freezer to firm it up while you make the frosting.

Scrumptious Apple Cake

3 egg whites

1½ cups sugar

1 cup unsweetened applesauce

1 teaspoon vanilla

2 cups all-purpose flour

2 teaspoons ground cinnamon

1 teaspoon baking soda

¼ teaspoon salt

4 cups cored peeled tart apple slices (McIntosh or Crispin)

Yogurt Glaze (recipe follows)

Preheat oven to 350°F. Beat egg whites until slightly foamy; add sugar, applesauce and vanilla. Combine flour, cinnamon, baking soda and salt in separate bowl; add to applesauce mixture. Spread apples in 13×9-inch pan or 9-inch round springform pan sprayed with nonstick cooking spray. Spread batter over apples. Bake 35 to 40 minutes or until wooden toothpick inserted in center comes out clean; cool on wire rack. Prepare Yogurt Glaze; spread over cooled cake.

Makes 15 to 20 servings

Yogurt Glaze: Combine 1½ cups plain or vanilla nonfat yogurt, 3 tablespoons brown sugar (or to taste) and 1 teaspoon vanilla or 1 teaspoon lemon juice. Stir together until smooth.

Favorite recipe from **New York Apple Association, Inc.**

Mom's Favorite White Cake

White Chocolate Pound Cake

3 cups flour

1 teaspoon CALUMET® baking powder

½ teaspoon salt

1 container (8 ounces) BREAKSTONE'S® or KNUDSEN® Sour Cream

1 can (8 ounces) crushed pineapple in juice, undrained

1 cup (2 sticks) butter, softened

2 cups sugar

5 eggs

1 package (6 squares) BAKER'S® Premium White Baking Chocolate, melted, cooled slightly

2 teaspoons vanilla

½ cup BAKER'S® ANGEL FLAKE® Coconut

HEAT oven to 350°F. Lightly grease and flour 12-cup fluted tube pan or 10-inch tube pan.

MIX flour, baking powder and salt; set aside. Mix sour cream and pineapple; set aside.

BEAT butter and sugar in large bowl with electric mixer on medium speed until light and fluffy. Add eggs, 1 at a time, beating well after each addition. Beat in melted chocolate and vanilla. Add flour mixture alternately with sour cream mixture. Beat in coconut. Pour into prepared pan.

BAKE 70 to 75 minutes or until toothpick inserted near center comes out clean. Cool in pan 10 minutes on wire rack. Loosen cake from side of pan with small knife or spatula. Invert cake onto rack; gently remove pan. Cool completely on wire rack. Sprinkle with powdered sugar, if desired.

Makes 12 to 16 servings

Prep Time: 20 minutes
Bake Time: 75 minutes

Kahlúa® Chocolate Decadence

½ cup butter

8 ounces (8 squares) semisweet baking chocolate, divided

3 extra large eggs

¾ cup granulated sugar

1¼ cups finely ground walnuts or pecans

2 tablespoons all-purpose flour

5 tablespoons KAHLÚA® Liqueur, divided

1 teaspoon vanilla

Sifted powdered sugar

Strawberries, chocolate nonpareil candy or coffee beans for garnish

Preheat oven to 325°F. In small saucepan over medium heat, or in microwave-safe bowl on HIGH (100% power), melt butter and 6 ounces chocolate, stirring until blended. Remove from heat; cool. In large bowl, beat eggs and granulated sugar at high speed of electric mixer about 3 minutes or until light and lemon colored. Stir together walnuts and flour; gradually beat into egg mixture.

Stir 3 tablespoons Kahlúa® and vanilla into cooled chocolate mixture; gradually beat into egg mixture until well combined. Pour batter into 9-inch springform pan. Bake 35 to 45 minutes or until top is set. Cool cake in pan.

Remove side of pan; place cake on serving plate. Sprinkle top with powdered sugar. Melt remaining 2 ounces chocolate as previously directed. Stir together melted chocolate and remaining 2 tablespoons Kahlúa®; drizzle over cake. Decorate with strawberries, if desired.

Makes 1 (9-inch) cake

White Chocolate Pound Cake

Raspberry Tortoni Cake Roll

Raspberry Tortoni Filling (recipe follows)

3 eggs, separated

¾ cup granulated sugar

¼ cup fat-free (skim) milk

1 teaspoon vanilla

¾ cup all-purpose flour

1½ teaspoons baking powder

¼ teaspoon salt

¼ teaspoon cream of tartar

1 tablespoon powdered sugar

¼ cup fresh raspberries (optional)

Mint sprigs (optional)

1. Prepare Raspberry Tortoni Filling. Set aside.

2. Lightly grease 15×10×1-inch jelly-roll pan and line with waxed paper; lightly grease and flour paper. Preheat oven to 400°F. Beat egg yolks in medium bowl with electric mixer at high speed 1 minute; gradually beat in granulated sugar until yolks are thick and lemon colored, about 5 minutes. Beat in milk and vanilla; mix in flour, baking powder and salt.

3. Beat egg whites in medium bowl at high speed until foamy; add cream of tartar and beat until stiff peaks form. Fold about one-third egg white mixture into cake batter; gently fold cake batter into remaining egg white mixture. Spread batter evenly in prepared pan.

4. Bake 8 to 10 minutes or until cake begins to brown. Immediately invert onto clean towel that has been sprinkled with powdered sugar. Peel off waxed paper; roll cake up in towel and cool on wire rack only 10 minutes.

5. Gently unroll cake and spread with Raspberry Tortoni Filling. Roll cake up; wrap in plastic wrap or foil and freeze until firm, at least 8 hours or overnight.

6. Remove cake from freezer; unwrap and trim ends, if uneven. Place cake on serving plate. Sprinkle with additional powdered sugar, fresh raspberries and mint, if desired.

Makes 12 servings

Raspberry Tortoni Filling

2 cups fresh or frozen unsweetened raspberries, thawed, drained and divided

1 tablespoon sugar

2 envelopes (1.3 ounces each) whipped topping mix

1 cup low-fat (1%) milk

½ teaspoon rum or sherry extract (optional)

¼ cup coarsely chopped pistachio nuts or blanched almonds

1. Place 1 cup raspberries in food processor or blender; process until smooth. Strain and discard seeds. Sprinkle sugar over remaining 1 cup raspberries.

2. Beat whipped topping mix with milk in medium bowl at high speed until stiff peaks form; fold in raspberry purée and rum, if desired. Fold in sugared raspberries and nuts.

Makes 4 cups

Angel Food Cake

1¼ cups cake flour, sifted
1⅓ cups plus ½ cup sugar, divided
12 egg whites
1¼ teaspoons cream of tartar
¼ teaspoon salt (optional)
1½ teaspoons vanilla
   Fresh strawberries for garnish
   (optional)

1. Preheat oven to 350°F.

2. Sift together flour with ½ cup sugar.

3. Beat egg whites with cream of tartar, salt and vanilla in large bowl at high speed with electric mixer until stiff peaks form.

4. Gradually add remaining 1⅓ cups sugar, beating well after each addition. Fold in flour mixture.

5. Pour into *ungreased* 10-inch tube pan.

6. Bake 35 to 40 minutes or until cake springs back when lightly touched.

7. Invert pan; place on top of clean empty bottle. Allow cake to cool completely before removing from pan.

8. Serve with strawberries, if desired.

Makes one 10-inch tube cake

Angel Food Cake

Lemon Poppy Seed Bundt Cake

Lemon Poppy Seed Bundt Cake

1 cup granulated sugar

½ cup (1 stick) butter, softened

1 egg, at room temperature

2 egg whites, at room temperature

¾ cup low-fat (1%) milk

2 teaspoons vanilla

2 cups all-purpose flour

2 tablespoons poppy seeds

1 tablespoon grated lemon peel

2 teaspoons baking powder

¼ teaspoon salt

4½ teaspoons powdered sugar

1. Preheat oven to 350°F. Grease and flour Bundt pan; set aside.

2. Beat granulated sugar, butter, egg and egg whites in large bowl with electric mixer at medium speed until well blended. Add milk and vanilla; mix well. Add flour, poppy seeds, lemon peel, baking powder and salt; beat about 2 minutes or until smooth.

3. Pour into prepared pan. Bake 30 minutes or until toothpick inserted into center comes out clean. Gently loosen cake from pan with knife and turn out onto wire rack; cool completely. Sprinkle with powdered sugar. Garnish as desired.

Makes 16 servings

Orange Baba Cake

2½ cups cake flour
1 teaspoon baking soda
¼ teaspoon salt
½ cup margarine, softened
1 cup reduced-fat sour cream
¾ cup granulated sugar
3 egg whites
1 tablespoon grated orange peel
⅓ cup fat-free (skim) milk
Orange Baba Syrup (recipe follows)
Powdered sugar (optional)

1. Preheat oven to 350°F. Grease and flour 6-cup bundt pan. Combine flour, baking soda and salt in medium bowl. Beat margarine in separate medium bowl with electric mixer at medium speed until fluffy. Beat in sour cream and granulated sugar until smooth. Beat in egg whites and orange peel. Beat in flour mixture, alternately with milk, beginning and ending with flour mixture.

2. Pour into prepared pan. Tap pan on countertop to remove air bubbles. Bake 45 to 50 minutes or until lightly browned and wooden pick inserted in cake comes out clean. Cool on wire rack 15 to 20 minutes. Meanwhile, prepare Orange Baba Syrup.

3. Pierce top of cake generously with wooden skewer; loosen side and center of cake with long, thin knife. Carefully spoon Orange Baba Syrup over cake, gently pressing cake away from side of pan with large spoon to allow syrup to flow to bottom of pan. Let stand 1 hour; invert onto serving plate. Garnish with powdered sugar, if desired.   *Makes 12 servings*

Orange Baba Syrup: Combine 1 cup sugar and ½ cup orange juice. Bring to a boil over high heat, stirring to dissolve sugar. Let stand until cool enough to handle. Makes about ¾ cup.

Golden Chiffon Cake

5 eggs, separated
¼ teaspoon cream of tartar
2¼ cups all-purpose flour
1⅓ cups sugar
1 tablespoon baking powder
1 teaspoon salt
¾ cup water
½ cup vegetable oil
1 teaspoon vanilla
½ teaspoon orange extract
Fresh fruit and whipped cream for garnish

1. Preheat oven to 325°F.

2. Beat egg whites and cream of tartar in large bowl until stiff peaks form; set aside. Sift flour, sugar, baking powder and salt into large bowl. Make a well in flour mixture. Add egg yolks, water, oil, vanilla and orange extract; mix well. Fold in egg white mixture.

3. Immediately spread in ungreased 10-inch tube pan. Bake 55 minutes. *Increase oven temperature to 350°F.* Continue baking 10 minutes or until cakes springs back when lightly touched with finger. Invert pan and allow cake to cool completely before removing from pan. Garnish with fresh fruit and whipped cream, if desired.

Makes one 10-inch tube cake

Orange Baba Cake

Hershey's "Perfectly Chocolate" Chocolate Cake

    2 cups sugar
1¾ cups all-purpose flour
    ¾ cup HERSHEY'S Cocoa or
       HERSHEY'S Dutch Processed
       Cocoa
1½ teaspoons baking powder
1½ teaspoons baking soda
    1 teaspoon salt
    2 eggs
    1 cup milk
    ½ cup vegetable oil
    2 teaspoons vanilla extract
    1 cup boiling water
       "Perfectly Chocolate" Chocolate
       Frosting (recipe follows)

1. Heat oven to 350°F. Grease and flour two 9-inch round baking pans.*

2. Stir together sugar, flour, cocoa, baking powder, baking soda and salt in large bowl. Add eggs, milk, oil and vanilla; beat on medium speed of mixer 2 minutes. Stir in water. (Batter will be thin.) Pour batter evenly into prepared pans.

3. Bake 30 to 35 minutes or until wooden pick inserted in center comes out clean. Cool 10 minutes; remove from pans to wire racks. Cool completely.

4. Prepare "Perfectly Chocolate" Chocolate Frosting; spread between layers and over top and sides of cake.   *Makes 8 to 10 servings*

One 13×9×2-inch baking pan may be substituted for 9-inch round baking pans. Prepare as directed above. Bake 35 to 40 minutes. Cool completely in pan on wire rack. Frost as desired.

"Perfectly Chocolate" Chocolate Frosting

    ½ cup (1 stick) butter or margarine
    ⅔ cup HERSHEY'S Cocoa
    3 cups powdered sugar
    ⅓ cup milk
    1 teaspoon vanilla extract

1. Melt butter. Stir in cocoa. Alternately add powdered sugar and milk, beating to spreading consistency.

2. Add small amount additional milk, if needed. Stir in vanilla.

Makes about 2 cups frosting

Oven-Tested Tips

Cake batter should not sit before baking, because baking powder and baking soda begin working as soon as they are mixed with liquids and will begin to dissipate. That's why it's important to prepare pans before mixing the batter. If you are baking two or more pans for a layer cake, allow at least an inch of space between the pans and two inches between the pans and the walls of the oven for proper heat circulation.

Pear-Ginger Upside-Down Cake

2 unpeeled Bosc or Anjou pears, cored and sliced ¼-inch thick

3 tablespoons fresh lemon juice

1 to 2 tablespoons melted butter

1 to 2 tablespoons packed brown sugar

1 cup all-purpose flour

1 teaspoon baking powder

¼ teaspoon baking soda

1 teaspoon ground cinnamon

⅛ teaspoon salt

⅓ cup fat-free (skim) milk

3 tablespoons no-sugar-added apricot spread

1 egg

1 tablespoon vegetable oil

1 tablespoon minced fresh ginger

1. Preheat oven to 375°F. Spray 10-inch deep-dish pie pan with nonstick cooking spray.

2. Toss pears in lemon juice; drain. Brush butter evenly onto bottom of prepared pan; sprinkle sugar over butter. Arrange pears in dish; bake 10 minutes.

3. Meanwhile, combine flour, baking powder, baking soda, cinnamon and salt in small bowl; set aside. Combine milk, apricot spread, egg, oil and ginger in medium bowl; mix well. Add flour mixture; stir until well mixed (batter is very thick). Carefully spread batter over pears to edges of pan.

4. Bake 20 to 25 minutes or until golden brown and toothpick inserted in center comes out clean.

5. Cool 5 minutes; use knife to loosen cake from sides of pan. Place 10-inch plate over top of pan; quickly turn over to transfer cake to plate. Place any pears left in pan on top of cake. Serve warm.

Makes 8 servings

Honey-Orange Spicecake

¾ cup honey

⅓ cup oil

¼ cup orange juice

2 eggs

1½ cups all-purpose flour

1 teaspoon baking powder

1 teaspoon ground cinnamon

½ teaspoon baking soda

¼ teaspoon ground cloves

Orange Syrup

¼ cup honey

¼ cup orange juice

2 teaspoons freshly grated orange peel

Using electric mixer, beat together honey, oil and orange juice; beat in eggs. Combine dry ingredients; gradually add to honey mixture, mixing until well blended.

Pour into lightly greased and floured 9×9-inch baking pan. Bake at 350°F for 25 to 30 minutes or until toothpick inserted in center comes out clean.

Meanwhile make syrup. In small saucepan, combine honey, orange juice and peel. Bring just to a boil. Remove from heat.

Remove cake from oven and immediately cut into squares. Pour hot syrup evenly over cake in pan. Cool in pan on wire rack.

Makes 9 servings

Favorite recipe from **National Honey Board**

Pear-Ginger Upside-Down Cake

Carrot Cake

¼ cup walnuts, chopped
1 cup whole wheat flour
1 cup all-purpose flour
2 teaspoons baking soda
2 teaspoons ground cinnamon
½ teaspoon salt
1 whole egg
3 egg whites
1½ cups granulated sugar
¾ cup buttermilk
½ cup unsweetened applesauce
¼ cup vegetable oil
3 teaspoons vanilla, divided
2 cups grated peeled carrots
1 can (8 ounces) crushed pineapple
    in juice, drained
1½ cups powdered sugar
1 tablespoon fat-free (skim) milk
1 tablespoon water

1. Preheat oven to 350°F. Spray 13×9×2-inch baking pan with nonstick cooking spray. Toast walnuts 8 to 10 minutes or until golden brown. Set aside. *Do not turn off oven.*

2. Sift both flours, baking soda, cinnamon and salt together in large bowl; set aside. Lightly beat egg and egg whites in another large bowl. Add granulated sugar, buttermilk, applesauce, oil and 2 teaspoons vanilla; mix well. Stir in flour mixture, carrots, pineapple and walnuts.

3. Pour batter into prepared pan. Bake 45 to 50 minutes or until wooden pick inserted in center comes out clean. Cool completely in pan on wire rack.

4. Combine powdered sugar, milk, water and remaining 1 teaspoon vanilla in medium bowl. Stir until smooth. Spread glaze over cooled cake.   *Makes 15 servings*

Carrot Cake

Flourless Chocolate Cake with Raspberry Sauce

Flourless Chocolate Cake with Raspberry Sauce

Cake

> 7 ounces semisweet baking
>   chocolate, broken into pieces
> ¾ cup (1½ sticks) unsalted butter
> 5 eggs, separated
> 1 teaspoon vanilla
> ⅓ cup sugar
> 2 tablespoons unsweetened cocoa
>   powder
> ⅛ teaspoon salt

Raspberry Sauce

> 1 package (12 ounces) frozen
>   unsweetened raspberries, thawed
> ⅓ to ½ cup sugar
>   Additional cocoa powder for
>   garnish

1. For cake, preheat oven to 350°F. Grease 9-inch springform pan. Heat chocolate and butter in medium saucepan over low heat until melted, stirring frequently. Remove from heat; whisk in egg yolks and vanilla. Blend in sugar, 2 tablespoons cocoa and salt.

2. Beat egg whites to soft peaks in large bowl. Stir about one fourth of egg whites into chocolate mixture. Fold chocolate mixture into remaining egg whites.

3. Spread batter evenly in prepared pan. Bake about 30 minutes or until toothpick inserted in center comes out clean and edge of cake begins to pull away from side of pan. Cool cake in pan on wire rack 2 to 3 minutes; carefully loosen edge of cake with sharp knife and remove side of pan. Cool cake completely. Cover and refrigerate overnight or up to 3 days, or wrap well and freeze up to 3 months.

4. For sauce, blend raspberries in blender or food processor until smooth. Strain sauce and discard seeds; stir in sugar to taste. Cut cake into wedges. (If frozen, allow at least 24 hours to defrost before cutting.) Sift additional cocoa over cake; serve with sauce. *Makes 8 to 10 servings*

Chocolate Almond Torte

4 eggs, separated

½ cup (1 stick) butter or margarine, softened

1 cup sugar

1 teaspoon almond extract

1 teaspoon vanilla extract

1 cup finely chopped toasted almonds

¾ cup all-purpose flour

½ cup unsweetened cocoa

½ teaspoon baking powder

½ teaspoon baking soda

⅔ cup milk

Chocolate Almond Frosting (recipe follows)

1. Line 2 (8- or 9-inch) round cake pans with waxed paper. Preheat oven to 350°F. In small mixing bowl, beat egg whites until soft peaks form; set aside.

2. In large mixing bowl, beat butter and sugar until fluffy. Add egg yolks and extracts; mix well.

3. In medium mixing bowl, combine almonds, flour, cocoa, baking powder and baking soda; add alternately with milk to butter mixture, beating well after each addition.

4. Fold in beaten egg whites. Pour into prepared pans. Bake 18 to 20 minutes or until wooden picks inserted near centers come out clean. Cool 10 minutes; remove from pans. Cool completely.

5. Prepare Chocolate Almond Frosting. Split each cake layer; fill and frost with frosting. Garnish as desired. Store covered in refrigerator. *Makes one 4-layer cake*

Prep Time: 30 minutes
Bake Time: 18 to 20 minutes

Chocolate Almond Frosting

2 (1-ounce) squares semi-sweet chocolate, chopped

1 (14-ounce) can EAGLE® BRAND Sweetened Condensed Milk (NOT evaporated milk)

1 teaspoon almond extract

1. In heavy saucepan over medium heat, melt chocolate with Eagle Brand. Cook and stir until mixture thickens, about 10 minutes.

2. Remove from heat; cool 10 minutes. Stir in almond extract; cool.

Sunny Lemon Cake

1½ cups sugar

1 cup vegetable oil

2 tablespoons grated lemon peel

1 tablespoon lemon juice

6 eggs

1⅔ cups plus 1 tablespoon all-purpose flour, divided

2 teaspoons baking powder

¼ teaspoon salt

⅓ cup sunflower kernels

1. Preheat oven to 300°F. Grease and flour two (9×5-inch) loaf pans.

2. Beat together sugar, oil, lemon peel and lemon juice in large bowl. Add eggs, one at a time, beating after each addition. Mix in 1⅔ cups flour, baking powder and salt. Toss remaining 1 tablespoon flour with sunflower kernels in small bowl; stir into batter.

3. Pour batter into prepared pans. Bake 1 hour or until toothpick inserted in centers comes out clean. Cool in pans on wire racks 10 minutes; remove from pans to cool completely. *Makes two 9×5-inch loaves*

Brandy Pecan Cake

    1 cup (2 sticks) butter, softened
1¼ cups granulated sugar
    ¾ cup packed brown sugar
    5 eggs
    1 cup sour cream
    ½ cup brandy
2¼ cups all-purpose flour
    ½ cup cornmeal
    2 teaspoons baking powder
    1 teaspoon ground cinnamon
    ¼ teaspoon ground nutmeg
    1 cup chopped pecans
       Brandy Glaze (recipe follows)
       Pecan halves for garnish

1. Preheat oven to 325°F. Generously grease and flour 10-inch tube pan.

2. Beat together butter and sugars in large bowl until light and fluffy. Add eggs, one at a time, beating well after each addition. Blend in sour cream and brandy.

3. Sift together dry ingredients. Add to butter mixture, mixing until well blended. Stir in pecans. Pour into prepared pan, spreading evenly to edges.

4. Bake 65 to 70 minutes or until wooden toothpick inserted in center comes out clean. (Surface will appear slightly wet in center.)

5. Cool cake in pan on wire rack 10 minutes. Loosen edges and remove to rack to cool completely.

6. Prepare Brandy Glaze.

7. Drizzle cake with Brandy Glaze. Garnish, if desired. Store tightly covered.

Makes one 10-inch tube cake

Brandy Glaze

    2 tablespoons butter
    1 cup powdered sugar
    1 teaspoon brandy
    4 to 5 teaspoons milk

1. Heat butter in medium saucepan over medium heat until melted and golden brown; cool slightly.

2. Add powdered sugar, brandy and milk; beat until smooth.

Oven-Tested Tips

A tube pan is a round pan with a deep side and hollow center. Bundt pans were originally a trademarked name for a type of tube pan with fluted sides. Now Bundt pan refers to any tube pan with a design molded into it. Tube and Bundt pans allow the cook to make a beautifully tall cake without the worry of layers. The hollow center helps the cake bake evenly. Always be sure to thoroughly grease the nooks and crannies in Bundt pans so you can unmold the cake easily.

Chocolate Strawberry Whipped Cream Cake

3 eggs
1 cup granulated sugar
⅓ cup water
1 teaspoon vanilla extract
¾ cup all-purpose flour
¼ cup HERSHEY'S Cocoa or HERSHEY'S Dutch Processed Cocoa
1 teaspoon baking powder
½ teaspoon salt
Powdered sugar
Strawberry Whipped Cream Filling (recipe follows)
Royal Glaze (recipe follows)

1. Heat oven to 375°F. Grease 15½×10½×1-inch jelly-roll pan. Line with wax paper; grease paper.

2. Beat eggs in large bowl on high speed of mixer until very thick and cream colored, about 5 minutes; gradually beat in granulated sugar. With mixer on low speed, beat in water and vanilla. Stir together flour, cocoa, baking powder and salt; gradually add to egg mixture, beating just until blended. Pour into prepared pan.

3. Bake 10 to 13 minutes or until wooden pick inserted in center comes out clean. Immediately invert pan onto towel sprinkled with powdered sugar; carefully peel off wax paper. Invert cake onto wire rack covered with wax paper. Cool completely.

4. Prepare Strawberry Whipped Cream Filling. Cut cake crosswise into four equal pieces, each about 10×3½ inches. Divide filling into thirds; spread evenly on three rectangles, leaving one plain rectangle for top. Cover and refrigerate until firm. To assemble, stack layers on top of each other with plain cake layer on top. Prepare Royal Glaze; spread over top. Refrigerate until serving. Cut into slices; refrigerate leftover cake. *Makes 8 to 10 servings*

Strawberry Whipped Cream Filling

1 cup rinsed, hulled and sliced fresh strawberries
¼ cup HERSHEY'S Strawberry Flavored Syrup
1 envelope unflavored gelatin
1 cup (½ pint) cold whipping cream

1. Purée strawberries with syrup in food processor or blender; sprinkle gelatin over mixture. Let stand until gelatin is softened, about 2 minutes; purée again for several seconds. Pour into medium microwave-safe bowl; microwave at HIGH (100%) 30 seconds to 1 minute, until mixture is hot, not boiling, and gelatin is dissolved. Cool to room temperature.

2. Beat whipping cream in small bowl on high speed of mixer until stiff; fold in strawberry mixture.

Royal Glaze

⅔ cup HERSHEY'S Semi-Sweet Chocolate Chips
¼ cup whipping cream

1. Place chocolate chips and whipping cream in small microwave-safe bowl. Microwave at HIGH (100%) 30 seconds; stir. If necessary, microwave at HIGH an additional 15 seconds at a time, stirring after each heating, just until chips are melted when stirred. Cool slightly until thickened, 5 to 10 minutes.

Chocolate Strawberry Whipped Cream Cake

Lady Baltimore Cake

2¼ cups sugar

1¼ cups shortening

2 teaspoons vanilla

3¼ cups all-purpose flour

4½ teaspoons baking powder

1½ teaspoons salt

1½ cups milk

8 egg whites, at room temperature

Filling (recipe follows)

Frosting (recipe follows)

1. Preheat oven to 350°F. Grease three (9-inch) round cake pans. Line bottom of pans with waxed paper.

2. Beat together sugar and shortening in large bowl until light and fluffy. Blend in vanilla.

3. Sift together dry ingredients. Add to sugar mixture alternately with milk, beating well after each addition.

4. Beat egg whites in separate bowl at high speed with electric mixer until stiff peaks form; fold into batter. Pour evenly into prepared pans.

5. Bake 30 minutes or until wooden pick inserted in centers comes out clean. Cool layers in pans on wire racks 10 minutes. Loosen edges and remove to racks to cool completely. Prepare filling and frosting.

6. To assemble, spread two cake layers with Filling; stack on cake plate. Top with remaining cake layer. Frost with Frosting.

Makes one 3-layer cake

Filling

½ cup (1 stick) butter

1 cup sugar

½ cup water

⅓ cup bourbon or brandy*

10 egg yolks, lightly beaten

1 cup finely chopped raisins

¾ cup chopped pecans

½ cup drained chopped maraschino cherries

½ cup flaked coconut

¾ teaspoon vanilla

Bourbon may be omitted. Increase water to ¾ cup. Add 1 tablespoon rum extract with vanilla.

1. Melt butter in medium saucepan. Stir in sugar, water and bourbon. Bring to a boil over medium-high heat, stirring occasionally to dissolve sugar.

2. Stir small amount of hot mixture into egg yolks; gradually add egg yolk mixture to remaining hot mixture in saucepan.

3. Cook over low heat until thickened; remove from heat.

4. Stir in raisins, pecans, cherries and coconut. Blend in vanilla. Cool completely.

Frosting

1½ cups sugar

½ cup water

2 egg whites**

2 teaspoons corn syrup or
   ¼ teaspoon cream of tartar

Dash salt

1 teaspoon vanilla

**Use clean, uncracked eggs.

1. Combine sugar, water, egg whites, corn syrup and salt in top of double boiler. Beat 30 seconds.

2. Place on top of range; cook, stirring occasionally, over simmering water 7 minutes.

3. Remove from heat; add vanilla. Beat 3 minutes or until frosting is of spreading consistency.

Mocha Marble Pound Cake

2 cups all-purpose flour

2 teaspoons baking powder

1 teaspoon baking soda

½ teaspoon salt

1 cup sugar

¼ cup FLEISCHMANN'S® Original Margarine, softened

1 teaspoon vanilla extract

½ cup EGG BEATERS® Healthy Real Egg Product

1 (8-ounce) container low-fat coffee yogurt

¼ cup unsweetened cocoa

Mocha Yogurt Glaze (recipe follows)

In small bowl, combine flour, baking powder, baking soda and salt; set aside.

In large bowl, with electric mixer at medium speed, beat sugar, margarine and vanilla until creamy. Add Egg Beaters®; beat until smooth. With mixer at low speed, add yogurt alternately with flour mixture, beating well after each addition. Remove half of batter to medium bowl. Add cocoa to batter remaining in large bowl; beat until blended. Alternately spoon coffee and chocolate batters into greased 9×5×3-inch loaf pan. With knife, cut through batters to create marbled effect.

Bake at 325°F for 60 to 65 minutes or until toothpick inserted in center comes out clean. Cool in pan on wire rack for 10 minutes. Remove from pan; cool completely on wire rack. Frost with Mocha Yogurt Glaze.   *Makes 16 servings*

Mocha Yogurt Glaze: In small bowl, combine ½ cup powdered sugar, 1 tablespoon unsweetened cocoa and 1 tablespoon low-fat coffee yogurt until smooth; add more yogurt, if necessary, to make spreading consistency.

Prep Time: 20 minutes
Bake Time: 65 minutes

Oven-Tested Tips

Traditionally, a proper pound cake was made from a pound of butter, a pound of flour, a pound of eggs and a pound of sugar. Modern cooks have modified this formula to make it healthier and more flavorful. Pound cakes of all kinds are still favorites with bakers since they're easy to make and they keep well.

Start with a Mix

Whether you're looking for a showstopping dessert for a dinner party or just baking with the kids on a rainy afternoon, starting with a mix puts you way ahead of the game. Turn an ordinary cake mix into Chocolate-Orange Bavarian Torte or transform a baking mix into Peanut Butter Surprise Cookies. These recipes offer lots of ways to mix up some magic.

Cheddar and Apple Muffins

2 cups buttermilk baking mix
½ to 1 teaspoon ground red pepper
½ teaspoon salt
⅔ cup milk
1 egg, lightly beaten
1 medium apple, peeled, cored and grated
1 cup (4 ounces) shredded sharp Cheddar cheese

1. Preheat oven to 375°F. Spray 12 (2½-inch) muffin cups with nonstick cooking spray.

2. Combine baking mix, red pepper and salt in large bowl. Add milk and egg; mix until just moistened. *Do not overmix.* Fold in apple and cheese.

3. Spoon batter into muffin cups until three-fourths full. Bake 20 to 25 minutes or until golden brown. Cool 5 minutes in pan. Loosen sides of muffins with knife; remove from pan to wire rack. Serve warm.

Makes 12 muffins

Chocolate-Chocolate Cake

1 package (8 ounces) PHILADELPHIA® Cream Cheese, softened
1 cup BREAKSTONE'S® or KNUDSEN® Sour Cream
½ cup coffee-flavored liqueur or water
2 eggs
1 package (2-layer size) chocolate cake mix
1 package (4-serving size) JELL-O® Chocolate Flavor Instant Pudding & Pie Filling
1 cup BAKER'S® Semi-Sweet Real Chocolate Chunks

MIX cream cheese, sour cream, liqueur and eggs with electric mixer on medium speed until well blended. Add cake mix and pudding mix; beat until well blended. Fold in chocolate chunks. (Batter will be stiff.)

POUR into greased and floured 12-cup fluted tube pan.

BAKE at 325°F for 1 hour to 1 hour and 5 minutes or until toothpick inserted near center comes out clean. Cool 5 minutes. Remove from pan. Cool completely on wire rack. Sprinkle with powdered sugar before serving. Garnish, if desired.

Makes 10 to 12 servings

Prep Time: 10 minutes plus cooling
Bake Time: 1 hour 5 minutes

Cinnamon-Raisin Rolls

1 package (16 ounces) hot roll mix plus ingredients to prepare mix
⅓ cup raisins
4 tablespoons butter, softened and divided
¼ cup granulated sugar
2 teaspoons ground cinnamon
½ teaspoon ground nutmeg
1½ cups powdered sugar
1 to 2 tablespoons fat-free (skim) milk
½ teaspoon vanilla

1. Preheat oven to 375°F. Spray 13×9-inch baking pan with nonstick cooking spray.

2. Prepare hot roll mix according to package directions; mix in raisins. Knead dough on lightly floured surface until smooth and elastic, about 5 minutes. Cover dough with plastic wrap; let stand 5 minutes.

3. Roll out dough on floured surface to 16×10-inch rectangle. Spread dough with 2 tablespoons butter. Combine granulated sugar, cinnamon and nutmeg in small bowl; sprinkle evenly over dough. Roll up dough starting at long end. Pinch edge of dough to seal.

4. Gently stretch sealed dough until 18 inches long. Cut dough into 1-inch pieces; place, cut side up, in prepared pan. Cover pan loosely with towel. Let stand 20 to 30 minutes or until doubled in size.

5. Bake 20 to 25 minutes or until golden. Cool in pan on wire rack 2 to 3 minutes. Remove from pan; cool on wire rack.

6. Combine powdered sugar, remaining 2 tablespoons butter, 1 tablespoon milk and vanilla in medium bowl. Add additional 1 tablespoon milk to make thin glaze, if needed. Spread glaze over warm rolls.

Makes 1½ dozen rolls

Chocolate-Chocolate Cake

Angel Food Roll with Strawberry Sauce

1 box (16 ounces) angel food cake mix

¼ cup plus 2 tablespoons powdered sugar

1 quart strawberry low-fat frozen yogurt

1 container (10 ounces) frozen sliced strawberries with sugar, thawed

1 tablespoon lemon juice

1½ teaspoons cornstarch

1. Preheat oven to 350°F. Line bottom of 15×10-inch jelly-roll pan with waxed paper. Prepare cake mix according to package directions; pour evenly into prepared pan. Bake about 20 minutes or until cake is golden brown and springs back when lightly touched.

2. Cool on wire rack 15 minutes. Lay clean kitchen towel on flat surface. Sift ¼ cup powdered sugar over towel; invert cake on top of sugar. Carefully peel off waxed paper. Starting at short end, roll cake up with towel, jelly-roll style. Cool 30 minutes, seam side down, on wire rack.

3. While cake is cooling, remove frozen yogurt from freezer to soften. Carefully unroll cake. Using rubber spatula, place pieces of frozen yogurt on top of cake; spread to edges with table knife. Reroll filled cake; cover tightly with plastic wrap. Freeze at least 3 hours or overnight.

4. To prepare strawberry sauce, combine strawberries, lemon juice and cornstarch in small saucepan; bring to a boil over medium heat. Reduce heat to low; cook and stir 2 to 3 minutes until sauce has thickened. Let cool; refrigerate until ready to serve.

5. To complete recipe, remove cake from freezer 15 minutes before serving. Dust with remaining 2 tablespoons powdered sugar. Cut into slices with serrated knife; serve with strawberry sauce.   *Makes 8 servings*

Make-Ahead Time: at least 3 hours or up to 24 hours before serving
Final Prep Time: 20 minutes

Tomato Cheese Bread

1 can (14.5 ounces) CONTADINA® Recipe Ready Diced Tomatoes

2 cups buttermilk baking mix

2 teaspoons dried oregano leaves, crushed, divided

¾ cup (3 ounces) shredded Cheddar cheese

¾ cup (3 ounces) shredded Monterey Jack cheese

1. Drain tomatoes, reserving juice.

2. Combine baking mix, 1 teaspoon oregano and ⅔ cup reserved tomato juice in medium bowl.

3. Press dough evenly to edge of 11×7×2-inch greased baking dish. Sprinkle Cheddar cheese and remaining oregano over batter. Distribute tomato pieces evenly over cheese; sprinkle with Jack cheese.

4. Bake in preheated 375°F oven 25 minutes, or until edges are golden brown and cheese is bubbly. Cool 5 minutes before cutting into squares to serve.   *Makes 12 servings*

Angel Food Roll with Strawberry Sauce

Della Robbia Cake

1 package DUNCAN HINES® Angel
    Food Cake Mix
1½ teaspoons grated lemon peel
  1 cup water
  6 tablespoons granulated sugar
1½ tablespoons cornstarch
  1 tablespoon lemon juice
  ½ teaspoon vanilla extract
    Few drops red food coloring
  6 cling peach slices
  6 medium strawberries, sliced

Preheat oven to 375°F.

Prepare cake mix as directed on package, adding lemon peel. Bake and cool cake as directed on package.

Combine water, sugar and cornstarch in small saucepan. Cook on medium-high heat until mixture thickens and clears. Remove from heat. Stir in lemon juice, vanilla extract and food coloring.

Alternate peach slices with strawberry slices around top of cake. Pour glaze over fruit and top of cake. *Makes 12 to 16 servings*

Tip: For angel food cakes, always use a totally grease-free cake pan to get the best volume.

Della Robbia Cake

Chocolate Peanut Butter Cups

Chocolate Peanut Butter Cups

1 package DUNCAN HINES® Moist Deluxe® Swiss Chocolate Cake Mix

1 container DUNCAN HINES® Creamy Home-Style Classic Vanilla Frosting

½ cup creamy peanut butter

15 miniature peanut butter cup candies, wrappers removed, cut in half vertically

1. Preheat oven to 350°F. Place 30 (2½-inch) paper liners in muffin cups.

2. Prepare, bake and cool cupcakes following package directions for basic recipe.

3. Combine vanilla frosting and peanut butter in medium bowl. Stir until smooth. Frost one cupcake. Decorate with peanut butter cup candy, cut side down. Repeat with remaining cupcakes and candies.

Makes 30 servings

Tip: You may substitute DUNCAN HINES® Moist Deluxe® Devil's Food, Dark Chocolate Fudge or Butter Recipe Fudge Cake Mix flavors for Swiss Chocolate Cake Mix.

Peanut Butter Surprise Cookies

24 miniature peanut butter cups
1 can (14 ounces) sweetened condensed milk (not evaporated milk)
¾ cup JIF® Creamy Peanut Butter
¼ Butter Flavor CRISCO® Stick or ¼ cup Butter Flavor CRISCO® all-vegetable shortening
1 egg
1 teaspoon vanilla
2 cups regular all-purpose baking mix

1. Remove wrappers from peanut butter cups. Cut candy into quarters.

2. Combine condensed milk, peanut butter, ¼ cup shortening, egg and vanilla in large bowl. Beat at medium speed of electric mixer until smooth. Add baking mix. Beat until well blended. Stir in candy pieces with spoon. Cover. Refrigerate 1 hour.

3. Heat oven to 350°F. Place sheets of foil on countertop for cooling cookies.

4. Drop dough by slightly rounded teaspoonfuls 2 inches apart onto ungreased baking sheet. Shape into balls with spoon.

5. Bake at 350°F for 7 to 9 minutes or until light brown around edges and center is just set. *Do not overbake*. Cool 2 minutes on baking sheet. Remove cookies to foil to cool completely.   *Makes about 4 dozen cookies*

Variation: Shape dough into 1¼-inch balls. Place 2 inches apart onto ungreased baking sheet. Dip fork in flour; flatten dough slightly in crisscross pattern.

Strawberry Streusel Squares

1 package (about 18 ounces) yellow cake mix, divided
3 tablespoons uncooked old-fashioned oats
1 tablespoon margarine
1½ cups sliced strawberries
¾ cup plus 2 tablespoons water, divided
¾ cup diced strawberries
3 egg whites
⅓ cup unsweetened applesauce
½ teaspoon ground cinnamon
⅛ teaspoon ground nutmeg

1. Preheat oven to 350°F. Spray 13×9-inch baking pan with nonstick cooking spray; lightly coat with flour.

2. Combine ½ cup cake mix and oats in small bowl. Cut in margarine until mixture resembles coarse crumbs; set aside.

3. Place 1½ cups sliced strawberries and 2 tablespoons water in blender or food processor. Process until smooth. Transfer to small bowl and stir in ¾ cup diced strawberries. Set aside.

4. Place remaining cake mix in large bowl. Add ¾ cup water, egg whites, applesauce, cinnamon and nutmeg. Blend 30 seconds at low speed or just until moistened. Beat at medium speed 2 minutes. Pour batter into prepared pan.

5. Spoon strawberry mixture evenly over batter, spreading lightly. Sprinkle evenly with oat mixture. Bake 31 to 34 minutes or until wooden toothpick inserted into center comes out clean. Cool completely in pan on wire rack.   *Makes 12 servings*

Orange Chocolate Chip Bread

½ cup nonfat milk

½ cup plain nonfat yogurt

⅓ cup sugar

¼ cup orange juice

1 egg, slightly beaten

1 tablespoon freshly grated orange peel

3 cups all-purpose biscuit baking mix

½ cup **HERSHEY'S MINI CHIPS™ Semi-Sweet Chocolate Chips**

1. Heat oven to 350°F. Grease 9×5×3-inch loaf pan or spray with vegetable cooking spray.

2. Stir together milk, yogurt, sugar, orange juice, egg and orange peel in large bowl; add baking mix. With spoon, beat until well blended, about 1 minute. Stir in small chocolate chips. Pour into prepared pan.

3. Bake 45 to 50 minutes or until wooden pick inserted in center comes out clean. Cool 10 minutes; remove from pan to wire rack. Cool completely before slicing. Garnish as desired. Wrap leftover bread in foil or plastic wrap. Store at room temperature or freeze for longer storage.

Makes 1 loaf (16 slices)

Orange Chocolate Chip Bread

Chocolate-Orange Bavarian Torte

1 package (about 9 ounces) chocolate cake mix (1 layer size)
2¼ cups water
2 tablespoons vegetable oil
3 eggs
½ teaspoon orange extract
½ teaspoon almond extract
Orange Bavarian (recipe follows)
Chocolate Glaze (recipe follows)

1. Preheat oven to 350°F. Grease and flour one 9-inch round baking pan.

2. Combine cake mix, water, oil, eggs and extracts in large bowl. Beat at low speed of electric mixer until blended. Beat at medium speed 2 to 3 minutes or until well blended. Pour into prepared pan.

3. Bake 30 to 35 minutes or until wooden toothpick inserted into center of cake comes out clean. Cool in pan on wire rack 10 minutes. Remove cake from pan; cool completely.

4. Prepare Orange Bavarian. Place cake layer on serving plate; invert bavarian on top of cake. Prepare Chocolate Glaze; pour over torte. *Makes 10 to 12 servings*

Orange Bavarian

1 envelope unflavored gelatin
¾ cup milk
½ cup plus 2 tablespoons sugar, divided
2 eggs, separated and at room temperature
½ cup frozen orange juice concentrate, thawed and undiluted
1 tablespoon grated orange peel
1 teaspoon vanilla extract
½ cup whipping cream

1. Grease 6-cup fluted pan.

2. Pour milk into medium saucepan. Sprinkle gelatin over milk; let stand several minutes to soften. Add ½ cup sugar and 2 egg yolks to gelatin mixture; mix well. Cook over medium-low heat, stirring constantly, until mixture thickens slightly. *Do not boil.* Remove from heat; set aside.

3. Combine orange juice concentrate, orange peel and vanilla in small bowl; mix well. Add orange juice mixture to gelatin mixture. Cool mixture in refrigerator, stirring occasionally, until it begins to set.

4. Meanwhile, beat egg whites in small bowl until soft peaks form. Add remaining 2 tablespoons sugar and beat until stiff peaks form. Gently fold into orange-gelatin mixture. Beat whipping cream in chilled bowl until stiff peaks form. Gently fold into orange mixture. Pour into prepared pan; refrigerate until set.

5. Dip bottom of mold briefly into warm water. Place serving plate on top of mold. Invert mold and plate and shake to loosen gelatin. Gently remove mold.

Chocolate Glaze

3 tablespoons butter
3 tablespoons light corn syrup
2 tablespoons water
1 cup semisweet chocolate chips

Combine butter, corn syrup and water in small saucepan. Heat over medium-high heat until mixture begins to boil. Remove from heat and stir in chocolate chips until melted. Blend until smooth; cool to room temperature.

Chocolate-Orange Bavarian Torte

Easy Lemon Pudding Cookies

1 cup BISQUICK® Original Baking Mix

1 package (4-serving size) JELL-O® Lemon Flavor Instant Pudding & Pie Filling

½ teaspoon ground ginger (optional)

1 egg, lightly beaten

¼ cup vegetable oil

Sugar

3 squares BAKER'S® Premium White Baking Chocolate, melted

HEAT oven to 350°F.

STIR baking mix, pudding mix and ginger in medium bowl. Mix in egg and oil until well blended. (Mixture will be stiff.) With hands, roll cookie dough into 1-inch diameter balls. Place balls 2 inches apart on lightly greased cookie sheets. Dip flat-bottom glass into sugar. Press glass onto each dough ball and flatten into ¼-inch-thick cookie.

BAKE 10 minutes or until edges are golden brown. Immediately remove from cookie sheets. Cool on wire racks. Drizzle cookies with melted white chocolate.

Makes about 20 cookies

How To Melt Chocolate: Microwave 3 squares BAKER'S® Premium White Baking Chocolate in heavy zipper-style plastic sandwich bag on HIGH 1 to 1½ minutes or until chocolate is almost melted. Gently knead bag until chocolate is completely melted. Fold down top of bag; snip tiny piece off 1 corner from bottom. Holding top of bag tightly, drizzle chocolate through opening across tops of cookies.

Prep Time: 10 minutes
Bake Time: 10 minutes

Kahlúa® Black Forest Cake

1 package (18¼ ounces) chocolate fudge cake mix with pudding

3 eggs

¾ cup water

½ cup KAHLÚA® Liqueur

⅓ cup vegetable oil

1 can (16 ounces) vanilla or chocolate frosting

1 can (21 ounces) cherry pie filling

Chocolate sprinkles or chocolate shavings for garnish (optional)

Preheat oven to 350°F. Grease and flour 2 (9-inch) cake pans; set aside. In large mixer bowl, prepare cake mix using 3 eggs, ¾ cup water, Kahlúa® and ⅓ cup oil. Pour batter into prepared pans. Bake 25 to 35 minutes or until toothpick inserted in center comes out clean. Cool cake in pans 10 minutes; turn layers out onto wire racks to cool completely.

Place one cake layer, bottom side up, on serving plate. Spread thick layer of frosting in circle, 1½ inches around outer edge of cake. Spoon half of cherry filling into center of cake layer to frosting edge. Top with second cake layer, bottom side down. Repeat with frosting and remaining cherry filling. Spread remaining frosting around side of cake. Decorate with chocolate sprinkles or shavings, if desired.

Makes 1 (9-inch) cake

Quick Cinnamon Sticky Buns

1 cup packed light brown sugar, divided

10 tablespoons butter, softened and divided

1 package (16-ounce) hot roll mix

2 tablespoons granulated sugar

1 cup hot water (120° to 130°F)

1 egg

1⅔ cups (10-ounce package) HERSHEY'S Cinnamon Chips

1. Lightly grease two 9-inch round baking pans. Combine ½ cup brown sugar and 4 tablespoons softened butter in small bowl with pastry blender; sprinkle mixture evenly on bottom of prepared pans. Set aside.

2. Combine contents of hot roll mix package, including yeast packet, and granulated sugar in large bowl. Using spoon, stir in water, 2 tablespoons butter and egg until dough pulls away from sides of bowl. Turn dough onto lightly floured surface. With lightly floured hands, shape into ball. Knead 5 minutes or until smooth, using additional flour if necessary.

3. To shape: Using lightly floured rolling pin, roll into 15×12-inch rectangle. Spread with remaining 4 tablespoons butter. Sprinkle with remaining ½ cup brown sugar and cinnamon chips, pressing lightly into dough. Starting with 12-inch side, roll tightly as for jelly roll; seal edges.

4. Cut into 1-inch-wide slices with floured knife. Arrange 6 slices, cut sides down, in each prepared pan. Cover with towel; let rise in warm place until doubled, about 30 minutes.

5. Heat oven to 350°F. Uncover rolls. Bake 25 to 30 minutes or until golden brown. Cool 2 minutes in pan; with knife, loosen around edges of pan. Invert onto serving plates. Serve warm or at room temperature.

Makes 12 cinnamon buns

Quick Cinnamon Sticky Buns

Dump Cake

1 (20-ounce) can crushed pineapple with juice, undrained

1 (21-ounce) can cherry pie filling

1 package DUNCAN HINES® Moist Deluxe® Yellow Cake Mix

1 cup chopped pecans or walnuts

½ cup (1 stick) butter or margarine, cut into thin slices

Preheat oven to 350°F. Grease 13×9-inch pan.

Dump pineapple with juice into pan. Spread evenly. Dump in pie filling. Spread evenly. Sprinkle cake mix evenly over cherry layer. Sprinkle pecans over cake mix. Dot with butter. Bake 50 minutes or until top is lightly browned. Serve warm or at room temperature.   *Makes 12 to 16 servings*

Tip: You can use DUNCAN HINES® Moist Deluxe® Pineapple Supreme Cake Mix in place of Moist Deluxe® Yellow Cake Mix.

Dump Cake

Black and White Pistachio Cake

Cake

1 package (about 18 ounces) marble cake mix

3 eggs

1¼ cups water

⅓ cup vegetable oil

½ teaspoon vanilla

Filling

2 packages (4-serving size each) pistachio instant pudding and pie filling mix

3 cups milk

⅓ cup chopped maraschino cherries, drained

¼ cup chopped pistachio nuts

Frosting

1¼ cups cold milk

1 package (4-serving size) pistachio instant pudding and pie filling mix

2 envelopes whipped topping mix

Additional marachino cherries and pistachio nuts (optional)

Cake

Preheat oven to 350°F. Grease and flour two 8-inch round cake pans.

Combine cake mix, eggs, water, oil and vanilla in large bowl. Mix according to package directions. Spread half of batter in one pan. Stir contents of chocolate packet into remaining batter. Spread chocolate batter in second pan. Bake and cool according to package directions.

Filling

Prepare pudding mix using 3 cups milk. Stir in cherries and pistachios. Refrigerate until ready to use.

Frosting

Combine milk, pudding mix and whipped topping mix in large bowl. Beat at low speed with electric mixer until blended. Beat at high speed 2 to 3 minutes or until stiff, scraping sides of bowl often.

To assemble cake, split each cake layer in half. Alternate chocolate cake layer with white cake layer, spreading filling between each layer. Frost top and side of cake with frosting. Garnish with marachino cherries and pistachios, if desired.

Makes one 4-layer cake

Oreo® Brownie Treats

15 OREO® Chocolate Sandwich Cookies, coarsely chopped

1 (21½-ounce) package deluxe fudge brownie mix, batter prepared according to package directions

2 pints ice cream, any flavor

1. Stir cookie pieces into prepared brownie batter. Pour into greased 13×9-inch baking pan.

2. Bake according to brownie mix package directions for time and temperature. Cool.

3. To serve, cut into 12 squares and top each with a scoop of ice cream.

Makes 12 servings

Oven-Tested Tips

To split cake layers, tightly loop a piece of unflavored dental floss horizontally around the center of the cake. Cross the ends, then pull gently and slowly.

Black and White Pistachio Cake

Heavenly Lemon Muffins

1 (16-ounce) package angel food cake mix

3 cups all-purpose flour

4 teaspoons baking powder

½ teaspoon salt

1 cup granulated sugar

⅔ cup skim milk

⅔ cup MOTT'S® Natural Apple Sauce

¼ cup vegetable oil

2 egg whites

2 tablespoons grated lemon peel

2 teaspoons lemon extract

4 drops yellow food coloring (optional)

2 tablespoons powdered sugar (optional)

1. Preheat oven to 375°F. Line 24 (2½-inch) muffin cups with paper liners or spray with nonstick cooking spray.

2. In large bowl, prepare angel food cake mix according to package directions.

3. In another large bowl, combine flour, baking powder and salt.

4. In medium bowl, combine granulated sugar, milk, apple sauce, oil, egg whites, lemon peel, lemon extract and food coloring, if desired.

5. Stir apple sauce mixture into flour mixture just until moistened.

6. Fill each muffin cup ⅓ full with apple sauce batter. Top with angel food cake batter, filling each cup almost full.*

7. Bake 20 minutes or until golden and puffed. Immediately remove from pan; cool completely on wire rack. Sprinkle tops with powdered sugar, if desired.

Makes 24 servings

There will be some angel food cake batter remaining.

Heavenly Strawberry Muffins: Substitute strawberry extract for lemon extract and red food coloring for yellow food coloring, if desired. Eliminate lemon peel.

Heavenly Lemon Muffin

Pretty-in-Pink Peppermint Cupcakes

Pretty-in-Pink Peppermint Cupcakes

1 package (about 18 ounces) white
    cake mix

1⅓ cups water

3 large egg whites

2 tablespoons vegetable oil or melted
    butter

½ teaspoon peppermint extract

3 to 4 drops red liquid food coloring
    or ¼ teaspoon gel food coloring

1 container (16 ounces) prepared
    vanilla frosting

½ cup crushed peppermint candies
    (about 16 candies)

1. Preheat oven to 350°F. Line 30 regular-size (2½-inch) muffin pan cups with pink or white paper muffin cup liners.

2. Beat cake mix, water, egg whites, oil, peppermint extract and food coloring with electric mixer at low speed 30 seconds. Beat at medium speed 2 minutes.

3. Spoon batter into prepared cups filling ¾ full. Bake 20 to 22 minutes or until toothpick inserted into centers comes out clean. Cool in pans on wire racks 10 minutes. Remove cupcakes to racks; cool completely. (At this point, cupcakes may be frozen up to 3 months. Thaw at room temperature before frosting.)

4. Spread cooled cupcakes with frosting; top with crushed candies. Store at room temperature up to 24 hours or cover and refrigerate up to 3 days before serving.

Makes about 30 cupcakes

Cappuccino Cupcakes

1 package (about 18 ounces) dark chocolate cake mix

1⅓ cups strong brewed or instant coffee at room temperature

⅓ cup vegetable oil or melted butter

3 large eggs

1 container (16 ounces) prepared vanilla frosting

2 tablespoons coffee liqueur

Grated chocolate*

Additional coffee liqueur (optional)

Chocolate-covered coffee beans (optional)

*Grate half of a 3- or 4-ounce milk, dark chocolate or espresso chocolate candy bar on the large holes of a standing grater.

1. Preheat oven to 350°F. Line 24 regular-size (2½-inch) muffin cups with paper muffin cup liners.

2. Beat cake mix, coffee, oil and eggs with electric mixer at low speed 30 seconds. Beat at medium speed 2 minutes.

3. Spoon batter into prepared muffin cups filling ⅔ full. Bake 18 to 20 minutes or until toothpick inserted in centers comes out clean. Cool in pans on wire racks 10 minutes. Remove cupcakes to racks; cool completely. (At this point, cupcakes may be frozen up to 3 months. Thaw at room temperature before frosting.)

4. Combine frosting and 2 tablespoons liqueur in small bowl; mix well. Before frosting, poke about 10 holes in cupcake with toothpick. Pour 1 to 2 teaspoons liqueur over top of each cupcake, if desired. Frost and sprinkle with chocolate. Garnish with chocolate-covered coffee beans, if desired. *Makes 24 cupcakes*

Peanut Butter Chip & Banana Mini Muffins

2 cups all-purpose biscuit baking mix

¼ cup sugar

2 tablespoons butter or margarine, softened

1 egg

1 cup mashed very ripe bananas (2 to 3 medium)

1 cup REESE'S® Peanut Butter Chips

Quick Glaze (recipe follows, optional)

1. Heat oven to 400°F. Grease small muffin cups (1¾ inches in diameter).

2. Stir together baking mix, sugar, butter and egg in medium bowl; with fork, beat vigorously for 30 seconds. Stir in bananas and peanut butter chips. Fill muffin cups ⅔ full with batter.

3. Bake 12 to 15 minutes or until golden brown. Meanwhile, prepare Quick Glaze, if desired. Immediately remove muffins from pan; dip tops of warm muffins into glaze. Serve warm.

Makes about 4 dozen small muffins

Quick Glaze

1½ cups powdered sugar

2 tablespoons water

Stir together powdered sugar and water in small bowl until smooth and of desired consistency. Add additional water, ½ teaspoon at a time, if needed.

Cappuccino Cupcakes

Chocolate Toffee Cream Cake

1 package DUNCAN HINES® Moist Deluxe® Dark Chocolate Fudge Cake Mix

3 eggs

1⅓ cups water

½ cup vegetable oil

1 (6-ounce) package milk chocolate English toffee chips, divided

1 (12-ounce) container extra creamy non-dairy whipped topping, thawed

Preheat oven to 350°F. Grease and flour two 9-inch round cake pans.

Blend cake mix, eggs, water and oil in large mixing bowl until moistened. Beat at medium speed with electric mixer for 4 minutes. Pour into prepared pans. Bake 30 to 33 minutes or until toothpick inserted in center comes out clean. Cool in pans 15 minutes. Remove from pans. Cool completely. Reserve ¼ cup toffee chips; fold remaining chips into whipped topping. Place one cake layer on serving plate; spread with ¾ cup topping mixture. Top with remaining layer. Frost sides and top with remaining topping mixture; garnish with reserved chips. Refrigerate until ready to serve. *Makes 12 to 16 servings*

Tip: If chocolate toffee chips are not available, 4 chocolate covered toffee candy bars can be substituted. Chop bars in a food processor until small pieces form.

Apple-Gingerbread Mini Cakes

1 large Cortland or Jonathan apple, cored and quartered

1 package (about 14 ounces) gingerbread cake and cookie mix

1 cup water

1 egg

Powdered sugar

Microwave Directions

1. Lightly grease 10 (6- to 7-ounce) custard cups; set aside. Grate apple in food processor or with hand-held grater. Combine grated apple, cake mix, water and egg in medium bowl; stir until well blended. Spoon about ⅓ cup mix into each custard cup, filling cups half full.

2. Arrange 5 cups in microwave. Microwave at HIGH 2 minutes. Rotate cups ½ turn. Microwave 1 minute more or until cakes are springy when touched and look slightly moist on top. Cool on wire rack. Repeat with remaining cakes.

3. To unmold cakes, run a small knife around edge of custard cups to loosen cakes while still warm. Invert on cutting board and tap lightly until cake drops out. Place on plates. When cool enough, dust with powdered sugar, if desired. Serve warm or at room temperature. *Makes 10 cakes*

Serving Suggestion: Serve with vanilla ice cream, whipped cream or crème anglaise.

Prep and Cook Time: 20 minutes

Cookie Jar Classics

Who could resist Cocoa Pecan Crescents or Chocolate Chip Shortbread? Cookies are easy to make, quick to bake and fun to eat. Be sure to make a double batch of whatever dough you're mixing up, because most cookies also keep well. That way you'll have plenty to sample hot from the oven and enough left to stock the cookie jar.

Choco-Scutterbotch

⅔ **Butter Flavor CRISCO® Stick or ⅔ cup Butter Flavor CRISCO® all-vegetable shortening**
½ **cup firmly packed brown sugar**
2 **eggs**
1 **package (18¼ ounces) deluxe yellow cake mix**
1 **cup toasted rice cereal**
½ **cup butterscotch chips**
½ **cup milk chocolate chunks**
½ **cup semisweet chocolate chips**
½ **cup coarsely chopped walnuts or pecans**

1. Heat oven to 375°F. Place sheets of foil on countertop for cooling cookies.

2. Combine ⅔ cup shortening and brown sugar in large bowl. Beat at medium speed with electric mixer until well blended. Beat in eggs.

3. Add cake mix gradually at low speed. Mix until well blended. Stir in cereal, butterscotch chips, chocolate chunks, chocolate chips and nuts. Stir until well blended.

4. Shape dough into 1¼-inch balls. Place 2 inches apart on ungreased baking sheet. Flatten slightly. Shape sides to form circle, if necessary.

5. Bake for 7 to 9 minutes or until lightly browned around edges. *Do not overbake.* Cool 2 minutes on baking sheet. Remove cookies to foil to cool completely. *Makes 3 dozen cookies*

Crispy's Irresistible Peanut Butter Marbles

1 package (18 ounces) refrigerated peanut butter cookie dough

2 cups "M&M's"® Milk Chocolate Mini Baking Bits, divided

1 cup crisp rice cereal, divided (optional)

1 package (18 ounces) refrigerated sugar cookie dough

¼ cup unsweetened cocoa powder

In large bowl combine peanut butter dough, 1 cup "M&M's"® Milk Chocolate Mini Baking Bits and ½ cup cereal, if desired.

Remove dough to small bowl; set aside. In large bowl combine sugar dough and cocoa powder until well blended. Stir in remaining 1 cup "M&M's"® Milk Chocolate Mini Baking Bits and remaining ½ cup cereal, if desired. Remove half the dough to small bowl; set aside. Combine half the peanut butter dough with half the chocolate dough by folding together just enough to marble. Shape marbled dough into 8×2-inch log. Wrap log in plastic wrap. Repeat with remaining doughs. Refrigerate logs 2 hours. To bake, preheat oven to 350°F. Cut dough into ¼-inch-thick slices. Place about 2 inches apart on ungreased cookie sheets. Bake 12 to 14 minutes. Cool 1 minute on cookie sheets; cool completely on wire racks. Store in tightly covered container.

Makes 5 dozen cookies

Crispy's Irresistible Peanut Butter Marbles

Butterscotch Blondies

Butterscotch Blondies

¾ cup (1½ sticks) butter or
  margarine, softened

¾ cup packed light brown sugar

½ cup granulated sugar

2 eggs

2 cups all-purpose flour

1 teaspoon baking soda

½ teaspoon salt

1⅔ cups (10-ounce package)
  HERSHEY'S Butterscotch Chips

1 cup chopped nuts (optional)

1. Heat oven to 350°F. Grease 13×9×2-inch baking pan.

2. Beat butter, brown sugar and granulated sugar in large bowl until creamy. Add eggs; beat well. Stir together flour, baking soda and salt; gradually add to butter mixture, blending well. Stir in butterscotch chips and nuts, if desired. Spread into prepared pan.

3. Bake 30 to 35 minutes or until top is golden brown and center is set. Cool completely in pan on wire rack. Cut into bars. *Makes about 36 bars*

Chocolate Sugar Cookies

2 cups flour
1 teaspoon baking soda
¼ teaspoon salt
3 squares BAKER'S® Unsweetened Baking Chocolate
1 cup (2 sticks) butter or margarine
1 cup sugar
1 egg
1 teaspoon vanilla
Additional sugar

HEAT oven to 375°F. Mix flour, baking soda and salt in medium bowl.

MICROWAVE chocolate and butter in large microwavable bowl on HIGH 2 minutes or until butter is melted. Stir until chocolate is completely melted.

STIR 1 cup sugar into melted chocolate mixture until well blended. Mix in egg and vanilla until completely blended. Stir in flour mixture until well blended. Refrigerate dough about 15 minutes or until easy to handle.

SHAPE dough into 1-inch balls; roll in additional sugar. Place on ungreased cookie sheets.

BAKE 8 to 10 minutes or until set. (If flatter, crisper cookies are desired, flatten with bottom of glass before baking.) Remove from cookie sheets. Cool on wire racks. Store in tightly covered container.

Makes about 3½ dozen cookies

Jam-Filled Chocolate Sugar Cookies: Prepare Baker's® Chocolate Sugar Cookie dough as directed. Roll in finely chopped nuts in place of sugar. Make indentation in each ball; fill center with your favorite jam. Bake as directed.

Chocolate-Caramel Sugar Cookies: Prepare Baker's® Chocolate Sugar Cookie dough as directed. Roll in finely chopped nuts in place of sugar. Make indentation in each ball; bake as directed. Microwave 1 package (14 ounces) KRAFT® Caramels with 2 tablespoons milk in microwavable bowl on HIGH 3 minutes or until melted, stirring after 2 minutes. Fill centers of cookies with caramel mixture. Drizzle with melted Baker's® Semi-Sweet Chocolate.

Prep Time: 20 minutes plus refrigerating
Bake Time: 10 minutes

Cashew-Lemon Shortbread Cookies

½ cup roasted cashews
1 cup (2 sticks) butter, softened
½ cup sugar
2 teaspoons lemon extract
1 teaspoon vanilla
2 cups all-purpose flour
Additional sugar

1. Preheat oven to 325°F. Place cashews in food processor; process until finely ground. Add butter, sugar, lemon extract and vanilla; process until well blended. Add flour; process using on/off pulsing action until dough is well blended and begins to form a ball.

2. Shape dough into 1½-inch balls; roll in additional sugar. Place about 2 inches apart on ungreased baking sheets; flatten.

3. Bake cookies 17 to 19 minutes or just until set and edges are lightly browned. Remove cookies from baking sheets to wire rack to cool.

Makes 2 to 2½ dozen cookies

Prep & Bake Time: 30 minutes

Chocolate Sugar Cookies, Jam-Filled Chocolate Sugar Cookies and Chocolate-Caramel Sugar Cookies

Soft Molasses Spice Cookies

2¼ cups all-purpose flour

1 teaspoon baking soda

1 teaspoon ground cinnamon

½ teaspoon ground ginger

¼ teaspoon ground nutmeg

⅛ teaspoon salt

⅛ teaspoon ground cloves

½ cup plus 2 tablespoons butter, softened and divided

½ cup packed dark brown sugar

1 egg

½ cup molasses

1¼ teaspoons vanilla, divided

¼ cup plus 2 to 3 tablespoons milk, divided

¾ cup raisins (optional)

2 cups powdered sugar

1. Preheat oven to 350°F. Grease cookie sheets. Combine flour, baking soda, cinnamon, ginger, nutmeg, salt and cloves in medium bowl.

2. Beat ½ cup butter in large bowl with electric mixer at medium speed until smooth and creamy. Gradually beat in brown sugar until blended; increase speed to high and beat until light and fluffy. Beat in egg until fluffy. Beat in molasses and 1 teaspoon vanilla until smooth. Beat in flour mixture at low speed alternately with ¼ cup milk until blended. Stir in raisins, if desired.

3. Drop rounded tablespoonfuls of dough about 1½ inches apart onto prepared cookie sheets. Bake 12 minutes or until set. Let cookies stand on cookie sheets 5 minutes; transfer to wire racks to cool completely.

4. For icing, melt remaining 2 tablespoons butter in small saucepan over medium-low heat. Remove from heat; add powdered sugar and stir until blended. Add remaining 2 tablespoons milk and ¼ teaspoon vanilla; stir until smooth. If icing is too thick, add milk, 1 teaspoon at a time, until desired consistency.

5. Spread icing over tops of cookies. Let stand 15 minutes or until icing is set. Store in airtight container.

Makes about 3 dozen cookies

Honey Shortbread

1 cup butter

⅓ cup honey

1 teaspoon vanilla

2½ cups all-purpose flour

¾ cup chopped pecans

Preheat oven to 300°F. Beat butter, honey and vanilla in large bowl with electric mixer at medium speed until mixture is light and fluffy. Add flour, 1 cup at a time, beating well after each addition. If dough becomes too stiff to stir, knead in remaining flour by hand. Knead in nuts. Pat dough into shortbread mold or ungreased 9-inch cast iron skillet. Score surface with knife so it can be divided into 24 wedges. With fork, prick deeply into the scores.

Bake 35 to 40 minutes. Cool in pan on wire rack 10 minutes. Remove from pan. Cut into wedges while warm.

Makes 2 dozen wedges

Favorite recipe from **National Honey Board**

Chocolate Chip Shortbread

½ cup (1 stick) butter, softened
½ cup sugar
1 teaspoon vanilla
1 cup all-purpose flour
¼ teaspoon salt
½ cup mini semisweet chocolate chips

1. Preheat oven to 375°F.

2. Beat butter and sugar in large bowl with electric mixer at medium speed until light and fluffy. Beat in vanilla. Add flour and salt; beat at low speed. Stir in chips.

3. Divide dough in half. Press each half into *ungreased* 8-inch round cake pan.

Bake 12 minutes or until edges are golden brown. Score shortbread with sharp knife, taking care not to cut completely through shortbread. Make 8 triangles per pan.

4. Let pans stand on wire racks 10 minutes. Invert shortbread onto wire racks; cool completely. Break into triangles.

Makes 16 cookies

Chocolate Chip Shortbread

Classic Refrigerator Sugar Cookies

Classic Refrigerator Sugar Cookies

1 cup (2 sticks) butter, softened

1 cup sugar

1 egg

1 teaspoon vanilla

2 cups all-purpose flour

2 teaspoons baking powder

Dash nutmeg

¼ cup milk

Colored sprinkles or melted semisweet chocolate chips* (optional)

To dip 24 cookies, melt 1 cup chocolate chips in small saucepan over very low heat until smooth.

1. Beat butter in large bowl with electric mixer at medium speed until smooth. Add sugar; beat until well blended. Add egg and vanilla; beat until well blended.

2. Combine flour, baking powder and nutmeg in medium bowl. Add flour mixture and milk alternately to butter mixture, beating at low speed after each addition until well blended.

3. Shape dough into 2 logs, each about 2 inches in diameter and 6 inches long. Roll logs in colored sprinkles, if desired, coating evenly (about ¼ cup sprinkles per roll). Or, leave logs plain and decorate cookies with melted chocolate after baking. Wrap each log in plastic wrap. Refrigerate 2 to 3 hours or overnight.

4. Preheat oven to 350°F. Grease cookie sheets. Cut logs into ¼-inch-thick slices; place 1 inch apart on prepared cookie sheets. (Keep unbaked logs and sliced cookies chilled until ready to bake.)

5. Bake 8 to 10 minutes or until edges are golden brown. Transfer to wire racks to cool.

6. Dip plain cookies in melted chocolate, or drizzle chocolate over cookies with fork or spoon, if desired. Set cookies on wire racks until chocolate is set. Store in airtight container.   *Makes about 4 dozen cookies*

Tiny Mini Kisses Peanut Blossoms

¾ cup REESE'S® Creamy Peanut Butter
½ cup shortening
⅓ cup granulated sugar
⅓ cup packed light brown sugar
1 egg
3 tablespoons milk
1 teaspoon vanilla extract
1½ cups all-purpose flour
½ teaspoon baking soda
½ teaspoon salt
   Granulated sugar
   HERSHEY'S MINI KISSES™ Semi-Sweet or Milk Chocolates

1. Heat oven to 350°F.

2. Beat peanut butter and shortening in large bowl with mixer until well mixed. Add ⅓ cup granulated sugar and brown sugar; beat well. Add egg, milk and vanilla; beat until fluffy. Stir together flour, baking soda and salt; gradually add to peanut butter mixture, beating until blended. Shape into ½-inch balls. Roll in granulated sugar; place on ungreased cookie sheet.

3. Bake 5 to 6 minutes or until set. Immediately press Mini Kiss™ into center of each cookie. Remove from cookie sheet to wire rack. *Makes about 14 dozen cookies*

Variation: For larger cookies, shape dough into 1-inch balls. Roll in granulated sugar. Place on ungreased cookie sheet. Bake 10 minutes or until set. Immediately place 3 Mini Kisses™ in center of each cookie, pressing down slightly. Remove from cookie sheet to wire rack. Cool completely.

Nancy's Dishpan Cookies

2 Butter Flavor CRISCO® Sticks or 2 cups Butter Flavor CRISCO® all-vegetable shortening plus additional for greasing
2 cups firmly packed light brown sugar
2 eggs
1 tablespoon vanilla
2 cups all-purpose flour
2 cups oats (quick or old-fashioned, uncooked)
1 teaspoon salt
1 teaspoon baking soda
1 teaspoon ground cinnamon
2 cups semisweet chocolate chips
1⅔ cups butterscotch chips
2 cups large pecan halves

1. Heat oven to 375°F. Grease baking sheet with shortening. Place sheets of foil on countertop for cooling cookies.

2. Combine shortening and brown sugar in very large bowl. Beat at medium speed of electric mixer until well blended. Beat in eggs and vanilla.

3. Combine flour, oats, salt, baking soda and cinnamon. Add gradually to creamed mixture at low speed. Finish mixing with spoon. Stir in chocolate chips, butterscotch chips and nuts. Fill ice cream scoop that holds ¼ cup with dough, rounding slightly (or use ¼-cup measure). Drop 3 inches apart onto prepared baking sheet.

4. Bake at 375°F for 12 to 15 minutes or until light brown and just set. *Do not overbake*. Cool 2 minutes on baking sheet. Remove cookies to foil to cool completely. *Makes about 2½ dozen cookies*

Baker's® Premium Chocolate Chunk Cookies

1¾ cups flour

¾ teaspoon baking soda

¼ teaspoon salt

¾ cup (1½ sticks) butter or margarine, softened

½ cup granulated sugar

½ cup firmly packed brown sugar

1 egg

1 teaspoon vanilla

1 package (12 ounces) BAKER'S® Semi-Sweet Chocolate Chunks

1 cup chopped nuts (optional)

HEAT oven to 375°F.

MIX flour, baking soda and salt in medium bowl; set aside.

BEAT butter and sugars in large bowl with electric mixer on medium speed until light and fluffy. Add egg and vanilla; beat well. Gradually beat in flour mixture. Stir in chocolate chunks and nuts. Drop by heaping tablepoonfuls onto ungreased cookie sheets.

BAKE 11 to 13 minutes or just until golden brown. Cool on cookie sheets 1 minute. Remove to wire racks and cool completely.

Makes about 3 dozen cookies

Bar Cookies: Spread dough in greased foil-lined 15×10×1-inch baking pan. Bake at 375°F for 18 to 20 minutes or until golden brown. (Or, bake in 13×9-inch pan for 20 to 22 minutes.) Cool completely in pan on wire rack. Makes 3 dozen.

Chocolate Chunkoholic Cookies: Omit nuts. Stir in 2 packages (12 ounces each) BAKER'S® Semi-Sweet Chocolate Chunks. Drop by scant ¼ cupfuls onto cookie sheets. Bake at 375°F for 12 to 14 minutes. Makes about 22 large cookies.

Freezing Cookie Dough: Freeze heaping tablespoonfuls of cookie dough on cookie sheet 1 hour. Transfer to airtight plastic container or freezer zipper-style plastic bag. Freeze dough up to 1 month. Bake frozen cookie dough at 375°F for 15 to 16 minutes or just until golden brown.

Prep Time: 15 minutes
Bake Time: 11 to 13 minutes

Marvelous Macaroons

1 can (8 ounces) DOLE® Crushed Pineapple

1 can (14 ounces) sweetened condensed milk

1 package (7 ounces) flaked coconut

½ cup margarine, melted

½ cup chopped almonds, toasted

1 teaspoon grated lemon peel

¼ teaspoon almond extract

1 cup all-purpose flour

1 teaspoon baking powder

• Preheat oven to 350°F. Drain crushed pineapple well, pressing out excess juice with back of spoon. In large bowl, combine drained pineapple, milk, coconut, margarine, almonds, lemon peel and almond extract.

• In small bowl, combine flour and baking powder. Beat into pineapple mixture until blended. Drop heaping tablespoonfuls of dough 1 inch apart onto greased cookie sheets.

• Bake 13 to 15 minutes or until lightly browned. Garnish with whole almonds, if desired. Cool on wire racks. Store in covered container in refrigerator.

Makes about 3½ dozen cookies

Baker's® Premium Chocolate Chunk Cookies

Hikers' Bar Cookies

¾ cup all-purpose flour

½ cup packed brown sugar

½ cup uncooked quick oats

¼ cup toasted wheat germ

¼ cup unsweetened applesauce

¼ cup margarine or butter, softened

⅛ teaspoon salt

½ cup cholesterol-free egg substitute

¼ cup raisins

¼ cup dried cranberries

¼ cup sunflower kernels

1 tablespoon grated orange peel

1 teaspoon ground cinnamon

1. Preheat oven to 350°F. Lightly coat 13×9-inch baking pan with nonstick cooking spray; set aside.

2. Beat flour, sugar, oats, wheat germ, applesauce, margarine and salt in large bowl with electric mixer at medium speed until well blended. Add egg substitute, raisins, cranberries, sunflower kernels, orange peel and cinnamon. Spread into pan.

3. Bake 15 minutes or until firm to touch. Cool completely in pan. Cut into 24 squares. *Makes 24 servings*

Hikers' Bar Cookies

Chewy Oatmeal-Apricot-Date Bars

Cookies

1¼ cups firmly packed brown sugar

¾ plus 4 teaspoons Butter Flavor CRISCO® Stick or ¾ cup plus 4 teaspoons Butter Flavor CRISCO® all-vegetable shortening plus additional for greasing

3 eggs

2 teaspoons vanilla

2 cups quick oats, uncooked, divided

½ cup all-purpose flour

2 teaspoons baking powder

1 teaspoon cinnamon

¼ teaspoon nutmeg

¼ teaspoon salt

1 cup finely grated carrots

1 cup finely minced dried apricots

1 cup minced dates

1 cup finely chopped walnuts

⅔ cup vanilla chips

Frosting

2½ cups confectioners' sugar

1 (3-ounce) package cream cheese, softened

¼ Butter Flavor CRISCO® Stick or ¼ cup Butter Flavor CRISCO® all-vegetable shortening

1 to 2 teaspoons milk

¾ teaspoon lemon extract

½ teaspoon vanilla

½ teaspoon finely grated lemon peel

⅓ cup finely chopped walnuts

1. Heat oven to 350°F. Place cooling rack on countertop. Grease 13×9-inch baking pan. Flour lightly.

2. For cookies, combine brown sugar and ¾ cup plus 4 teaspoons shortening in large bowl. Beat at medium speed of electric mixer until fluffy. Add eggs, 1 at a time, and 2 teaspoons vanilla. Beat until well blended and fluffy.

3. Process ½ cup oats in food processor or blender until finely ground. Combine ground oats with flour, baking powder, cinnamon, nutmeg and salt in medium bowl. Add oat mixture gradually to creamed mixture at low speed. Add remaining 1½ cups oats, carrots, apricots, dates, 1 cup nuts and vanilla chips. Mix until partially blended. Finish mixing with spoon. Spread in prepared pan.

4. Bake 35 to 45 minutes or until center is set and cookie starts to pull away from sides of pan. Toothpick inserted in center should come out clean. *Do not overbake.* Cool completely on cooling rack.

5. For frosting, combine confectioners' sugar, cream cheese, ¼ cup shortening, milk, lemon extract, vanilla and lemon peel in medium bowl. Beat at low speed until blended. Increase speed to medium-high. Beat until fluffy. Stir in ⅓ cup nuts. Spread on baked surface. Cut into bars about 2¼×2 inches. Refrigerate.   *Makes about 24 bars*

Oven-Tested Tips

When making bar cookies, be sure to use the pan size called for in the recipe. A larger pan will produce thin, dry cookies; a smaller one will leave them undercooked and gummy in the center. If you are using a glass pan instead of a metal one, reduce oven temperature by 25°F.

Honey Ginger Snaps

2 cups all-purpose flour

1 tablespoon ground ginger

2 teaspoons baking soda

⅛ teaspoon salt

⅛ teaspoon ground cloves

½ cup shortening

¼ cup (½ stick) butter, softened

1½ cups sugar, divided

¼ cup honey

1 egg

1 teaspoon vanilla

Preheat oven to 350°F. Grease cookie sheets. Combine flour, ginger, baking soda, salt and cloves in medium bowl.

Beat shortening and butter in large bowl with electric mixer at medium speed until smooth. Gradually beat in 1 cup sugar until blended; increase speed to high and beat until light and fluffy. Beat in honey, egg and vanilla until fluffy. Gradually stir in flour mixture until blended.

Shape mixture into 1-inch balls. Place remaining ½ cup sugar in shallow bowl; roll balls in sugar to coat. Place 2 inches apart on prepared cookie sheets.

Bake 10 minutes or until golden brown. Let cookies stand on cookie sheets 5 minutes; transfer to wire racks to cool completely. Store in airtight container up to 1 week.

Makes 3½ dozen cookies

Oven-Tested Tips

Before measuring honey (or other sticky ingredients), lightly oil the measuring cup, or spray with nonstick cooking spray. The honey will slide out easily.

Oatmeal Toffee Bars

1 cup (2 sticks) butter or margarine, softened

½ cup packed light brown sugar

½ cup granulated sugar

2 eggs

1 teaspoon vanilla extract

1½ cups all-purpose flour

1 teaspoon baking soda

½ teaspoon ground cinnamon

½ teaspoon salt

3 cups quick-cooking or regular rolled oats

1¾ cups (10-ounce package) SKOR® English Toffee Bits *or* 1¾ cups HEATH® BITS 'O BRICKLE™, divided

1. Heat oven to 350°F. Grease 13×9×2-inch baking pan.

2. Beat butter, brown sugar and granulated sugar in large bowl until well blended. Add eggs and vanilla; beat well. Stir together flour, baking soda, cinnamon and salt; gradually add to butter mixture, beating until well blended. Stir in oats and 1⅓ cups toffee bits (mixture will be stiff). Spread mixture into prepared pan.

3. Bake 25 minutes or until wooden pick inserted in center comes out clean. Immediately sprinkle remaining toffee bits over surface. Cool completely in pan on wire rack. Cut into bars.

Makes about 36 bars

Tip: Bar cookies can be cut into different shapes for variety. To cut into triangles, cut cookie bars into 2- to 3-inch squares, then diagonally cut each square in half. To make diamond shapes, cut parallel lines 2 inches apart across the length of the pan, then cut diagonal lines 2 inches apart.

Peanutty Cranberry Bars

½ cup (1 stick) butter or margarine, softened

½ cup granulated sugar

¼ cup packed light brown sugar

1 cup all-purpose flour

1 cup quick-cooking rolled oats

¼ teaspoon baking soda

¼ teaspoon salt

1 cup REESE'S® Peanut Butter Chips

1½ cups fresh or frozen whole cranberries

⅔ cup light corn syrup

½ cup water

1 teaspoon vanilla extract

1. Heat oven to 350°F. Grease 8-inch square baking pan.

2. Beat butter, granulated sugar and brown sugar in medium bowl until fluffy. Stir together flour, oats, baking soda and salt; gradually add to butter mixture, mixing until mixture is consistency of coarse crumbs. Stir in peanut butter chips.

3. Reserve 1½ cups mixture for crumb topping. Firmly press remaining mixture evenly into prepared pan. Bake 15 minutes or until set. Meanwhile, in medium saucepan, combine cranberries, corn syrup and water. Cook over medium heat, stirring occasionally, until mixture boils. Reduce heat; simmer 15 minutes, stirring occasionally. Remove from heat. Stir in vanilla. Spread evenly over baked layer. Sprinkle reserved 1½ cups crumbs evenly over top.

4. Return to oven. Bake 15 to 20 minutes or until set. Cool completely in pan on wire rack. Cut into bars.   *Makes about 16 bars*

Chocolate-Dipped Cinnamon Thins

1¼ cups all-purpose flour

1½ teaspoons ground cinnamon

¼ teaspoon salt

1 cup unsalted butter, softened

1 cup powdered sugar

1 egg

1 teaspoon vanilla

4 ounces broken bittersweet chocolate candy bar, melted

1. Combine flour, cinnamon and salt in small bowl; set aside. Beat butter in large bowl with electric mixer at medium speed until light and fluffy. Add powdered sugar; beat well. Add egg and vanilla. Gradually add flour mixture. Beat at low speed just until blended.

2. Place dough on sheet of waxed paper. Using waxed paper to hold dough, roll it back and forth to form a log, about 12 inches long and 2½ inches wide. Securely wrap log in plastic wrap. Refrigerate at least 2 hours or until firm. (Log may be frozen up to 3 months; thaw in refrigerator before baking.)

3. Preheat oven to 350°F. Cut dough into ¼-inch-thick slices. Place 2 inches apart on ungreased cookie sheets. Bake 10 minutes or until set. Let cookies stand on cookie sheets 2 minutes. Remove cookies with spatula to wire racks; cool completely.

4. Dip each cookie into chocolate, coating 1 inch up sides. Transfer to wire racks or waxed paper; let stand at cool room temperature about 40 minutes or until chocolate is set.

5. Store cookies between sheets of waxed paper at cool room temperature or in refrigerator. These cookies do not freeze well.   *Makes about 2 dozen cookies*

Autumn Apple Bars

Crust

> **Milk**
> **1 egg yolk (reserve egg white)**
> **2½ cups all-purpose flour**
> **1 teaspoon salt**
> **1 cup (2 sticks) butter, softened**

Filling

> **1 cup graham cracker crumbs**
> **8 cups tart cooking apples, peeled, cored and sliced to ¼-inch thickness (about 8 to 10 medium)**
> **1 cup plus 2 tablespoons granulated sugar, divided**
> **2½ teaspoons ground cinnamon, divided**
> **¼ teaspoon ground nutmeg**
> **1 egg white**

Drizzle

> **1 cup powdered sugar**
> **1 to 2 tablespoons milk**
> **½ teaspoon vanilla**

1. Preheat oven to 350°F. For crust, add enough milk to egg yolk to measure ⅔ cup; set aside. Combine flour and salt in medium bowl. Cut in butter until crumbly using pastry blender or two knives. With fork, stir in milk mixture until dough forms ball; divide into 2 halves. Roll out half to 15×10-inch rectangle on lightly floured surface. Place on bottom of *ungreased* 15×10×1-inch jelly-roll pan.

2. For filling, sprinkle graham cracker crumbs over top of dough; layer apple slices over crumbs. Combine 1 cup granulated sugar, 1½ teaspoons cinnamon and nutmeg in small bowl; sprinkle over apples.

3. Roll out remaining dough into 15×10½-inch rectangle; place over apples. With fork, beat egg white in small bowl until foamy; brush over top crust. Stir together remaining 2 tablespoons granulated sugar and remaining 1 teaspoon cinnamon in another small bowl; sprinkle over crust. Bake 45 to 60 minutes or until lightly browned.

4. For drizzle, stir together all ingredients in small bowl. Drizzle over top; cut into bars.

Makes about 3 dozen bars

Cocoa Pecan Crescents

> **1 cup (2 sticks) butter or margarine, softened**
> **⅔ cup granulated sugar**
> **1½ teaspoons vanilla extract**
> **1¾ cups all-purpose flour**
> **⅓ cup HERSHEY'S Cocoa**
> **⅛ teaspoon salt**
> **1½ cups ground pecans**
> **Powdered sugar**

1. Beat butter, granulated sugar and vanilla in large bowl until fluffy. Stir together flour, cocoa and salt. Add to butter mixture; blend well. Stir in pecans. Refrigerate dough 1 hour or until firm enough to handle.

2. Heat oven to 375°F. Shape scant 1 tablespoon dough into log about 2½ inches long; place on ungreased cookie sheet. Shape each log into crescent, tapering ends.

3. Bake 13 to 15 minutes or until set. Cool slightly; remove from cookie sheet to wire rack. Cool completely. Roll in powdered sugar.

Makes about 3½ dozen cookies

Tropical Chunk Cookies

1 package (12 ounces) BAKER'S® White Chocolate Chunks, divided

1¾ cups flour

1½ cups BAKER'S® ANGEL FLAKE® Coconut, toasted

¾ teaspoon baking soda

¼ teaspoon salt

½ cup (1 stick) butter or margarine, softened

⅓ cup firmly packed brown sugar

1 egg

1 teaspoon vanilla

1 cup chopped macadamia nuts

HEAT oven to 375°F.

MICROWAVE 1 cup of the chocolate chunks in microwavable bowl on HIGH 2 minutes until almost melted. Stir until chocolate is completely melted; cool slightly. Mix flour, coconut, baking soda and salt in medium bowl; set aside.

BEAT butter and sugar in large bowl with electric mixer on medium speed until light and fluffy. Add egg and vanilla; beat well. Stir in melted chocolate. Gradually beat in flour mixture. Stir in remaining chocolate chunks and nuts. Drop by heaping tablespoonfuls onto ungreased cookie sheets.

BAKE 11 to 13 minutes or just until golden brown. Cool on cookie sheets 1 minute. Remove to wire racks and cool completely.

Makes about 3 dozen cookies

Great Substitute: Substitute toasted, slivered almonds for the macadamia nuts.

Tip: Store in tightly covered container up to 1 week.

Prep Time: 15 minutes
Bake Time: 11 to 13 minutes

Raspberry Pecan Thumbprints

2 cups all-purpose flour

1 cup pecan pieces, finely chopped and divided

½ teaspoon ground cinnamon

¼ teaspoon ground allspice

⅛ teaspoon salt

1 cup (2 sticks) butter, softened

½ cup packed light brown sugar

2 teaspoons vanilla

⅓ cup seedless raspberry jam

1. Preheat oven to 350°F. Combine flour, ½ cup pecans, cinnamon, allspice and salt in medium bowl.

2. Beat butter in large bowl until smooth. Gradually beat in brown sugar; beat until light and fluffy. Beat in vanilla until blended. Beat in flour mixture just until blended.

3. Form dough into 1-inch balls; flatten slightly and place on ungreased cookie sheets. Press down with thumb in center of each ball to form indentation. Pinch together any cracks in dough. Fill each indentation with generous ¼ teaspoon jam. Sprinkle filled cookies with remaining ½ cup pecans.

4. Bake 14 minutes or until just set. Let cookies stand on cookie sheets 5 minutes; transfer to wire racks to cool completely. Store in airtight container at room temperature. Cookies are best the day after baking.

Makes 3 dozen cookies

Triple Layer Peanut Butter Bars

Base

**1¼ cups firmly packed light brown
   sugar**

¾ cup JIF® Creamy Peanut Butter

**½ CRISCO® Stick or ½ cup CRISCO®
   all-vegetable shortening plus
   additional for greasing**

3 tablespoons milk

1 tablespoon vanilla

1 egg

1¾ cups all-purpose flour

¾ teaspoon baking soda

¾ teaspoon salt

Peanut Butter Layer

1½ cups confectioners' sugar

**2 tablespoons JIF® Creamy Peanut
   Butter**

**1 tablespoon Butter Flavor CRISCO®
   Stick or 1 tablespoon Butter
   Flavor CRISCO® all-vegetable
   shortening**

3 tablespoons milk

Chocolate Glaze

**2 squares (1 ounce each)
   unsweetened baking chocolate**

**2 tablespoons Butter Flavor
   CRISCO® Stick or 2 tablespoons
   Butter Flavor CRISCO® all-
   vegetable shortening**

1. Heat oven to 350°F. Grease 9×13-inch baking pan. Place cooling rack on counter.

2. For base, place brown sugar, peanut butter, shortening, milk and vanilla in a large bowl. Beat at medium speed of electric mixer until well blended. Add egg; beat just until blended.

3. Combine flour, baking soda and salt. Add to shortening mixture; beat at low speed just until blended.

4. Press mixture evenly onto bottom of prepared pan.

5. Bake at 350°F for 18 to 20 minutes or until toothpick inserted in center comes out clean. *Do not overbake.* Cool completely on cooling rack.

6. For peanut butter layer, place confectioners' sugar, peanut butter, shortening and milk in medium bowl. Beat at low speed of electric mixer until smooth. Spread over base. Refrigerate 30 minutes.

7. For chocolate glaze, place chocolate and shortening in small microwave-safe bowl. Microwave at 50% (MEDIUM) for 1 to 2 minutes or until shiny and soft. Stir until smooth. Cool slightly. Spread over peanut butter layer. Refrigerate about 1 hour or until glaze is set. Cut into 3×1½-inch bars. Let stand 15 to 20 minutes at room temperature before serving.

Makes about 2 dozen bars

Oven-Tested Tips

For easier cutting and cleanup when making bar cookies, line the baking pan with foil, allowing the foil to overhang each end by about 3 inches. Grease the foil if the recipe directions recommend greasing the pan. After baking and cooling, remove the cookies from the pan using the foil overhangs as handles. Peel off the foil. Place the cookies on a cutting board and cut into bars, triangles or diamonds.

Triple Layer Peanut Butter Bars

Brownie Points

Win them over with Ooey Gooey Peanut Butter and Fudge Brownies or classic and easy-to-make Hershey's Best Brownies. Brownies are the perfect treats for almost any occasion. Take a batch to a soccer game, a dinner party or a bake sale. Brownies make friends wherever they go.

Hershey's Best Brownies

1 cup (2 sticks) butter or margarine
2 cups sugar
2 teaspoons vanilla extract
4 eggs
¾ cup HERSHEY'S Cocoa or HERSHEY'S Dutch Processed Cocoa
1 cup all-purpose flour
½ teaspoon baking powder
¼ teaspoon salt
1 cup chopped nuts (optional)

1. Heat oven to 350°F. Grease 13×9×2-inch baking pan.

2. Place butter in large microwave-safe bowl. Microwave at HIGH (100%) 2 to 2½ minutes or until melted. Stir in sugar and vanilla. Add eggs, one at a time, beating well with spoon after each addition. Add cocoa; beat until well blended. Add flour, baking powder and salt; beat well. Stir in nuts, if desired. Pour batter into prepared pan.

3. Bake 30 to 35 minutes or until brownies begin to pull away from sides of pan. Cool completely in pan on wire rack. Cut into bars.   *Makes about 36 brownies*

Brownie Cake Delight

1 package reduced-fat fudge brownie mix

⅓ cup strawberry all-fruit spread

2 cups thawed frozen reduced-fat nondairy whipped topping

¼ teaspoon almond extract

2 cups strawberries, stems removed, halved

¼ cup chocolate sauce

1. Prepare brownies according to package directions, substituting 11×7-inch baking pan. Cool completely in pan.

2. Whisk fruit spread in small bowl until smooth.

3. Combine whipped topping and almond extract in medium bowl.

4. Cut brownie horizontally in half. Place half of brownie on serving dish. Spread with fruit spread and 1 cup whipped topping. Place second half of brownie, cut side down, over bottom layer. Spread with remaining whipped topping. Arrange strawberries on whipped topping. Drizzle chocolate sauce over cake before serving. Garnish with fresh mint, if desired. *Makes 16 servings*

White Chocolate & Almond Brownies

12 ounces white chocolate, broken into pieces

1 cup unsalted butter

3 eggs

¾ cup all-purpose flour

1 teaspoon vanilla

½ cup slivered almonds

1. Preheat oven to 325°F. Grease and flour 9-inch square pan. Melt white chocolate and butter in large saucepan over low heat, stirring constantly. (Do not be concerned if the white chocolate separates.) Remove from heat when chocolate is just melted.

2. With electric mixer, beat in eggs until mixture is smooth. Beat in flour and vanilla. Spread batter evenly in prepared pan. Sprinkle almonds evenly over top. Bake 30 to 35 minutes or just until set in center. Cool completely in pan on wire rack. Cut into 2-inch squares. *Makes about 16 brownies*

Coconut-Topped Brownies

1 package (19 to 21 ounces) brownie mix, plus ingredients to prepare

½ cup semisweet chocolate chunks or chocolate chips

½ cup packed brown sugar

2 tablespoons butter or margarine, softened

1 tablespoon all-purpose flour

⅔ cup chopped pecans

⅔ cup flaked coconut

1. Preheat oven to 350°F. Grease 13×9-inch baking pan.

2. Prepare brownie mix according to package directions; stir in chocolate chunks. Spread into prepared pan.

3. Combine brown sugar, butter and flour in small bowl. Mix until well blended. Stir in pecans and coconut. Sprinkle mixture over batter. Bake 28 to 30 minutes or until topping is lightly browned. Cool completely in pan. Cut into bars. *Makes 30 brownies*

Philadelphia® Cheesecake Brownies

1 package (19.8 ounces) brownie mix (do not use mix that includes syrup pouch)

1 package (8 ounces) PHILADELPHIA® Cream Cheese, softened

⅓ cup sugar

1 egg

½ teaspoon vanilla

PREPARE brownie mix as directed on package. Pour into greased 13×9-inch baking pan.

BEAT cream cheese with electric mixer on medium speed until smooth. Mix in sugar until blended. Add egg and vanilla; mix just until blended. Pour cream cheese mixture over brownie batter; cut through batter with knife several times for marble effect.

BAKE at 350°F for 35 to 40 minutes or until cream cheese mixture is lightly browned. Cool. Cut into squares.

Makes 2 dozen

Special Extras: For extra chocolate flavor, sprinkle 1 cup BAKER'S® Semi-Sweet Real Chocolate Chunks over top of brownies before baking.

Prep Time: 20 minutes
Bake Time: 40 minutes

Chocolate Espresso Brownies

4 squares (1 ounce each) unsweetened chocolate

1 cup sugar

¼ cup Dried Plum Purée (recipe follows) or prepared dried plum butter

3 egg whites

1 to 2 tablespoons instant espresso coffee powder

1 teaspoon baking powder

1 teaspoon salt

1 teaspoon vanilla

½ cup all-purpose flour

Powdered sugar (optional)

Preheat oven to 350°F. Coat 8-inch square baking pan with vegetable cooking spray. In small heavy saucepan, melt chocolate over very low heat, stirring until melted and smooth. Remove from heat; cool. In mixer bowl, beat chocolate and remaining ingredients except flour and powdered sugar at medium speed until well blended; mix in flour. Spread batter evenly in prepared pan. Bake in center of oven about 30 minutes until pick inserted into center comes out clean. Cool completely in pan on wire rack. Dust with powdered sugar. Cut into 1⅓-inch squares. *Makes 36 brownies*

Dried Plum Purée: Combine 1⅓ cups (8 ounces) pitted dried plums and 6 tablespoons hot water in container of food processor or blender. Pulse on and off until dried plums are finely chopped and smooth. Store leftovers in a covered container in the refrigerator for up to two months. Makes 1 cup.

Favorite recipe from **California Dried Plum Board**

Philadelphia® Cheesecake Brownies

Raspberry Fudge Brownies

½ cup (1 stick) butter

3 squares (1 ounce each) bittersweet chocolate*

1 cup sugar

12 eggs

1 teaspoon vanilla

¾ cup all-purpose flour

¼ teaspoon baking powder

Dash salt

½ cup sliced or slivered almonds

½ cup raspberry preserves

1 cup (6 ounces) milk chocolate chips

*One square unsweetened chocolate plus two squares semisweet chocolate may be substituted.

1. Preheat oven to 350°F. Grease and flour 8-inch square baking pan.

2. Melt butter and bittersweet chocolate in small, heavy saucepan over low heat. Remove from heat; cool. Beat sugar, eggs and vanilla in large bowl until light. Beat in chocolate mixture. Stir in flour, baking powder and salt until just blended. Spread ¾ of batter in prepared pan; sprinkle almonds over top.

3. Bake 10 minutes. Remove from oven; spread preserves over almonds. Carefully spoon remaining batter over preserves, smoothing top. Bake 25 to 30 minutes or just until top feels firm.

4. Remove from oven; sprinkle chocolate chips over top. Let stand 1 to 2 minutes or until chips melt, then spread evenly over brownies. Cool completely in pan on wire rack. When chocolate is set, cut into 2-inch squares.
Makes 16 brownies

Easy Microwave Brownies

1 cup granulated sugar

¼ cup packed light brown sugar

½ cup vegetable oil

2 eggs

2 tablespoons light corn syrup

1½ teaspoons vanilla

1 cup all-purpose flour

½ cup unsweetened cocoa powder

¼ teaspoon baking powder

¼ teaspoon salt

½ cup powdered sugar

Microwave Directions

1. Lightly grease 8×8-inch microwaveable baking pan.

2. Combine granulated sugar, brown sugar, oil, eggs, corn syrup and vanilla in large bowl. Combine flour, cocoa, baking powder and salt in medium bowl. Add flour mixture to sugar mixture; blend well. Spread batter in prepared pan.

3. Microwave at MEDIUM-HIGH (70% power) 3 minutes. Rotate pan ½ turn; microwave at MEDIUM-HIGH 3 minutes or until brownies begin to pull away from sides of pan and surface has no wet spots. (If brownies are not done, rotate pan ¼ turn and continue to microwave at MEDIUM-HIGH, checking for doneness at 30-second intervals.) Let brownies stand 20 minutes. When cool, sprinkle with powdered sugar and cut into squares.
Makes about 16 brownies

Creamy Filled Brownies

½ cup (1 stick) butter or margarine
⅓ cup HERSHEY'S Cocoa
2 eggs
1 cup sugar
½ cup all-purpose flour
¼ teaspoon baking powder
¼ teaspoon salt
1 teaspoon vanilla extract
1 cup finely chopped nuts
  Creamy Filling (recipe follows)
  MiniChip Glaze (recipe follows)
½ cup sliced almonds or chopped
   nuts (optional)

1. Heat oven to 350°F. Line 15½×10½×1-inch jelly roll pan with foil; grease foil.

2. Melt butter in small saucepan; remove from heat. Stir in cocoa until smooth. Beat eggs in medium bowl; gradually add sugar, beating until fluffy. Stir together flour, baking powder and salt; add to egg mixture.

Add cocoa mixture and vanilla; beat well. Stir in nuts. Spread batter into prepared pan.

3. Bake 12 to 14 minutes or until top springs back when touched lightly in center. Cool completely in pan on wire rack; remove from pan to cutting board. Remove foil; cut brownie in half crosswise. Spread one half with Creamy Filling; top with second half. Spread MiniChip Glaze over top; sprinkle with almonds, if desired. After glaze has set cut into bars. *Makes about 24 brownies*

Creamy Filling: Beat 1 package (3 ounces) softened cream cheese, 2 tablespoons softened butter or margarine and 1 teaspoon vanilla extract in small bowl. Gradually add 1½ cups powdered sugar, beating until of spreading consistency.

Filling Variations: Coffee: Add 1 teaspoon powdered instant coffee. Orange: Add ½ teaspoon freshly grated orange peel and 1 or 2 drops orange food color. Almond: Add ¼ teaspoon almond extract.

MiniChip Glaze: Heat ¼ cup sugar and 2 tablespoons water to boiling in small saucepan. Remove from heat. Immediately add ½ cup HERSHEY'S MINICHIPS™ Semi-Sweet Chocolate, stirring until melted.

Creamy Filled Brownie

Toffee Chunk Brownie Cookies

1 cup butter

4 ounces unsweetened chocolate, coarsely chopped

1½ cups sugar

2 eggs

1 tablespoon vanilla

3 cups all-purpose flour

⅛ teaspoon salt

1½ cups coarsely chopped chocolate-covered toffee bars

1. Preheat oven to 350°F. Melt butter and chocolate in large saucepan over low heat, stirring until smooth. Remove from heat; cool slightly.

2. Stir sugar into chocolate mixture until smooth. Stir in eggs until well blended. Stir in vanilla until smooth. Stir in flour and salt just until mixed. Fold in chopped toffee bars.

3. Drop heaping tablespoonfuls of dough 1½ inches apart onto ungreased cookie sheets.

4. Bake 12 minutes or until just set. Let cookies stand on cookie sheets 5 minutes; transfer to wire racks to cool completely. Store in airtight container.

Makes 36 cookies

Oven-Tested Tips

Save those cookie or brownie crumbs! They make a delicious topping for ice cream or pudding. You can even use them to make a cookie-crumb crust for a pie or cheesecake.

Devil's Fudge Brownies

½ cup (1 stick) butter or margarine, softened

1 cup granulated sugar

2 large eggs

2 tablespoons *Frank's*® *RedHot*® Cayenne Pepper Sauce

1 teaspoon vanilla extract

⅔ cup all-purpose flour

½ cup unsweetened cocoa

¼ teaspoon baking soda

1 cup chopped pecans

½ cup mini chocolate chips

Pecan halves

Confectioners' sugar

Ice cream (optional)

Fudge sauce (optional)

Microwave Directions

Beat butter, granulated sugar, eggs, ***Frank's RedHot*** Sauce and vanilla in large bowl of electric mixer on medium speed until light and fluffy. Blend in flour, cocoa and baking soda. Beat until smooth. Stir in chopped nuts and mini chips. Spread into greased deep-dish 9-inch microwave-safe pie plate. Arrange pecan halves on top.

Place pie plate on top of inverted custard cup in microwave oven. Microwave, uncovered, on HIGH 6 minutes or until toothpick inserted in center comes out clean, turning once. (Brownie may appear moist on surface. Do not overcook.) Cool completely on wire rack.

Dust top with confectioners' sugar. Cut into wedges. Serve with ice cream and fudge sauce, if desired.   *Makes 8 servings*

Prep Time: 20 minutes
Cook Time: 6 minutes

Double-Decker Confetti Brownies

¾ cup (1½ sticks) butter or margarine, softened

1 cup granulated sugar

1 cup firmly packed light brown sugar

3 large eggs

1 teaspoon vanilla extract

2½ cups all-purpose flour, divided

2½ teaspoons baking powder

½ teaspoon salt

⅓ cup unsweetened cocoa powder

1 tablespoon butter or margarine, melted

1 cup "M&M's"® Semi-Sweet Chocolate Mini Baking Bits, divided

Preheat oven to 350°F. Lightly grease 13×9×2-inch baking pan; set aside. In large bowl cream ¾ cup butter and sugars until light and fluffy; beat in eggs and vanilla. In medium bowl combine 2¼ cups flour, baking powder and salt; blend into creamed mixture. Divide batter in half. Blend together cocoa powder and melted butter; stir into one half of the dough. Spread cocoa dough evenly into prepared baking pan. Stir remaining ¼ cup flour and ½ cup "M&M's"® Semi-Sweet Chocolate Mini Baking Bits into remaining dough; spread evenly over cocoa dough in pan. Sprinkle with remaining ½ cup "M&M's"® Semi-Sweet Chocolate Mini Baking Bits. Bake 25 to 30 minutes or until edges start to pull away from sides of pan. Cool completely. Cut into bars. Store in tightly covered container.

Makes 24 brownies

Double-Decker Confetti Brownies

Ooey Gooey Peanut Butter and Fudge Brownies

Batter

    PAM® No-Stick Cooking Spray

    3 cups sugar

    1 cup (2 sticks) butter, softened

    ½ cup WESSON® Vegetable Oil

    1 tablespoon plus 1½ teaspoons vanilla

    6 eggs, at room temperature

    2¼ cups all-purpose flour

    1¼ cups unsweetened cocoa powder

    1½ teaspoons baking powder

    ¾ teaspoon salt

    1 (10-ounce) bag peanut butter chips

Filling

    1½ cups PETER PAN® Creamy Peanut Butter

    ⅓ cup WESSON® Vegetable Oil

    ½ cup sugar

    3 tablespoons all-purpose flour

    3 eggs, at room temperature

    1 tablespoon vanilla

Frosting

    3 (1-ounce) squares unsweetened chocolate

    3 tablespoons PETER PAN® Creamy Peanut Butter

    2⅔ cups powdered sugar

    ¼ cup water

    1 teaspoon vanilla

    ¼ teaspoon salt

Batter

Preheat oven to 350°F. Spray two 13×9×2-inch baking pans with PAM® Cooking Spray. In a large bowl, beat sugar and butter until creamy. Add Wesson® Oil and vanilla. Add eggs, one at a time, beating well after *each* addition. In a small bowl, combine flour, cocoa, baking powder and salt; blend well. While beating, gradually add flour mixture to creamed mixture; mix well. Fold in peanut butter chips. Evenly spread ¼ of batter into 1 pan.

Filling

In a small bowl, cream together Peter Pan® Peanut Butter and Wesson® Oil. Add sugar and flour; blend well. Add eggs and vanilla; beat until smooth. Carefully spread ½ of filling mixture evenly over batter in pan. Top filling with an additional ¼ of batter and spread evenly. Gently cut through layers to create a marble effect throughout the brownies. Repeat process with *remaining* pan and *remaining* batter and *remaining* filling. Bake for 30 minutes. *Do not overbake.*

Frosting

Meanwhile, in a medium saucepan, melt chocolate and peanut butter over low heat, stirring constantly. Remove from heat and stir in *remaining* ingredients; mix until smooth. If frosting is too thick, add an additional 1 to 3 tablespoons water. Spread frosting over brownies *immediately* after baking. Cool in pans on wire racks.

Makes 3 dozen brownies

Oven-Tested Tips

Unsweetened chocolate is also known as baking or bitter chocolate. It is pure chocolate: no sugar or flavorings have been added. Used for baking rather than eating, it is usually available in packages of individually wrapped one-ounce squares. Bittersweet chocolate and semisweet chocolate both have sugar added and can be used interchangeably.

Brownie Pizza

4 squares BAKER'S® Unsweetened
    Baking Chocolate

¾ cup (1½ sticks) margarine or
    butter

2¼ cups sugar, divided

5 eggs, divided

1½ teaspoons vanilla, divided

1 cup flour

1 package (8 ounces)
    PHILADELPHIA® Cream
    Cheese, softened

Assorted sliced fruit

2 squares BAKER'S® Semi-Sweet
    Baking Chocolate, melted

LINE 12-inch pizza pan with foil; grease foil.

MICROWAVE unsweetened chocolate and margarine in large microwavable bowl on HIGH 2 minutes or until margarine is melted. (Stir until chocolate is completely melted.)

STIR 2 cups of the sugar into melted chocolate mixture. Mix in 4 eggs and 1 teaspoon of the vanilla until well blended. Stir in flour. Spread into prepared pan. Bake at 350°F for 30 minutes.

BEAT cream cheese, remaining ¼ cup sugar, remaining egg and remaining ½ teaspoon vanilla in same bowl until well blended. Pour over baked brownie crust.

BAKE an additional 10 minutes or until toothpick inserted in center comes out with fudgy crumbs. Do not overbake. Cool in pan. Lift brownie pizza out of pan; peel off foil. Place brownie pizza on serving plate. Arrange fruit over cream cheese layer. Drizzle with melted semi-sweet chocolate.

Makes 12 servings

Prep Time: 30 minutes
Bake Time: 40 minutes

Irish Brownies

4 squares (1 ounce each) semisweet
    baking chocolate, coarsely
    chopped

½ cup butter

½ cup sugar

2 eggs

¼ cup Irish cream liqueur

1 cup all-purpose flour

½ teaspoon baking powder

¼ teaspoon salt

Irish Cream Frosting (recipe
    follows)

Preheat oven to 350°F. Grease 8-inch square baking pan. Melt chocolate and butter in medium, heavy saucepan over low heat, stirring constantly. Remove from heat. Stir in sugar. Beat in eggs, 1 at a time, with wire whisk. Whisk in liqueur. Combine flour, baking powder and salt in small bowl; stir into chocolate mixture until just blended. Spread batter evenly in prepared pan.

Bake 22 to 25 minutes or until center is set. Remove pan to wire rack; cool completely. Prepare Irish Cream Frosting; spread over cooled brownies. Chill at least 1 hour or until frosting is set. Cut into 2-inch squares.

Makes about 16 brownies

Irish Cream Frosting

¼ cup (2 ounces) cream cheese,
    softened

2 tablespoons butter or margarine,
    softened

2 tablespoons Irish cream liqueur

1½ cups powdered sugar

Beat cream cheese and butter in small bowl with electric mixer at medium speed until smooth. Beat in liqueur. Gradually beat in powdered sugar until smooth. Makes about ⅔ cup frosting.

Brownie Pizza

Bittersweet Pecan Brownies with Caramel Sauce

Brownies

- ¾ cup all-purpose flour
- ¼ teaspoon baking soda
- 4 squares (1 ounce each) bittersweet or unsweetened chocolate, coarsely chopped
- ½ cup (1 stick) plus 2 tablespoons I CAN'T BELIEVE IT'S NOT BUTTER!® Spread
- ¾ cup sugar
- 2 eggs
- ½ cup chopped pecans

Caramel Sauce

- ¾ cup firmly packed light brown sugar
- 6 tablespoons I CAN'T BELIEVE IT'S NOT BUTTER!® Spread
- ⅓ cup whipping or heavy cream
- ½ teaspoon apple cider vinegar or fresh lemon juice

For brownies, preheat oven to 325°F. Line 8-inch square baking pan with aluminum foil, then grease and flour foil; set aside.

In small bowl, combine flour and baking soda; set aside.

In medium microwave-safe bowl, microwave chocolate and I Can't Believe It's Not Butter! Spread at HIGH (Full Power) 1 minute or until chocolate is melted; stir until smooth. With wooden spoon, beat in sugar, then eggs. Beat in flour mixture. Evenly spread into prepared pan; sprinkle with pecans.

Bake 31 minutes or until toothpick inserted in center comes out clean. On wire rack, cool completely. To remove brownies, lift edges of foil. Cut brownies into 4 squares, then cut each square into 2 triangles.

For caramel sauce, in medium saucepan, bring brown sugar, I Can't Believe It's Not Butter! Spread and cream just to a boil over high heat, stirring frequently. Cook 3 minutes. Stir in vinegar. To serve, pour caramel sauce around brownie and top with vanilla or caramel ice cream, if desired.

Makes 8 servings

Sensational Peppermint Pattie Brownies

- 24 small (1½-inch) YORK® Peppermint Patties
- 1½ cups (3 sticks) butter or margarine, melted
- 3 cups sugar
- 1 tablespoon vanilla extract
- 5 eggs
- 2 cups all-purpose flour
- 1 cup HERSHEY'S Cocoa
- 1 teaspoon baking powder
- 1 teaspoon salt

1. Heat oven to 350°F. Remove wrappers from peppermint patties. Grease 13×9×2-inch baking pan.

2. Stir together butter, sugar and vanilla in large bowl. Add eggs; beat until well blended. Stir together flour, cocoa, baking powder and salt; gradually add to butter mixture, blending well. Reserve 2 cups batter. Spread remaining batter into prepared pan. Arrange peppermint patties about ½ inch apart in single layer over batter. Spread reserved batter over patties.

3. Bake 50 to 55 minutes or until brownies pull away from sides of pan. Cool completely in pan on wire rack.

Makes about 36 brownies

Bittersweet Pecan Brownies with Caramel Sauce

Fudgy Mocha Brownies with a Crust

1¼ cups all-purpose flour, divided
¼ cup sugar
½ cup cold butter or margarine
1 can (14 ounces) sweetened condensed milk (not evaporated milk)
½ cup HERSHEY'S Cocoa
1 egg
2 tablespoons coffee-flavored liqueur *or* 1 teaspoon instant coffee dissolved in 1 tablespoon hot water
1 teaspoon vanilla extract
½ teaspoon baking powder
¾ cup chopped nuts
Fudgy Mocha Frosting (recipe follows)

1. Heat oven to 350°F.

2. Combine 1 cup flour and sugar in medium bowl. Cut in cold butter with pastry blender or 2 knives until mixture resembles fine crumbs. Press firmly onto bottom of 13×9-inch baking pan. Bake 15 minutes.

3. Meanwhile, beat sweetened condensed milk, cocoa, egg, remaining ¼ cup flour, liqueur, vanilla and baking powder in large bowl until well blended. Stir in nuts. Spread evenly over baked crust.

4. Bake 20 minutes or until center is set. Cool. Spread with Fudgy Mocha Frosting. Store tightly covered at room temperature.

Makes 24 to 36 brownies

Fudgy Mocha Frosting: Melt 3 tablespoons butter or margarine in small saucepan, over low heat; add 3 tablespoons HERSHEY'S Cocoa and 1 tablespoon water, stirring constantly until mixture thickens (do not boil). Remove from heat; add 2 tablespoons coffee-flavored liqueur.

Gradually add in 1½ cups powdered sugar, beating with whisk until smooth. Add additional water, 1 teaspoon at a time, until of desired consistency. Makes about 1 cup.

Butterscotch Brownies

1 cup butterscotch chips
½ cup packed light brown sugar
¼ cup butter, softened
2 eggs
½ teaspoon vanilla
1 cup all-purpose flour
½ teaspoon baking powder
¼ teaspoon salt
1 cup semisweet chocolate chips

1. Preheat oven to 350°F. Grease 9-inch square baking pan. Melt butterscotch chips in small saucepan over low heat, stirring constantly; set aside.

2. Beat brown sugar and butter in large bowl until light and fluffy. Beat in eggs, one at a time, scraping down side of bowl after each addition. Beat in melted butterscotch chips and vanilla. Combine flour, baking powder and salt in small bowl; add to butter mixture. Beat until well blended. Spread batter evenly in prepared pan.

3. Bake 20 to 25 minutes or until golden brown and center is set. Remove pan from oven and immediately sprinkle with chocolate chips. Let stand about 4 minutes or until chocolate is melted. Spread chocolate evenly over top. Place pan on wire rack; cool completely. Cut into 2¼-inch squares.

Makes about 16 brownies

Fabulous Blonde Brownies

1¾ cups all-purpose flour

1 teaspoon baking powder

¼ teaspoon salt

1 cup (6 ounces) white chocolate chips

1 cup (4 ounces) blanched whole almonds, coarsely chopped

1 cup toffee baking pieces

1½ cups packed light brown sugar

⅔ cup butter, softened

2 eggs

2 teaspoons vanilla

Preheat oven to 350°F. Lightly grease 13×9-inch baking pan.

Combine flour, baking powder and salt in small bowl; mix well. Combine white chocolate chips, almonds and toffee pieces in medium bowl; mix well.

Beat brown sugar and butter in large bowl with electric mixer at medium speed until light and fluffy. Beat in eggs and vanilla. Add flour mixture; beat at low speed until well blended. Stir in ¾ cup of white chocolate chip mixture. Spread evenly in prepared pan.

Bake 20 minutes. Immediately sprinkle remaining white chocolate chip mixture evenly over brownies. Press lightly. Bake 15 to 20 minutes or until toothpick inserted into center comes out clean. Cool brownies completely in pan on wire rack. Cut into 2×1½-inch bars.

Makes 3 dozen brownies

Fabulous Blonde Brownies

Brownie Berry Parfaits

1 box (10 ounces) BIRDS EYE®
  frozen Raspberries*

4 large prepared brownies, cut into
  cubes

1 pint vanilla or chocolate ice cream

4 tablespoons chocolate syrup

2 tablespoons chopped walnuts

*Or, substitute Birds Eye® frozen Strawberries.

• Thaw raspberries according to package
directions.

• Divide half the brownie cubes among four
parfait glasses. Top with half the ice cream
and raspberries. Repeat layers with
remaining brownie cubes, ice cream and
raspberries.

• Drizzle chocolate syrup over each dessert;
sprinkle with walnuts.   *Makes 4 servings*

Prep Time: 10 minutes

Oven-Tested Tips

*Parfait means perfect in French—the
perfect name for this easy and elegant
dessert. Invest in a set of parfait glasses,
which are simply tall, narrow v-shaped
glasses like the kind used for sundaes at
the ice cream shop, then invent your
own combinations. Try layering cake,
cookies, fruit, whipped cream, ice
cream, nuts, whatever you like.*

Miniature Brownie Cups

6 tablespoons butter or margarine,
  melted

¾ cup sugar

½ teaspoon vanilla extract

 2 eggs

½ cup all-purpose flour

¼ cup HERSHEY'S Cocoa or
  HERSHEY'S Dutch Processed
  Cocoa

¼ teaspoon baking powder
  Dash salt

¼ cup finely chopped nuts

1. Heat oven to 350°F. Line small muffin
cups (1¾ inches in diameter) with paper
bake cups. Stir together butter, sugar and
vanilla in medium bowl. Add eggs; beat well
with spoon.

2. Stir together flour, cocoa, baking powder
and salt; gradually add to butter mixture,
beating with spoon until well blended. Fill
muffin cups ½ full with batter; sprinkle nuts
over top.

3. Bake 12 to 15 minutes or until wooden
pick inserted in center comes out almost
clean. Cool slightly; remove brownies from
pan to wire rack. Cool completely.

Makes about 24 brownies

Tip: HERSHEY'S Dutch Processed Cocoa
involves a process which neutralizes the natural
acidity found in cocoa powder. This results in a
darker cocoa with a more mellow flavor than
natural cocoa.

Prep Time: 20 minutes
Bake Time: 12 minutes
Cool Time: 25 minutes

Rocky Road Brownies

½ cup (1 stick) butter
½ cup unsweetened cocoa powder
1 cup sugar
½ cup all-purpose flour
¼ cup buttermilk
1 egg
1 teaspoon vanilla
1 cup miniature marshmallows
1 cup coarsely chopped walnuts
1 cup (6 ounces) semisweet
   chocolate chips

Preheat oven to 350°F. Lightly grease 8-inch square pan. Combine butter and cocoa in medium saucepan over low heat, stirring constantly until smooth. Remove from heat; stir in sugar, flour, buttermilk, egg and vanilla. Mix until smooth. Spread batter evenly in prepared pan. Bake 25 minutes or until center feels dry. *Do not overbake or brownies will be dry.* Remove from oven; sprinkle with marshmallows, walnuts and chocolate chips. Return to oven for 3 to 5 minutes or just until topping is warmed enough to melt. Cool in pan on wire rack. Cut into 2-inch squares.

Makes 16 brownies

Brownie Fudge

4 squares (1 ounce each)
   unsweetened chocolate
1 cup butter
2 cups sugar
4 eggs
1 cup all-purpose flour
1 cup chopped walnuts
2 teaspoons vanilla
   Fudge Topping (recipe follows)

1. Preheat oven to 350°F. Grease 13×9-inch baking pan. Melt chocolate and butter in small, heavy saucepan over low heat, stirring until completely melted; cool.

2. Beat sugar and eggs in large bowl with electric mixer until light and fluffy. Gradually blend chocolate mixture into egg mixture. Stir in flour, walnuts and vanilla. Spread evenly in prepared pan.

3. Bake 25 to 35 minutes or just until set. *Do not overbake.* Meanwhile, prepare Fudge Topping. Remove brownies from oven. Immediately pour topping evenly over hot brownies. Cool in pan on wire rack. Place in freezer until firm. Cut into 1-inch squares.

Makes about 9 dozen brownies

Fudge Topping

4½ cups sugar
1 can (12 ounces) evaporated milk
⅓ cup butter
1 jar (7 ounces) marshmallow creme
1 package (12 ounces) semisweet
   chocolate chips
1 package (12 ounces) milk
   chocolate chips
2 teaspoons vanilla
2 cups walnuts, coarsely chopped

Combine sugar, evaporated milk and butter in large saucepan. Bring to a boil over medium heat; boil 5 minutes, stirring constantly. Remove from heat; add marshmallow creme, chocolate chips and vanilla. Beat with wooden spoon until smooth. Stir in walnuts.

P.B. Chips Brownie Cups

1 cup (2 sticks) butter or margarine
2 cups sugar
2 teaspoons vanilla extract
4 eggs
¾ cup HERSHEY'S Cocoa or HERSHEY'S Dutch Processed Cocoa
1¾ cups all-purpose flour
½ teaspoon baking powder
½ teaspoon salt
1⅔ cups (10-ounce package) REESE'S® Peanut Butter Chips, divided

1. Heat oven to 350°F. Line 18 muffin cups (2½ inches in diameter) with paper or foil bake cups.

2. Place butter in large microwave-safe bowl. Microwave at HIGH (100%) 1 to 1½ minutes or until melted. Stir in sugar and vanilla. Add eggs; beat well. Add cocoa; beat until well blended. Add flour, baking powder and salt; beat well. Stir in 1⅓ cups peanut butter chips. Divide batter evenly into muffin cups; sprinkle with remaining ⅓ cup peanut butter chips.

3. Bake 25 to 30 minutes or until surface is firm; cool completely in pan on wire rack.

Makes about 1½ dozen brownie cups

Oven-Tested Tips

When melting butter in the microwave oven, cover the container with a piece of waxed paper to prevent spatters.

Orange Cappuccino Brownies

¾ cup (1½ sticks) butter
2 squares (1 ounce each) semisweet chocolate, coarsely chopped
2 squares (1 ounce each) unsweetened chocolate, coarsely chopped
1¾ cups granulated sugar
1 tablespoon instant espresso powder or instant coffee granules
3 eggs
¼ cup orange-flavored liqueur
2 teaspoons grated orange peel
1 cup all-purpose flour
1 package (12 ounces) semisweet chocolate chips
2 tablespoons shortening

1. Preheat oven to 350°F. Grease 13×9-inch baking pan.

2. Melt butter and chopped chocolates in large heavy saucepan over low heat, stirring constantly. Stir in granulated sugar and espresso powder. Remove from heat. Cool slightly. Beat in eggs, 1 at a time. Whisk in liqueur and orange peel. Beat flour into chocolate mixture just until blended. Spread batter evenly in prepared pan.

3. Bake 25 to 30 minutes or until center is just set. Remove pan to wire rack. Meanwhile, melt chocolate chips and shortening in small heavy saucepan over low heat, stirring constantly. Immediately, spread hot chocolate mixture over warm brownies. Cool completely in pan on wire rack. Cut into 2-inch squares.

Makes about 2 dozen brownies

P.B. Chips Brownie Cups

Coconutty "M&M's"® Brownies

6 squares (1 ounce each) semi-sweet chocolate

¾ cup granulated sugar

½ cup (1 stick) butter

2 large eggs

1 tablespoon vegetable oil

1 teaspoon vanilla extract

1¼ cups all-purpose flour

3 tablespoons unsweetened cocoa powder

1 teaspoon baking powder

½ teaspoon salt

1½ cups "M&M's"® Chocolate Mini Baking Bits, divided

Coconut Topping (recipe follows)

Preheat oven to 350°F. Lightly grease 8×8×2-inch baking pan; set aside. In small saucepan combine chocolate, sugar and butter over low heat; stir constantly until chocolate is melted. Remove from heat; let cool slightly. In large bowl beat eggs, oil and vanilla; stir in chocolate mixture until well blended. In medium bowl combine flour, cocoa powder, baking powder and salt; add to chocolate mixture. Stir in 1 cup "M&M's"® Chocolate Mini Baking Bits. Spread batter evenly in prepared pan. Bake 35 to 40 minutes or until toothpick inserted in center comes out clean. Cool completely on wire rack. Prepare Coconut Topping. Spread over brownies; sprinkle with remaining ½ cup "M&M's"® Chocolate Mini Baking Bits. Cut into bars. Store in tightly covered container.   *Makes 16 brownies*

Coconut Topping

½ cup (1 stick) butter

⅓ cup firmly packed light brown sugar

⅓ cup light corn syrup

1 cup sweetened shredded coconut, toasted*

¾ cup chopped pecans

1 teaspoon vanilla extract

*To toast coconut, spread evenly on cookie sheet. Toast in preheated 350°F oven 7 to 8 minutes or until golden brown, stirring occasionally.

In large saucepan melt butter over medium heat; add brown sugar and corn syrup, stirring constantly until thick and bubbly. Remove from heat and stir in remaining ingredients.

Marbled Cherry Brownies

Cherry Cream Filling (recipe follows)

½ cup (1 stick) butter or margarine, melted

⅓ cup HERSHEY'S Cocoa

2 eggs

1 cup sugar

1 teaspoon vanilla extract

½ cup all-purpose flour

½ teaspoon baking powder

¼ teaspoon salt

1. Prepare Cherry Cream Filling; set aside. Heat oven to 350°F. Grease 9-inch square baking pan.

2. Stir butter and cocoa in small bowl until well blended. Beat eggs in medium bowl until foamy. Gradually add sugar and vanilla, beating until well blended.

Stir together flour, baking powder and salt; add to egg mixture. Add cocoa mixture; stir until well blended.

3. Spread half of chocolate batter into prepared pan; cover with cherry filling. Drop spoonfuls of remaining chocolate batter over filling. With knife or spatula, gently swirl chocolate batter into filling for marbled effect.

4. Bake 35 to 40 minutes or until brownies begin to pull away from sides of pan. Cool; cut into squares. Cover; refrigerate leftover brownies. Bring to room temperature to serve. *Makes about 16 brownies*

Prep Time: 25 minutes
Bake Time: 35 minutes
Cool Time: 1½ hours

Cherry Cream Filling

1 package (3 ounces) cream cheese, softened
¼ cup sugar
1 egg
½ teaspoon vanilla extract
¼ teaspoon almond extract
⅓ cup chopped maraschino cherries, well drained
1 to 2 drops red food color (optional)

1. Beat cream cheese and sugar in small bowl on medium speed of mixer until blended. Add egg, vanilla and almond extract; beat well. (Mixture will be thin.)

2. Stir in cherries and food color, if desired.

Coconutty "M&M's"® Brownies

Dreamy Cheesecake

Some say that cheesecake originated in ancient Greece where it was served to Olympic athletes. Certainly, whoever invented it deserves a medal. Rich and creamy cheesecake is one dessert that is worth every calorie. From classic New York Cheesecake to elegant Black & White Cheesecake, you'll find the recipes for a taste of heaven right here.

New York Cheesecake

1 cup graham cracker crumbs

3 tablespoons sugar

3 tablespoons butter or margarine, melted

5 packages (8 ounces each) PHILADELPHIA® Cream Cheese, softened

1 cup sugar

3 tablespoons flour

1 tablespoon vanilla

3 eggs

1 cup BREAKSTONE'S® or KNUDSEN® Sour Cream

MIX crumbs, 3 tablespoons sugar and butter; press onto bottom of 9-inch springform pan. Bake at 350°F for 10 minutes.

MIX cream cheese, 1 cup sugar, flour and vanilla with electric mixer on medium speed until well blended. Add eggs, 1 at a time, mixing on low speed after each addition, just until blended. Blend in sour cream.

BAKE 1 hour or until center is almost set. Run knife or metal spatula around rim of pan to loosen cake; cool before removing rim of pan. Refrigerate 4 hours or overnight. Top with cherry pie filling and garnish, if desired.   *Makes 12 servings*

Prep Time: 15 minutes plus refrigerating
Bake Time: 1 hour

Dreamy Cheesecake ◆ 269

Mini Cheesecakes

1½ cups graham cracker or chocolate wafer crumbs

¼ cup sugar

¼ cup (½ stick) butter or margarine, melted

3 (8-ounce) packages cream cheese, softened

1 (14-ounce) can EAGLE® BRAND Sweetened Condensed Milk (NOT evaporated milk)

3 eggs

2 teaspoons vanilla extract

1. Preheat oven to 300°F. In small mixing bowl, combine crumbs, sugar and butter; press equal portions firmly on bottoms of 24 lightly greased or paper-lined muffin cups.

2. In large mixing bowl, beat cream cheese until fluffy. Gradually beat in Eagle Brand until smooth. Add eggs and vanilla; mix well. Spoon equal amounts of mixture (about 3 tablespoons) into prepared cups. Bake 20 minutes or until cakes spring back when lightly touched. Cool.* Chill. Garnish as desired. Refrigerate leftovers.

Makes 2 dozen mini cheesecakes

If greased muffin cups are used, cool baked cheesecakes. Freeze 15 minutes; remove with narrow spatula. Proceed as directed above.

Chocolate Mini Cheesecakes: Melt 1 cup (6 ounces) semi-sweet chocolate chips; mix into batter. Proceed as directed above, baking 20 to 25 minutes.

Prep Time: 20 minutes
Bake Time: 20 minutes

Mini Cheesecakes

Chocolate-Berry Cheesecake

1 cup chocolate wafer crumbs

1 container (12 ounces) fat-free cream cheese

1 package (8 ounces) reduced-fat cream cheese, softened

⅔ cup sugar

½ cup cholesterol-free egg substitute

3 tablespoons fat-free (skim) milk

1¼ teaspoons vanilla

1 cup mini semisweet chocolate chips

2 tablespoons raspberry all fruit spread

2½ cups fresh strawberries, hulled and halved

1. Preheat oven to 350°F. Spray bottom of 9-inch springform pan with nonstick cooking spray.

2. Press chocolate wafer crumbs firmly onto bottom of prepared pan. Bake 10 minutes. Remove from oven; cool. *Reduce oven temperature to 325°F.*

3. Combine cheeses in large bowl with electric mixer. Beat at medium speed until well blended. Beat in sugar until well blended. Beat in egg substitute, milk and vanilla until well blended. Stir in mini chips with spoon. Pour batter into pan.

4. Bake 40 minutes or until center is set. Remove from oven; cool 10 minutes in pan on wire rack. Carefully loosen cheesecake from edge of pan. Cool completely.

5. Remove side of pan from cake. Blend fruit spread and 2 tablespoons water in medium bowl until smooth. Add strawberries; toss to coat. Arrange strawberries on top of cake. Refrigerate 1 hour before serving.   *Makes 16 servings*

Decadent Turtle Cheesecake

2½ cups crushed chocolate cookies or vanilla wafers

¼ cup (½ stick) butter, melted

2 packages (8 ounces each) cream cheese, softened

1 cup sugar

1½ tablespoons all-purpose flour

1½ teaspoons vanilla

¼ teaspoon salt

3 eggs

2 tablespoons whipping cream

Caramel Topping (recipe follows)

Chocolate Topping (recipe follows)

1 cup chopped toasted pecans

1. Preheat oven to 450°F. Combine cookie crumbs and butter in medium bowl; press onto bottom of 9-inch springform pan.

2. Beat cream cheese in large bowl until creamy. Add sugar, flour, vanilla and salt; mix well. Add eggs, one at a time, beating well after each addition. Blend in cream. Pour over crust. Bake 10 minutes.

3. *Reduce oven temperature to 200°F.* Bake 35 to 40 minutes more or until set. Loosen cake from rim of pan; cool. Remove rim.

4. Prepare Toppings; drizzle over cheesecake; refrigerate. Sprinkle with pecans just before serving.   *Makes one 9-inch cheesecake*

Caramel Topping: Combine 7 ounces (½ bag) caramels and ⅓ cup whipping cream in small saucepan; stir over low heat until smooth.

Chocolate Topping: Combine 4 squares (1 ounce each) semisweet chocolate, 1 teaspoon butter and 3 tablespoons whipping cream in small saucepan; stir over low heat until smooth.

Lemon Cheesecake

Crust

> 35 vanilla wafers
> ¾ cup slivered almonds, toasted
> ⅓ cup sugar
> ¼ cup butter, melted

Filling

> 3 packages (8 ounces each) cream cheese, softened
> ¾ cup sugar
> 4 eggs
> ⅓ cup whipping cream
> ¼ cup lemon juice
> 1 tablespoon grated lemon peel
> 1 teaspoon vanilla

Topping

> 1 pint strawberries
> 2 tablespoons sugar

1. Preheat oven to 375°F. For crust, combine wafers, almonds and ⅓ cup sugar in food processor; process until fine crumbs are formed. Combine crumb mixture with melted butter in medium bowl. Press mixture evenly on bottom and 1 inch up side of 9-inch springform pan. Set aside.

2. For filling, beat cream cheese and ¾ cup sugar in large bowl on high speed of electric mixer 2 to 3 minutes or until fluffy. Add eggs one at a time, beating after each addition. Add whipping cream, lemon juice, lemon peel and vanilla; beat just until blended. Pour into prepared crust. Place springform pan on baking sheet. Bake 45 to 55 minutes or until set. Cool completely on wire rack. Cover and refrigerate at least 10 hours or overnight.

3. For topping, hull and slice strawberries. Combine with sugar in medium bowl. Let stand 15 minutes. Serve over cheesecake.

Makes 16 servings

Traditional Ricotta Cheesecake

Crust

> 1 cup finely crushed graham crackers
> ¼ cup sugar
> ¼ cup melted margarine

Filling

> 2 cups (15 ounces) SARGENTO® Light Ricotta Cheese
> ½ cup sugar
> ½ cup half-and-half
> 2 tablespoons all-purpose flour
> 1 tablespoon fresh lemon juice
> 1 teaspoon finely grated lemon peel
> ¼ teaspoon salt
> 2 eggs

Topping

> 1 cup light sour cream
> 2 tablespoons sugar
> 1 teaspoon vanilla

Combine graham crackers, ¼ cup sugar and margarine; mix well. Press over bottom and 1½ inches up side of 8- or 9-inch springform pan. Chill while preparing filling.

In bowl of electric mixer, combine ricotta cheese, ½ cup sugar, half-and-half, flour, lemon juice, lemon peel and salt; blend until smooth. Add eggs, one at a time; blend until smooth. Pour into crust. Bake at 350°F 50 minutes or until center is just set. Remove from oven.

Beat sour cream with 2 tablespoons sugar and vanilla. Gently spoon onto warm cheesecake; spread evenly over surface. Return to oven 10 minutes. Turn off oven; cool in oven with door propped open 30 minutes. Remove to wire cooling rack; cool completely. Chill at least 3 hours.

Makes 8 servings

Lemon Cheesecake

Dreamy Cheesecake ◆ 273

Currant Cheesecake Bars

Currant Cheesecake Bars

½ cup (1 stick) butter, softened

1 cup all-purpose flour

½ cup packed light brown sugar

½ cup finely chopped pecans

1 package (8 ounces) cream cheese, softened

¼ cup granulated sugar

1 egg

1 tablespoon milk

2 teaspoons grated lemon peel

⅓ cup currant jelly or seedless raspberry jam

Preheat oven to 350°F. Grease 9-inch square baking pan. Beat butter in medium bowl with electric mixer at medium speed until smooth. Add flour, brown sugar and pecans; beat at low speed until well blended. Press mixture into bottom and partially up sides of prepared pan.

Bake about 15 minutes or until light brown. If sides of crust have shrunk down, press back up and reshape with spoon. Let cool 5 minutes on wire rack.

Meanwhile, beat cream cheese in large bowl with electric mixer at medium speed until smooth. Add granulated sugar, egg, milk and lemon peel; beat until well blended.

Heat jelly in small saucepan over low heat 2 to 3 minutes or until smooth, stirring occasionally.

Pour cream cheese mixture over crust. Drizzle jelly in 7 to 8 horizontal strips across filling with spoon. Swirl jelly through filling with knife to create marbled effect.

Bake 20 to 25 minutes or until filling is set. Cool completely on wire rack before cutting into bars. Store in airtight container in refrigerator up to 1 week.

Makes about 32 bars

Black & White Cheesecake

2 (3-ounce) packages cream cheese, softened

1 (14-ounce) can EAGLE® BRAND Sweetened Condensed Milk (NOT evaporated milk)

1 egg

1 teaspoon vanilla extract

1 cup mini chocolate chips, divided

1 teaspoon all-purpose flour

1 (6-ounce) chocolate crumb pie crust

Chocolate Glaze (recipe follows)

1. Preheat oven to 350°F. In medium mixing bowl, beat cream cheese until fluffy. Gradually beat in Eagle Brand until smooth. Add egg and vanilla; mix well.

2. In small mixing bowl, toss ½ cup chips with flour to coat; stir into cheese mixture. Pour into crust.

3. Bake 35 minutes or until center springs back when lightly touched. Cool. Prepare Chocolate Glaze and spread over cheesecake. Serve chilled. Store covered in refrigerator. *Makes 6 to 8 servings*

Chocolate Glaze: In small saucepan over low heat, melt remaining ½ cup chips with ¼ cup whipping cream. Cook and stir until thickened and smooth. Use immediately.

Prep Time: 15 minutes
Bake Time: 35 minutes

Black & White Cheesecake

White Chocolate Cheesecake with Orange Sauce

3 packages (8 ounces each) cream cheese, softened

1 cup sour cream

¾ cup sugar

1 tablespoon cornstarch

1 teaspoon vanilla

4 eggs

8 squares (1 ounce each) white chocolate, melted

Orange Sauce (recipe follows)

Preheat oven to 325°F. Grease 9-inch springform pan.

Beat cream cheese in large bowl with electric mixer at medium speed until creamy. Add sour cream; beat until blended. Add sugar, cornstarch and vanilla; beat until blended. Add eggs, one at a time, beating well after each addition. Add chocolate; beat until just blended.

Pour cream cheese mixture into prepared pan. Bake 60 to 70 minutes or until set. Turn off oven. Let cheesecake cool in oven 1 hour with oven door slightly open. Cool cheesecake in pan on wire rack 2 hours. Loosen edge; cool completely before removing rim of pan. Refrigerate at least 6 hours before serving. Serve with Orange Sauce. *Makes 8 servings*

Orange Sauce

1 cup orange juice

½ cup matchstick-size orange peel slices (about 3 oranges)

½ cup corn syrup

¼ cup sugar

¼ cup orange-flavored liqueur

⅓ cup chopped macadamia nuts

Place juice, orange peel, corn syrup, sugar and liqueur in medium saucepan; stir until sugar dissolves. Bring to a boil over high heat. Reduce heat to medium; boil 20 minutes or until liquid becomes syrupy. Remove from heat; cool thoroughly. Stir in macadamia nuts.

Philadelphia® 3-Step® Tiramisu Cheesecake

2 packages (8 ounces each) PHILADELPHIA® Cream Cheese, softened

½ cup sugar

½ teaspoon vanilla

2 eggs

2 tablespoons brandy

12 ladyfingers, split

½ cup strong MAXWELL HOUSE® Coffee

1 cup thawed COOL WHIP® Whipped Topping

1 square BAKER'S® Semi-Sweet Baking Chocolate, shaved

1. **BEAT** cream cheese, sugar and vanilla with electric mixer on medium speed until well blended. Add eggs; mix just until blended. Stir in brandy. Arrange ladyfingers on bottom and up side of 9-inch pie plate; drizzle with coffee.

2. **POUR** batter into prepared pie plate.

3. **BAKE** at 350°F for 40 minutes or until center is almost set. Cool. Refrigerate 3 hours or overnight. Top with whipped topping and shaved chocolate just before serving. *Makes 8 servings*

Prep Time: 10 minutes plus refrigerating
Bake Time: 40 minutes

Heavenly Cheesecake

½ cup HONEY MAID® Graham
    Cracker Crumbs

4 packages (8 ounces each)
    PHILADELPHIA® Neufchâtel
    Cheese, ⅓ Less Fat than Cream
    Cheese

1 cup sugar

¼ teaspoon almond extract or
    1 teaspoon vanilla

3 egg whites

2 eggs

GREASE bottom of 9-inch springform pan.
Sprinkle with crumbs.

BEAT Neufchâtel cheese, sugar and extract
with electric mixer on medium speed until
well blended. Add 3 egg whites; mix well.
Add eggs, 1 at a time, mixing at low speed
after each addition just until blended. Pour
into prepared pan.

BAKE at 325°F for 45 to 50 minutes or
until center is almost set. Run knife or
metal spatula around rim of pan to loosen
cake; cool before removing rim of pan.
Refrigerate 4 hours or overnight.

GARNISH with raspberries, strawberries or
blueberries and mint leaves.

Makes 12 servings

Prep Time: 15 minutes
Bake Time: 50 minutes

Heavenly Cheesecake

Refreshing Choco-Orange Cheesecake

1 cup graham cracker crumbs

¼ cup (½ stick) butter or margarine, melted

2 cups sugar, divided

1 cup HERSHEY'S Semi-Sweet Chocolate Chips

3 packages (8 ounces each) cream cheese, softened

4 eggs

1½ cups dairy sour cream

2 teaspoons orange extract

1 teaspoon freshly grated orange peel

Whipped topping

1. Stir together graham cracker crumbs, melted butter and ¼ cup sugar in small bowl; pat firmly onto bottom of 9-inch springform pan.

2. Place chocolate chips in medium microwave-safe bowl. Microwave at HIGH (100%) 1 minute or just until chips are melted when stirred.

3. Beat cream cheese and remaining 1¾ cups sugar in large bowl; add eggs, one at a time, beating after each addition. Stir in sour cream and orange extract. Stir 3 cups cream cheese mixture into melted chocolate chips; pour into crust. Freeze 10 to 15 minutes or until chocolate sets.

4. Heat oven to 325°F. Stir orange peel into remaining cream cheese mixture; gently spread over chocolate mixture.

5. Bake 1 hour 15 minutes or until set except for 3-inch circle in center; turn off oven. Let stand in oven, with door ajar, 1 hour; remove from oven. With knife, loosen cheesecake from side of pan. Cool completely; remove side of pan. Cover; refrigerate. Garnish with whipped topping and orange wedges, if desired. Cover; refrigerate leftover cheesecake.

Makes 12 servings

Creamy Lemon Cheesecake

9 graham crackers, crushed into crumbs

⅓ cup blanched almonds, ground

6 tablespoons butter or margarine, melted

¾ cup plus 2 tablespoons sugar, divided

3 packages (8 ounces each) cream cheese, softened

1 container (15 ounces) ricotta cheese

4 eggs, lightly beaten

2 tablespoons finely grated lemon peel

1 teaspoon lemon extract

1 teaspoon vanilla

1. Preheat oven to 375°F.

2. Blend graham cracker crumbs, almonds, butter and 2 tablespoons sugar in small bowl. Press evenly on bottom and ½ inch up side of 9-inch springform pan. Bake 5 minutes. Remove; cool pan on wire rack. *Reduce oven to 325°F.*

3. Combine cream cheese, ricotta cheese, eggs, remaining ¾ cup sugar, lemon peel, lemon extract and vanilla in large bowl. Beat on low speed of electric mixer until blended. Increase mixer speed to high. Beat 4 to 5 minutes until smooth and creamy. Pour into prepared crust.

4. Bake 1 hour and 10 minutes or until just set in center. *Do not overbake.* Cool to room temperature on wire rack. Cover and refrigerate at least four hours or overnight.

Makes 12 servings

Refreshing Choco-Orange Cheesecake

Peach Blueberry Cheesecake

Crust

- 1½ cups crushed graham cracker crumbs
- ½ cup crushed gingersnap cookies
- 5 tablespoons butter, melted

Filling

- 2 packages (8 ounces each) cream cheese, softened
- ¾ cup sugar
- ½ cup GRANDMA'S® Molasses
- 7 egg yolks
- 2 tablespoons lemon juice
- 1½ teaspoons vanilla extract
- ½ teaspoon salt
- 3 cups sour cream

Topping:

- 1 can (16 ounces) peach slices, drained
- Fresh blueberries
- 2 tablespoons peach or apricot preserves, melted

1. Heat oven to 350°F. Grease 9-inch springform pan. In small bowl, combine crust ingredients; press over bottom and half way up side of pan. Refrigerate. Place large roasting pan filled with 1 inch hot water on middle rack of oven. In large bowl, beat cream cheese and sugar until very smooth, about 3 minutes. Beat in molasses. Add egg yolks, beating until batter is smooth. Add lemon juice, vanilla and salt; beat until well incorporated. Beat in sour cream just until blended. Pour batter into prepared crust.

2. Place cheesecake in roasting pan. Bake 45 minutes. Turn oven off without opening door and let cake cool 1 hour. Transfer to wire rack (center will be jiggly) and cool to room temperature, about 1 hour. Cover pan with plastic wrap and refrigerate overnight. Remove side of pan. Top with peach slices and blueberries. Brush fruit with preserves.

Makes 12 to 16 servings

Chocolate Turtle Cheesecake

- 24 chocolate sandwich cookies, ground (about 2¾ cups)
- 2 tablespoons butter, melted
- 2 packages (8 ounces each) cream cheese, softened
- ⅓ cup sugar
- ¼ cup sour cream
- 2 eggs
- 1 teaspoon vanilla
- ½ cup prepared caramel sauce
- ½ cup prepared fudge sauce
- ½ cup pecan halves

1. Preheat oven to 350°F. Combine ground cookies and butter in medium bowl; pat evenly on bottom and 1 inch up side of 9-inch springform pan. Place in freezer while preparing filling.

2. Beat cream cheese in large bowl with electric mixer until fluffy. Beat in sugar, sour cream, eggs and vanilla until smooth. Pour mixture into prepared crust.

3. Bake cheesecake 30 to 35 minutes or until almost set in center. Cool on wire rack. Refrigerate, loosely covered, 8 hours or up to 3 days.

4. To complete recipe, remove side of springform pan from cheesecake; place on serving plate. Drizzle caramel and fudge sauces over cake; cut cake into wedges. Top each serving with 2 to 3 pecan halves.

Makes 12 servings

Peach Blueberry Cheesecake

Dreamy Cheesecake ◆ 281

Jeweled Brownie Cheesecake

Jeweled Brownie Cheesecake

¾ cup (1½ sticks) butter or margarine

4 squares (1 ounce each) unsweetened baking chocolate

1½ cups sugar

4 large eggs

1 cup all-purpose flour

1¾ cups "M&M's"® Chocolate Mini Baking Bits, divided

½ cup chopped walnuts, optional

1 (8-ounce) package cream cheese, softened

1 teaspoon vanilla extract

Preheat oven to 350°F. Lightly grease 9-inch springform pan; set aside. Place butter and chocolate in large microwave-safe bowl. Microwave at HIGH 1 minute; stir. Microwave at HIGH an additional 30 seconds; stir until chocolate is completely melted. Add sugar and 3 eggs, one at a time, beating well after each addition; blend in flour. Stir in 1¼ cups "M&M's"® Chocolate Mini Baking Bits and nuts, if desired; set aside. In large bowl, beat cream cheese, remaining 1 egg and vanilla. Spread half of the chocolate mixture in prepared pan. Carefully spread cream cheese mixture evenly over chocolate mixture, leaving 1-inch border. Spread remaining chocolate mixture evenly over top, all the way to the edges. Sprinkle with remaining ½ cup "M&M's"® Chocolate Mini Baking Bits. Bake 40 to 45 minutes or until firm to the touch. Cool completely. Store in refrigerator in tightly covered container.

Makes 12 slices

Chocolate Chip Cheesecake

1 package DUNCAN HINES® Moist Deluxe® Devil's Food Cake Mix

½ cup vegetable oil

3 (8-ounce) packages cream cheese, softened

1½ cups granulated sugar

1 cup sour cream

1½ teaspoons vanilla extract

4 eggs, lightly beaten

¾ cup semisweet mini chocolate chips, divided

1 teaspoon all-purpose flour

1. Preheat oven to 350°F. Grease 10-inch springform pan.

2. Combine cake mix and oil in large bowl. Mix well. Press onto bottom of prepared pan. Bake 22 to 25 minutes or until set. Remove from oven. *Increase oven temperature to 450°F.*

3. Place cream cheese in large mixing bowl. Beat at low speed with electric mixer, adding sugar gradually. Add sour cream and vanilla extract, mixing until blended. Add eggs, mixing only until incorporated. Toss ½ cup chocolate chips with flour. Fold into cream cheese mixture. Pour filling onto crust. Sprinkle with remaining ¼ cup chocolate chips. Bake 5 to 7 minutes. *Reduce oven temperature to 250°F.* Bake 60 to 65 minutes or until set. Loosen cake from side of pan with knife or spatula. Cool completely in pan on cooling rack. Refrigerate until ready to serve. Remove side of pan. *Makes 12 to 16 servings*

Tip: Place pan of water on bottom shelf of oven during baking to prevent cheesecake from cracking.

Chocolate Chip Cheesecake

Espresso Swirl Cheesecake

- **1 package (9 ounces) chocolate wafer cookies**
- **1 tablespoon plus 1½ cups sugar**
- **6 tablespoons I CAN'T BELIEVE IT'S NOT BUTTER!® Spread**
- **3 tablespoons instant espresso coffee powder, divided**
- **4 packages (8 ounces each) cream cheese, softened**
- **⅓ cup all-purpose flour**
- **½ cup (1 stick) I CAN'T BELIEVE IT'S NOT BUTTER!® Spread, melted**
- **7 eggs, lightly beaten**
- **1 cup (½ pint) whipping or heavy cream**
- **2 teaspoons vanilla extract**
- **2 squares (1 ounce each) bittersweet chocolate *or* ⅓ cup semi-sweet chocolate chips**

On bottom rack in oven, place 13×9-inch pan filled halfway with water. Preheat oven to 350°F.

In food processor, process cookies and 1 tablespoon sugar until combined; set aside. In small saucepan, melt 6 tablespoons I Can't Believe It's Not Butter! Spread, then stir in 1 tablespoon instant coffee until dissolved. Remove from heat; stir in cookie mixture. In 9-inch springform pan, press crumb mixture onto bottom and up side.

In medium bowl, with electric mixer, beat cream cheese, remaining 1½ cups sugar, flour and melted ½ cup I Can't Believe It's Not Butter! Spread 2 minutes or until mixture is creamy. Gradually beat in eggs, cream and vanilla until smooth. Reserve 1 cup batter. Pour remaining batter into prepared pan.

In microwave-safe bowl, microwave chocolate at HIGH (Full Power) 1 minute or until chocolate is melted; stir until smooth. Stir in remaining 2 tablespoons instant coffee until dissolved. Stir chocolate mixture into reserved batter until blended. Drop mixture by 2 tablespoonfuls onto batter and swirl with knife.

Bake 1 hour 10 minutes or until edges are golden. Without opening the door, turn oven off and let cheesecake stand in oven 30 minutes. On wire rack, cool completely. Cover and refrigerate overnight. Best if made 1 day ahead.   *Makes 12 servings*

Oven-Tested Tips

One reason that a cheesecake cracks is that it loses too much moisture while baking. Placing a pan of water in the oven can help prevent this by increasing the oven's humidity. You can also prevent cracks by not overbeating the batter, baking in the wrong size pan or baking too long. Remember that cracks do NOT ruin a cheesecake. Hide them with a topping of berries, jam or slightly sweetened sour cream.

Espresso Swirl Cheesecake

Cheery Cheesecake Cookie Bars

4 bars (1 ounce each) HERSHEY'S Unsweetened Baking Chocolate, broken into pieces

1 cup (2 sticks) butter

2½ cups sugar, divided

4 eggs

1 teaspoon vanilla extract

2 cups all-purpose flour

1 package (8 ounces) cream cheese, softened

1¾ cups (10-ounce package) HERSHEY'S MINI KISSES™ Milk Chocolates or Semi-Sweet Chocolates, divided

½ cup chopped red or green maraschino cherries

½ teaspoon almond extract

Few drops red food color (optional)

1. Heat oven to 350°F. Grease 13×9×2-inch baking pan.

2. Place baking chocolate and butter in large microwave-safe bowl. Microwave at HIGH (100%) 2 to 2½ minutes, stirring after each minute, until mixture is melted. Beat in 2 cups sugar, 3 eggs and vanilla until blended. Stir in flour; spread batter into prepared pan.

3. Beat cream cheese, remaining ½ cup sugar and remaining 1 egg; stir in 1¼ cups Mini Kisses™, cherries, almond extract and red food color, if desired. Drop by spoonfuls over top of chocolate mixture in pan.

4. Bake 35 to 40 minutes or just until set. Remove from oven; immediately sprinkle remaining ½ cup Mini Kisses™ over top. Cool completely in pan on wire rack; cut into bars. Cover; refrigerate leftover bars.

Makes 36 bars

Pumpkin Cheesecake

⅓ cup graham cracker crumbs

1 can (16 ounces) solid pack pumpkin

2 cups low-fat ricotta cheese

1 cup sugar

3 tablespoons all-purpose flour

1 tablespoon nonfat dry milk powder

1 tablespoon ground cinnamon

1 teaspoon ground allspice

1 egg white

¾ cup canned evaporated skimmed milk

1 tablespoon vegetable oil

1 tablespoon vanilla

1. Preheat oven to 400°F. Spray 9-inch springform pan with nonstick cooking spray. Add graham cracker crumbs; shake to coat pan evenly. Set aside.

2. Combine pumpkin and ricotta cheese in food processor or blender; process until smooth. Add sugar, flour, milk powder, cinnamon, allspice, egg white, evaporated skimmed milk, oil and vanilla; process until smooth.

3. Pour mixture into prepared pan. Bake 15 minutes. *Reduce oven temperature to 275°F;* bake 1 hour and 15 minutes. Turn off oven; leave cheesecake in oven with door closed 1 hour. Remove from oven; cool completely on wire rack. Remove springform pan side. Cover cheesecake with plastic wrap; refrigerate at least 4 hours or up to 2 days. Garnish with fresh fruit, if desired.

Makes 16 servings

Cheery Cheesecake Cookie Bar

Creamy Baked Cheesecake

1¼ cups graham cracker crumbs

¼ cup sugar

⅓ cup (⅔ stick) butter or margarine, melted

2 (8-ounce) packages cream cheese, softened

1 (14-ounce) can EAGLE® BRAND Sweetened Condensed Milk (NOT evaporated milk)

3 eggs

¼ cup lemon juice from concentrate

1 (8-ounce) container sour cream, at room temperature

Raspberry Topping (recipe follows), if desired

1. Preheat oven to 300°F. In small mixing bowl, combine crumbs, sugar and butter; press firmly on bottom of ungreased 9-inch springform pan.

2. In large mixing bowl, beat cream cheese until fluffy. Gradually beat in Eagle Brand until smooth. Add eggs and lemon juice; mix well. Pour into prepared pan.

3. Bake 50 to 55 minutes or until set. Remove from oven; top with sour cream. Bake 5 minutes longer. Cool. Chill. Prepare Raspberry Topping, if desired, and serve with cheesecake. Store covered in refrigerator.   *Makes 1 (9-inch) cheesecake*

Prep Time: 20 minutes
Bake Time: 55 to 60 minutes
Chill Time: 4 hours

Raspberry Topping

1 (10-ounce) package frozen red raspberries in syrup, thawed

¼ cup red currant jelly or red raspberry jam

1 tablespoon cornstarch

1. Reserve ⅔ cup syrup from raspberries; set raspberries aside.

2. In small saucepan over medium heat, combine reserved syrup, jelly and cornstarch. Cook and stir until slightly thickened and clear. Cool. Stir in raspberries.

Prep Time: 5 minutes

New York Style Cheesecake: Increase cream cheese to 4 (8-ounce) packages and eggs to 4. Proceed as directed, adding 2 tablespoons flour after eggs. Bake 1 hour 10 minutes or until center is set. Omit sour cream. Cool. Chill. Serve and store as directed.

Oven-Tested Tips

To soften cream cheese quickly, remove it from the wrapper and place it in a medium microwavable container. Microwave at MEDIUM (50% power) 15 to 20 seconds or until slightly softened. For a smooth, creamy cheesecake, be sure to beat the cream cheese until light and fluffy before adding other ingredients.

Creamy Baked Cheesecake

Dreamy Cheesecake • 289

Crazy Kids' Stuff

Bake some family memories. Exercise the kids' creativity with Cookie Canvases. Share a giggle with Hot Dog Cookies. Make someone's birthday very special with an Enchanted Castle Cake. Whenever you gather kids (and fun-loving grown-ups!) in the kitchen to mix up a batter, decorate a cake or just lick the frosting bowl, good times are guaranteed.

Oreo® Muffins

1¾ cups all-purpose flour
½ cup sugar
1 tablespoon baking powder
½ teaspoon salt
¾ cup milk
⅓ cup sour cream
1 egg
¼ cup margarine or butter, melted
20 OREO® Chocolate Sandwich Cookies,
    coarsely chopped

1. Mix flour, sugar, baking powder and salt in medium bowl; set aside.

2. Blend milk, sour cream and egg in small bowl; stir into flour mixture with margarine or butter until just blended. Gently stir in cookie pieces. Spoon batter into 12 greased 2½-inch muffin-pan cups.

3. Bake at 400°F for 20 to 25 minutes or until toothpick inserted in center comes out clean. Remove from pan; cool on wire rack. Serve warm or cold.

Makes 1 dozen muffins

Hot Dog Cookies

Butter Cookie Dough (recipe
follows)
Liquid food colors
Sesame seeds
**Shredded coconut, red and green
decorator gels, frosting and
gummy candies**

1. Prepare Butter Cookie Dough. Cover;
refrigerate 4 hours or until firm. Grease
cookie sheets.

2. Reserve ⅓ of dough to make "hot dogs."
Refrigerate remaining dough. Mix food
colors in small bowl to get reddish-brown
color following chart on back of food color
box. Mix color throughout reserved dough.

3. Divide colored dough into 6 equal
sections. Roll each section into thin log
shape. Round edges; set aside.

4. To make "buns," divide remaining dough
into 6 equal sections. Roll sections into
thick logs. Make very deep indentation the
length of logs in centers; smooth edges to
create buns. Dip sides of buns in sesame
seeds. Place 3 inches apart on prepared
cookie sheets. Place hot dogs inside buns.
Freeze 20 minutes.

5. Preheat oven to 350°F. Bake 17 to
20 minutes or until bun edges are light
golden brown. Cool completely on cookie
sheets.

6. Top hot dogs with green-tinted shredded
coconut for "relish," white coconut for
"onions," red decorator gel for "ketchup"
and yellow-tinted frosting or whipped
topping for "mustard."

Makes 6 hot dog cookies

Butter Cookie Dough

¾ cup butter, softened
¼ cup granulated sugar
¼ cup packed light brown sugar
1 egg yolk
1¾ cups all-purpose flour
¾ teaspoon baking powder
⅛ teaspoon salt

1. Combine butter, granulated sugar, brown
sugar and egg yolk in medium bowl. Add
flour, baking powder and salt; mix well.

2. Cover; refrigerate about 4 hours or until
firm.

Oven-Tested Tips

*To pipe gels or frosting onto cookies, you
can use a resealable plastic sandwich bag
as a substitute for a pastry bag. Fold the
top of the bag down to form a cuff and
use a spatula to fill the bag half full with
gel or frosting. Unfold the top of the bag
and twist down against the filling. Snip a
tiny tip off one corner of the bag. Hold
the top of bag tightly and squeeze the
filling through the opening.*

Sugar-and-Spice Twists

1 tablespoon sugar

¼ teaspoon ground cinnamon

1 package (6) refrigerated breadsticks

1. Preheat oven to 350°F. Lightly grease baking sheet or line with parchment paper.

2. Stir together sugar and cinnamon. Place in shallow dish or plate.

3. Open package of breadsticks. Divide into 6 portions. Roll each portion into 12-inch rope. Roll in sugar mixture. Twist into pretzel shape. Place on prepared baking sheet. Bake 15 to 18 minutes or until lightly browned. Remove from baking sheet. Cool 5 minutes. Serve warm.

Makes 6 servings

Hint: Use colored sugar sprinkles in place of the sugar in this recipe for a fun 'twist' of color that's perfect for holidays, birthdays or simply everyday celebrations.

Sugar-and-Spice Twists

"Everything but the Kitchen Sink" Bar Cookies

1 package (18 ounces) refrigerated chocolate chip cookie dough

1 jar (7 ounces) marshmallow creme

½ cup creamy peanut butter

1½ cups toasted corn cereal

½ cup miniature candy-coated chocolate pieces

1. Preheat oven to 350°F. Grease 13×9-inch baking pan. Remove dough from wrapper according to package directions.

2. Press dough into prepared baking pan. Bake 13 minutes.

3. Remove baking pan from oven. Drop teaspoonfuls of marshmallow creme and peanut butter over hot cookie base.

4. Bake 1 minute. Carefully spread marshmallow creme and peanut butter over cookie base.

5. Sprinkle cereal and chocolate pieces over melted marshmallow and peanut butter mixture.

6. Bake 7 minutes. Cool completely on wire rack. Cut into 2-inch bars.

Makes 3 dozen bars

"Everything but the Kitchen Sink" Bar Cookies

Banana Split Cupcakes

1 package (about 18 ounces) yellow cake mix, divided

1 cup water

1 cup mashed ripe bananas

3 eggs

1 cup chopped drained maraschino cherries

1½ cups miniature semi-sweet chocolate chips, divided

1½ cups prepared vanilla frosting

1 cup marshmallow creme

1 teaspoon shortening

30 whole maraschino cherries, drained and patted dry

1. Preheat oven to 350°F. Line 30 regular-size (2½-inch) muffin cups with paper muffin cup liners.

2. Reserve 2 tablespoons cake mix. Combine remaining cake mix, water, bananas and eggs in large bowl. Beat at low speed of electric mixer until moistened, about 30 seconds. Beat at medium speed 2 minutes. Combine chopped cherries and reserved cake mix in small bowl. Stir chopped cherry mixture and 1 cup chocolate chips into batter.

3. Spoon batter into prepared muffin cups. Bake 15 to 20 minutes or until toothpick inserted in centers comes out clean. Cool in pans on wire racks 10 minutes. Remove to wire racks; cool completely.

4. Combine frosting and marshmallow creme in medium bowl until well blended. Frost each cupcake with frosting mixture.

5. Combine remaining ½ cup chocolate chips and shortening in small microwavable bowl. Microwave at HIGH 30 to 45 seconds, stirring after 30 seconds, or until smooth. Drizzle chocolate mixture over cupcakes. Place one whole cherry on each cupcake. *Makes 30 cupcakes*

Note: If desired, omit chocolate drizzle and top cupcakes with colored sprinkles.

Fruity Cookie Rings and Twists

1 package (20 ounces) refrigerated sugar cookie dough

3 cups fruit-flavored cereal, crushed and divided

1. Remove dough from wrapper according to package directions. Combine dough and ½ cup crushed cereal in large bowl. Divide dough into 32 balls. Refrigerate 1 hour.

2. Preheat oven to 375°F. Shape dough balls into 6- to 8-inch-long ropes. Roll ropes in remaining cereal to coat; shape into rings or fold in half and twist.

3. Place cookies 2 inches apart on ungreased cookie sheets.

4. Bake 10 to 11 minutes or until lightly browned. Remove to wire racks; cool completely. *Makes 32 cookies*

Tip: These cookie rings can be transformed into Christmas tree ornaments by poking a hole in each unbaked ring using a drinking straw. Bake cookies and decorate with colored gels and small candies to resemble wreaths. Loop thin ribbon through holes and tie together.

Banana Split Cupcakes

Enchanted Castle

5½ cups cake batter, divided

1 (15×15-inch) cake board, covered, or large platter

2 cans (16 ounces each) white frosting

4 sugar ice cream cones

50 chocolate-covered wafer cookies

9 square dark chocolate mints

Assorted candies, decors and fruit rollups

1. Preheat oven to 350°F. Grease and flour 9-inch square cake pan and medium muffin pan. Pour 3½ cups cake batter into cake pan; pour remaining cake batter into muffin pan (¼ cup batter per muffin cup). Bake cake in pan 35 to 45 minutes and cupcakes about 20 minutes or until toothpick inserted into centers comes out clean. Cool 15 minutes in pans. Loosen edges; invert onto wire racks and cool completely.

2. Trim top and sides of square cake to even out. Slice rounded tops off four cupcakes. (Reserve remaining cupcakes for another use.) Place cake on prepared cake board. Place one cupcake upside down on each corner of cake, attaching with small amount of frosting.

3. Tint 1 can frosting pink. Divide second can of frosting in half; tint half yellow and half purple.

4. Frost entire cake and cupcakes with pink frosting. Frost ice cream cones with yellow frosting.

5. Place frosted cones on top of cupcakes. Using medium writing tip and purple frosting, pipe decorative lines around tops and bottoms of cones, cupcakes and edges of square cake.

6. Place chocolate wafer cookies around sides of cake, alternating whole cookies with cookies cut down by one fourth to create castle wall.

7. Decorate castle with assorted candies, cookies, decors and fruit rollups cut into flag shapes. *Makes 14 to 16 servings*

Bird's Nest Cookies

1⅓ cups (3½ ounces) flaked coconut

1 cup (2 sticks) butter or margarine, softened

½ cup granulated sugar

1 large egg

½ teaspoon vanilla extract

2 cups all-purpose flour

¾ teaspoon salt

1¾ cups "M&M's"® Semi-Sweet Chocolate Mini Baking Bits, divided

Preheat oven to 300°F. Spread coconut on ungreased cookie sheet. Toast in oven, stirring until coconut just begins to turn light golden, about 25 minutes. Remove coconut from cookie sheet; set aside. Increase oven temperature to 350°F. In large bowl cream butter and sugar until light and fluffy; beat in egg and vanilla. In medium bowl combine flour and salt; blend into creamed mixture. Stir in 1 cup "M&M's"® Semi-Sweet Chocolate Mini Baking Bits. Form dough into 1¼-inch balls. Roll heavily in toasted coconut. Place 2 inches apart on lightly greased cookie sheets. Make indentation in center of each cookie with thumb. Bake 12 to 14 minutes or until coconut is golden brown. Remove cookies to wire racks; immediately fill indentations with remaining "M&M's"® Semi-Sweet Chocolate Mini Baking Bits, using scant teaspoonful for each cookie. Cool completely. *Makes about 3 dozen cookies*

Hershey's Milk Chocolate Chip Giant Cookie

Hershey's Milk Chocolate Chip Giant Cookies

6 tablespoons butter, softened
½ cup granulated sugar
¼ cup packed light brown sugar
½ teaspoon vanilla extract
1 egg
1 cup all-purpose flour
½ teaspoon baking soda
2 cups (11½-ounce package) HERSHEY'S Milk Chocolate Chips
Frosting (optional)
Ice cream (optional)

1. Heat oven to 350°F. Line two 9-inch round baking pans with foil, extending foil over edges of pans.

2. Beat butter, granulated sugar, brown sugar and vanilla until fluffy. Add egg; beat well. Stir together flour and baking soda; gradually add to butter mixture, beating until well blended. Stir in milk chocolate chips. Spread one half of batter into each prepared pan, spreading to 1 inch from edge. (Cookies will spread to edge when baking.)

3. Bake 18 to 22 minutes or until lightly browned. Cool completely; carefully lift cookies from pans and remove foil. Frost, if desired. Cut each cookie into wedges; serve topped with scoop of ice cream, if desired.

Makes about 12 to 16 servings

Tip: Bake cookies on the middle rack of the oven, one pan at a time. Uneven browning can occur if baking on more than one rack at the same time.

Soft Pretzels

1 package (16 ounces) hot roll mix plus ingredients to prepare mix

1 egg white

2 teaspoons water

2 tablespoons *each* **assorted coatings: coarse salt, grated Parmesan cheese, sesame seeds, poppy seeds, dried oregano leaves**

1. Prepare hot roll mix according to package directions.

2. Preheat oven to 375°F. Spray baking sheets with nonstick cooking spray; set aside.

3. Divide dough equally into 16 pieces; roll each piece with hands to form a rope, 7 to 10 inches long. Place on prepared cookie sheets; form into desired shape (hearts, wreaths, pretzels, snails, loops, etc.).

4. Beat together egg white and water in small bowl until foamy. Brush onto dough shapes; sprinkle each shape with 1½ teaspoons of one of the coatings.

5. Bake until golden brown, about 15 minutes. Serve warm or at room temperature. *Makes 8 servings*

Fruit Twists: Omit coatings. Prepare dough and roll into ropes as directed. Place ropes on lightly floured surface. Roll out, or pat, each rope into rectangle, ¼ inch thick; brush each rectangle with about 1 teaspoon spreadable fruit or preserves. Fold each rectangle lengthwise in half; twist into desired shape. Bake as directed.

Cheese Twists: Omit coatings. Prepare dough and roll into ropes as directed. Place ropes on lightly floured surface. Roll out, or pat, each rope into rectangle, ¼ inch thick. Sprinkle each rectangle with about 1 tablespoon shredded Cheddar or other flavor cheese. Fold each rectangle lengthwise in half; twist into desired shape. Bake as directed.

Soft Pretzels

Peanut Butter S'Mores

1½ cups all-purpose flour
½ teaspoon baking powder
½ teaspoon baking soda
¼ teaspoon salt
½ cup butter, softened
½ cup granulated sugar
½ cup packed brown sugar
½ cup creamy or chunky peanut butter
1 egg
1 teaspoon vanilla
½ cup chopped roasted peanuts (optional)
4 (1.55-ounce) milk chocolate candy bars
16 large marshmallows

1. Preheat oven to 350°F.

2. Combine flour, baking powder, baking soda and salt in small bowl; set aside. Beat butter, granulated sugar and brown sugar in large bowl with electric mixer at medium speed until light and fluffy. Beat in peanut butter, egg and vanilla until well blended. Gradually beat in flour mixture at low speed until blended. Stir in peanuts, if desired.

3. Roll dough into 1-inch balls; place 2 inches apart on ungreased cookie sheets. Flatten dough with tines of fork, forming criss-cross pattern. Bake about 14 minutes or until set and edges are light golden brown. Cool cookies 2 minutes on cookie sheets; transfer to wire cooling racks. Cool completely.

4. To assemble sandwiches, break each candy bar into four sections. Place 1 section of chocolate on flat side of 1 cookie. Place on microwavable plate; top with 1 marshmallow. Microwave at HIGH 10 to 12 seconds or until marshmallow is puffy. Immediately top with another cookie, flat side down. Press slightly on top cookie, spreading marshmallow to edges. Repeat with remaining cookies, marshmallows and candy pieces, one at a time. Cool completely.

Makes about 16 sandwich cookies

PB & J Cookie Sandwiches

½ cup butter or margarine, softened
½ cup creamy peanut butter
¼ cup solid vegetable shortening
1 cup firmly packed light brown sugar
1 large egg
1 teaspoon vanilla extract
1⅔ cups all-purpose flour
1 teaspoon baking soda
½ teaspoon baking powder
1 cup "M&M's"® Milk Chocolate Mini Baking Bits
½ cup finely chopped peanuts
½ cup grape or strawberry jam

Preheat oven to 350°F. In large bowl cream butter, peanut butter, shortening and sugar until light and fluffy; beat in egg and vanilla. In medium bowl combine flour, baking soda and baking powder; blend into creamed mixture. Stir in "M&M's"® Milk Chocolate Mini Baking Bits and nuts. Drop by rounded teaspoonfuls onto ungreased cookie sheets. Bake 8 to 10 minutes or until light golden brown. Let cool 2 minutes on cookie sheets; remove to wire racks to cool completely. Just before serving, spread ½ teaspoon jam on bottom of one cookie; top with second cookie. Store in tightly covered container.

Makes about 2 dozen sandwich cookies

Gingerbread Farm Animals in Corral

Gingerbread House Dough (recipe follows)
Royal Icing (recipe follows)
Assorted food colors
Shredded coconut, tinted green
Assorted small hard candies

Supplies
Cardboard and decorative paper

1. Preheat oven to 375°F. Prepare Gingerbread House Dough. Divide dough into 4 equal sections. To make fence, roll 1 section of dough directly onto large cookie sheet to ¼-inch thickness. Cut into 6 (6×2¾-inch) sections, leaving ½-inch space between sections. Bake 10 to 12 minutes or until edges are browned. Cool completely on wire racks.

2. Roll second section of dough directly onto cookie sheet to ¼-inch thickness. Cut into 4 (6×2¾ inch) sections and 2 (3-inch) sections, leaving ½-inch space between sections. Bake 10 to 12 minutes or until edges are browned. Cool on wire racks.

3. To make animals, roll remaining 2 sections of dough directly on cookie sheets to ⅛-inch thickness. Cut out animal shapes using animal-shaped cookie cutters. Bake 8 to 12 minutes or until edges are browned. Cool completely on wire racks.

4. Prepare 2 recipes Royal Icing. Tint small amounts of icing with food colors to decorate animals. Place remaining icing in small resealable plastic food storage bag. Cut off small corner of bag for piping.

5. Decorate animals and fence sections with icing and assorted candies according to photo. Cover 20-inch piece of cardboard with decorative paper and plastic wrap. Assemble fence by piping icing on bottom and side edges of fence sections. Use smaller sections to make 2 gates. Pipe icing on feet of animals; arrange so animals can be supported by fence or other animals. Sprinkle coconut around feet of animals for grass, if desired.

Makes 1 fence and 2 dozen animals

Gingerbread House Dough

5¼ cups all-purpose flour
1 tablespoon ground ginger
2 teaspoons baking soda
1½ teaspoons ground allspice
1 teaspoon salt
2 cups packed dark brown sugar
1 cup butter or margarine, softened
¾ cup dark corn syrup
2 eggs

1. Combine flour, ginger, baking soda, allspice and salt in medium bowl.

2. Beat brown sugar and butter in large bowl at medium speed of electric mixer until fluffy. Beat in corn syrup and eggs. Gradually add flour mixture. Beat at low speed until well blended. Cover; refrigerate about 2 hours or until firm.

Royal Icing

1 egg white,* at room temperature
2 to 2½ cups sifted powdered sugar
½ teaspoon almond extract

Use only grade A clean, uncracked egg.

1. Beat egg white in small bowl at high speed of electric mixer until foamy.

2. Gradually add 2 cups powdered sugar and almond extract. Beat at low speed until moistened. Increase mixer speed to high and beat until icing is stiff, adding additional powdered sugar if needed.

Gingerbread Farm Animals in Corral

Play Ball

2 cups plus 1 tablespoon all-purpose flour, divided

¾ cup granulated sugar

¾ cup packed brown sugar

1 tablespoon baking powder

1 teaspoon salt

½ teaspoon baking soda

½ cup shortening

1¼ cups milk

3 eggs

1½ teaspoons vanilla

½ cup mini semisweet chocolate chips

1 container (16 ounces) vanilla frosting

Assorted candies and food colorings

1. Preheat oven to 350°F. Line 24 regular-size (2½-inch) muffin pan cups with paper muffin cup liners.

2. Combine 2 cups flour, sugars, baking powder, salt and baking soda in medium bowl. Beat shortening, milk, eggs and vanilla in large bowl with electric mixer at medium speed until well combined. Add flour mixture; blend well. Beat at high speed 3 minutes, scraping side of bowl frequently. Toss mini chocolate chips with remaining 1 tablespoon flour; stir into batter. Divide evenly between prepared muffin cups.

3. Bake 20 minutes or until toothpick inserted into centers comes out clean. Cool in pan on wire racks 5 minutes. Remove cupcakes to racks; cool completely. Decorate with desired frostings and candies as shown in photo. *Makes 24 cupcakes*

Cinnamon Trail Mix

2 cups corn cereal squares

2 cups whole wheat cereal squares or whole wheat cereal squares with mini graham crackers

1½ cups fat-free oyster crackers

½ cup broken sesame snack sticks

2 tablespoons margarine or butter, melted

1 teaspoon ground cinnamon

¼ teaspoon ground nutmeg

½ cup bite-sized fruit-flavored candy pieces

1. Preheat oven to 350°F. Spray 13×9-inch baking pan with nonstick cooking spray.

2. Place cereals, oyster crackers and sesame sticks in prepared pan; mix lightly.

3. Combine margarine, cinnamon and nutmeg in small bowl; mix well. Drizzle evenly over cereal mixture; toss to coat.

4. Bake 12 to 14 minutes or until golden brown, stirring gently after 6 minutes. Cool completely. Stir in candies.

Makes 8 (¾-cup) servings

Oven-Tested Tips

If you don't use up an entire container of prepared frosting, cover and refrigerate leftovers for up to 30 days. Small amounts of frosting can easily be made into a glaze. Simply heat the frosting in a small saucepan over low heat stirring constantly until it reaches the desired consistency.

Cookie Canvases

1 package (20 ounces) refrigerated cookie dough, any flavor

All-purpose flour (optional)

Cookie Glaze (recipe follows)

Assorted liquid food colors

Supplies

1 (3½-inch) square cardboard template

1 (2½×4½-inch) rectangular cardboard template

Small, clean craft paintbrushes

1. Preheat oven to 350°F. Grease cookie sheets.

2. Remove dough from wrapper according to package directions. Cut dough in half. Wrap half of dough in plastic wrap and refrigerate.

3. Roll remaining dough on floured surface to ¼-inch thickness. Sprinkle with flour to minimize sticking, if necessary. Cut out cookie shapes using cardboard templates as guides. Place cookies 2 inches apart on prepared cookie sheets. Repeat steps with remaining dough.

4. Bake 8 to 10 minutes or until edges are lightly browned. Remove from oven and straighten cookie edges with spatula. Cool cookies completely on cookie sheets. Prepare Cookie Glaze.

5. Place cookies on wire racks set over waxed paper. Drizzle Cookie Glaze over cookies. Let stand at room temperature 40 minutes or until glaze is set. Place food colors in small bowls. Using small, clean craft paintbrushes, decorate cookies with food colors by "painting" designs such as rainbows, flowers and animals.

Makes 8 to 10 cookie canvases

Cookie Glaze: Combine 4 cups powdered sugar and 4 tablespoons milk in a small bowl. Stir; add 1 to 2 tablespoons more milk as needed to make a medium-thick, pourable glaze.

Ice Cream Cone Cakes

1 package (18¼ ounces) devil's food cake mix plus ingredients to prepare mix

⅓ cup sour cream

1 package (2⅝ ounces) flat-bottomed ice cream cones (about 18 cones)

1¼ cups nonfat frozen yogurt (any flavor)

Cake decorations or chocolate sprinkles

1. Preheat oven to 350°F. Grease and flour 8- or 9-inch round cake pan; set aside.

2. Prepare cake mix according to package directions, substituting sour cream for ⅓ cup of the water and decreasing oil to ¼ cup.

3. Spoon ½ of the batter (about 2⅓ cups) evenly into ice cream cones, using about 2 tablespoons batter for each. Pour remaining batter into prepared cake pan.

4. Stand cones on cookie sheet. Bake cones and cake layer until toothpick inserted into center of cake comes out clean, about 20 minutes for cones and about 35 minutes for cake layer. Cool on wire racks, removing cake from pan after 10 minutes. Reserve or freeze cake layer for another use.

5. Top each filled cone with ¼ cup scoop of frozen yogurt just before serving. Sprinkle with decorations as desired. Serve immediately.   *Makes 18 servings*

Puzzle Cookie

¾ cup shortening

½ cup packed light brown sugar

6 tablespoons dark molasses

2 egg whites

¾ teaspoon vanilla

2¼ cups all-purpose flour

2 teaspoons ground cinnamon

¾ teaspoon baking soda

¾ teaspoon salt

¾ teaspoon ground ginger

¼ teaspoon plus ⅛ teaspoon baking powder

Assorted colored frostings, colored sugars, colored decorator gels and assorted small candies

1. Beat shortening, brown sugar, molasses, egg whites and vanilla in large bowl at high speed of electric mixer until smooth.

2. Combine flour, cinnamon, baking soda, salt, ginger and baking powder in medium bowl. Add to shortening mixture; mix well. Shape dough into flat rectangle. Wrap in plastic wrap and refrigerate about 8 hours or until firm.

3. Preheat oven to 350°F. Grease 15½×10½-inch jelly-roll pan.

4. Sprinkle dough with additional flour. Place dough in center of prepared pan and roll evenly to within ½ inch of edge of pan. Cut shapes into dough using cookie cutters or free-hand using sharp knife, allowing at least 1 inch between each shape. Cut through dough, but do not remove shapes.

5. Bake 12 minutes or until edges begin to brown lightly. Remove from oven and retrace shapes with knife. Return to oven 5 to 6 minutes. Cool in pan 5 minutes. Carefully remove shapes to wire racks; cool completely.

6. Decorate shapes with frostings, sugars, decorator gels and small candies as shown in photo. Leave puzzle frame in pan. Decorate with frostings, colored sugars and gels to represent sky, clouds, grass and water, if desired. Return shapes to their respective openings to complete puzzle.

Makes 1 puzzle cookie

Handprints

1 package (20 ounces) refrigerated cookie dough, any flavor

All-purpose flour (optional)

Cookie glazes, frostings and assorted candies

1. Grease cookie sheets. Remove dough from wrapper; cut into 4 equal sections. Reserve 1 section; refrigerate remaining 3 sections.

2. Sprinkle reserved dough with flour to minimize sticking, if necessary. Roll dough on prepared cookie sheet to 5×7-inch rectangle.

3. Place hand, palm-side down, on dough. Carefully, cut around outline of hand with knife. Remove scraps. Separate fingers as much as possible using small spatula. Pat fingers outward to lengthen slightly. Repeat steps with remaining dough.

4. Freeze dough 15 minutes. Preheat oven to 350°F. Bake 7 to 13 minutes or until cookies are set and edges are golden brown. Cool completely on cookie sheets.

5. Decorate as desired.

Makes 5 adult handprint cookies

Tip: To get the kids involved, let them use their hands to make the handprints. Be sure that an adult is available to cut around the outline with a knife. The kids will enjoy seeing how their handprints bake into big cookies.

Gatherings & Gifts

The holidays bring out the baker in us all. Wow them at the cookie exchange with a brand new treat. Give a gift from the heart— homemade bread or cookies. You'll find the recipes here for classics like Orange Pecan Pie, as well as fresh ideas like Danish Cookie Rings. However you celebrate, home-baked treats will add to the warmth of the season.

Holiday Cheesecake Presents

1½ cups HONEY MAID® Graham Cracker Crumbs

⅓ cup butter or margarine, melted

3 tablespoons sugar

3 packages (8 ounces each) PHILADELPHIA® Cream Cheese, softened

¾ cup sugar

1 teaspoon vanilla

3 eggs

Decorations, such as decorating gels, colored sprinkles, nonpareils and small FARLEY'S Candies

MIX crumbs, butter and 3 tablespoons sugar; press onto bottom of 13×9-inch baking pan.*

BEAT cream cheese, ¾ cup sugar and vanilla with electric mixer on medium speed until well blended. Add eggs, 1 at a time, mixing just until blended after each addition. Pour over crust.

BAKE at 350°F for 30 minutes or until center is almost set. Cool. Refrigerate 3 hours or overnight. Cut into bars. Decorate with remaining ingredients as desired to resemble presents. Store leftover bars in refrigerator.

Makes 2 dozen bars

Line pan with foil before pressing crumb mixture onto bottom of pan for easy removal of bars.

Prep Time: 10 minutes plus refrigerating
Bake Time: 30 minutes

Holiday Fudge Torte

   1 cup all-purpose flour
   ¾ cup sugar
   ¼ cup HERSHEY'S Cocoa
   1½ teaspoons powdered instant coffee
   ¾ teaspoon baking soda
   ¼ teaspoon salt
   ½ cup (1 stick) butter or margarine, softened
   ¾ cup dairy sour cream
   1 egg
   ½ teaspoon vanilla extract
   Fudge Nut Glaze (recipe follows)

1. Heat oven to 350°F. Grease 9-inch round baking pan; line bottom with wax paper. Grease paper; flour paper and pan.

2. Stir together flour, sugar, cocoa, instant coffee, baking soda and salt in large bowl. Add butter, sour cream, egg and vanilla; beat on low speed of mixer until blended. Increase speed to medium; beat 3 minutes. Pour batter into prepared pan.

3. Bake 30 to 35 minutes or until wooden pick inserted in center comes out clean. Cool 10 minutes. Remove from pan to wire rack; gently peel off wax paper. Cool completely.

4. Prepare Fudge Nut Glaze. Place cake on serving plate; pour glaze evenly over cake, allowing some to run down sides. Refrigerate until glaze is firm, about 1 hour. Cover; refrigerate leftover torte.

Makes 8 to 10 servings

Fudge Nut Glaze

   ½ cup whipping cream
   ¼ cup sugar
   1 tablespoon butter
   1½ teaspoons light corn syrup
   ⅓ cup HERSHEY'S Semi-Sweet Chocolate Chips
   ¾ cup chopped hazelnuts, macadamia nuts or pecans
   ½ teaspoon vanilla extract

1. Combine all ingredients except nuts and vanilla in small saucepan. Cook over medium heat, stirring constantly, until mixture boils. Cook, stirring constantly, 5 minutes. Remove from heat.

2. Cool 10 minutes; stir in nuts and vanilla.

Scottish Shortbread

   5 cups all-purpose flour
   1 cup rice flour
   2 cups butter, softened
   1 cup sugar
   Candied fruit (optional)

Preheat oven to 325°F. Sift together flours. Beat butter and sugar in large bowl with electric mixer until creamy. Blend in ¾ of flour until mixture resembles fine crumbs. Stir in remaining flour by hand. Press dough firmly into ungreased 15½×10½×1-inch jelly-roll pan or two 9-inch fluted tart pans; crimp and flute edges of dough in jelly-roll pan, if desired. Bake 40 to 45 minutes or until light brown. Place pan on wire rack. Cut into bars or wedges while warm. Decorate with candied fruit, if desired. Cool completely. Store in airtight containers.

Makes about 4 dozen bars or 24 wedges

Holiday Fudge Torte

Santa Lucia Bread Wreath

Ingredients

1 to 1½ teaspoons ground cardamom

1 package (16 ounces) hot roll mix plus ingredients to prepare mix

½ recipe Cookie Glaze (recipe follows)

Red and green candied cherries

Supplies

Small custard cup

Artificial holly leaves* (optional)

5 (7- or 8-inch) candles

*Real holly leaves are toxic; do not use on food.

1. Stir cardamom into hot roll mix. Prepare mix according to package directions. Knead dough on lightly floured surface until smooth, about 5 minutes. Cover loosely; let stand in bowl about 15 minutes.

2. Grease large baking sheet and outside of custard cup. Place inverted custard cup in center of prepared baking sheet; set aside.

3. Punch down dough; divide into 3 equal pieces. On floured surface, roll and stretch 2 pieces of dough into 20-inch ropes. Braid ropes together; shape into 7-inch circle around custard cup.

4. Divide remaining dough piece in half. Place dough on floured surface; roll and stretch each piece into 12-inch rope. Braid 2 ropes together; shape into 5-inch circle. Place around custard cup, overlapping top of larger braid already on baking sheet.

5. To make holes for candles, shape small sheets of foil into 5 balls, each 1 inch in diameter. Insert balls between 2 braids, evenly spacing them around wreath. Cover dough loosely; let rise in warm place until doubled in size, 20 to 30 minutes.

6. Preheat oven to 375°F.

7. Uncover dough. Bake 25 to 30 minutes or until golden brown. Remove custard cup. Cool wreath on wire rack. Drizzle Cookie Glaze over wreath; decorate with cherries and artificial holly leaves, if desired. Before serving, remove balls of foil. Wrap bottoms of candles with small pieces of additional foil; insert candles into holes.

Makes 8 to 10 servings

Cookie Glaze: Combine 4 cups powdered sugar and 4 tablespoons milk in small bowl. Stir; add 1 to 2 tablespoons more milk as needed to make medium-thick, pourable glaze.

Oven-Tested Tips

Shaping dough can sometimes be frustrating. It seems like it just won't keep the shape you give it. Be patient. Don't try to force the dough to stretch or overwork it or you risk ending up with a dry, flat loaf. Every time shaping becomes difficult let the dough rest for 5 or 10 minutes in the refrigerator. This relaxes the dough and makes it easier to handle. In fact, it's a good idea to keep any portion of the dough you're not working with refrigerated until you're ready for it.

Banana Crescents

½ cup chopped almonds, toasted

6 tablespoons sugar, divided

½ cup margarine, cut into pieces

1½ cups plus 2 tablespoons all-purpose flour

⅛ teaspoon salt

1 extra-ripe, medium DOLE® Banana, peeled

2 to 3 ounces semisweet chocolate chips

• Pulverize almonds with 2 tablespoons sugar in blender.

• Beat margarine, almond mixture, remaining 4 tablespoons sugar, flour and salt.

• Purée banana in blender; add to almond mixture and mix until well blended.

• Roll tablespoonfuls of dough into logs, then shape into crescents. Place on ungreased cookie sheet. Bake at 375°F 25 minutes or until golden. Cool on wire rack.

• Melt chocolate in microwavable dish at MEDIUM (50% power) 1½ to 2 minutes, stirring once. Dip ends of cookies in chocolate. Refrigerate until chocolate is set.

Makes 2 dozen cookies

Banana Crescents

Orange Pecan Pie

Orange Pecan Pie

   3 eggs
½ cup GRANDMA'S® Molasses
½ cup light corn syrup
¼ cup orange juice
   1 teaspoon grated orange peel
   1 teaspoon vanilla
1½ cups whole pecan halves
   1 (9-inch) unbaked pie shell
   Whipped cream (optional)

Heat oven to 350°F. In large bowl, beat eggs. Add molasses, corn syrup, orange juice, orange peel and vanilla; beat until well blended. Stir in pecans. Pour into unbaked pie shell. Bake 30 to 45 minutes or until filling sets. Cool on wire rack. Serve with whipped cream, if desired.

Makes 8 servings

Gingerbread Log Cabin

7 cups all-purpose flour

4½ teaspoons ground ginger

2¾ teaspoons baking soda

2¼ teaspoons ground allspice

1¼ teaspoons salt

2⅔ cups packed brown sugar

1⅓ cups butter, softened

1 cup dark corn syrup

3 eggs

Royal Icing (recipe follows)

Assorted food colors

Assorted gumdrops and hard candies

Supplies

Cardboard

1. Draw patterns for house on cardboard, using diagrams on page 321; cut out patterns. Preheat oven to 375°F. Grease and flour large cookie sheet. Combine flour, ginger, baking soda, allspice and salt in medium bowl.

2. Beat brown sugar and butter in large bowl at medium speed of electric mixer until fluffy. Beat in corn syrup and eggs. Gradually add 6 cups flour mixture. Beat until well blended. Stir in remaining flour mixture with wooden spoon. Divide dough into 4 equal sections. Reserve 1 section; wrap and refrigerate remaining 3 sections.

3. To make sides of cabin, roll reserved dough directly onto prepared cookie sheet to ¼-inch thickness. Lay sheet of waxed paper over dough. Place patterns over waxed paper 2 inches apart. Cut dough around pattern with sharp knife; remove patterns and waxed paper. Reserve scraps to reroll with next dough section.

4. To make logs, roll dough into 12 (1-inch) balls. Roll each ball into 6-inch rope. Lay 6 logs parallel to one another on 1 prepared house side, leaving ¼-inch border at top and bottom of house side. Repeat steps with remaining 6 balls and second side. Freeze 15 minutes.

5. Bake 15 to 18 minutes or until no indentation remains when cookies are touched in center. While cookies are still hot, place cardboard pattern lightly over cookies; trim edges with sharp knife to straighten. Return to oven 2 minutes. Let stand on cookie sheets 5 minutes. Remove to wire racks; cool completely. Leave cookie pieces out uncovered overnight.

6. To make front and back walls, repeat step 3. To make logs for front and back, roll dough into 18 (1¼-inch) balls. Roll each ball into 7-inch log. Place 9 logs for front wall over cardboard pattern as a guide; cut out openings for windows. Lay logs parallel on front wall, leaving ¼-inch border at top and bottom of wall. Repeat steps with remaining 9 balls and back wall. Freeze 15 minutes. Bake and reserve as directed in step 5.

7. To make roof, repeat step 3. To make logs for roof, roll dough into 16 (1¼-inch) balls. Roll each ball into 7½-inch log. Lay logs parallel to one another on roof, leaving ¼-inch border at top and bottom of roof. Freeze 15 minutes. Bake and reserve as directed in step 5.

8. To make chimney, roll dough scraps into ball. Roll and cut out rectangle about 3×1¾-inches. Bake 10 to 12 minutes.

9. Cover 15-inch square piece of heavy cardboard with foil to use as base for cabin. Prepare Royal Icing. Place icing in small resealable plastic food storage bag. Cut off small corner of bag. Pipe icing on edges of all pieces including bottom; "glue" house together at seams and on base.

10. Position mug against outside of each wall and another at inside corner where 2 walls meet. Let dry at least 6 hours. When icing is set, remove mugs from inside walls. Pipe icing onto roof edges and attach to house. Place mug under each side of roof. Let dry at least 6 hours. Place chimney near top of one side of roof; attach with icing. Decorate with additional icing and candies as desired. *Makes 1 centerpiece*

Royal Icing: Beat 1 egg white in small bowl at high speed of electric mixer until foamy. Gradually add 2 cups powdered sugar and ½ teaspoon almond extract. Beat at low speed until moistened. Increase mixer speed to high and beat until icing is stiff, adding additional powdered sugar if needed.

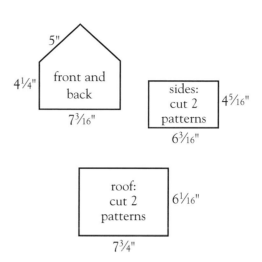

5"

4¼" front and back

7³⁄₁₆"

sides: cut 2 patterns 4⁵⁄₁₆"

6³⁄₁₆"

roof: cut 2 patterns 6¹⁄₁₆"

7¾"

Gingerbread Log Cabin

Holiday Chocolate Cake

2 cups sugar

1¾ cups all-purpose flour

¾ cup HERSHEY'S Cocoa

2 teaspoons baking soda

1 teaspoon baking powder

1 teaspoon salt

2 eggs

1 cup buttermilk or sour milk*

1 cup strong black coffee *or*
   2 teaspoons instant coffee
   dissolved in 1 cup hot water

½ cup vegetable oil

2 teaspoons vanilla extract

Ricotta Cheese Filling (recipe
   follows)

Chocolate Whipped Cream (recipe
   follows)

Vanilla Whipped Cream (recipe
   follows)

*To sour milk: Use 1 tablespoon white vinegar plus milk to equal 1 cup.

1. Heat oven to 350°F. Grease and flour two 9-inch round baking pans.

2. Stir together sugar, flour, cocoa, baking soda, baking powder and salt in large bowl. Add eggs, buttermilk, coffee, oil and vanilla; beat at medium speed of mixer 2 minutes (batter will be thin). Pour batter into prepared pans.

3. Bake 30 to 35 minutes or until wooden pick inserted into center of cakes comes out clean. Cool 10 minutes; remove from pans to wire racks. Cool completely.

4. Slice cake layers in half horizontally. Place bottom slice on serving plate; top with ⅓ Ricotta Cheese Filling. Alternate cake layers and filling, ending with cake on top. Frost cake with Chocolate Whipped Cream.

Decorate with Vanilla Whipped Cream and cherries, if desired. Cover; refrigerate leftover cake.   *Makes 10 to 12 servings*

Chocolate Whipped Cream: Stir together ⅓ cup powdered sugar and 2 tablespoons HERSHEY'S Cocoa in small bowl. Add 1 cup (½ pint) cold whipping cream and 1 teaspoon vanilla extract; beat until stiff.

Vanilla Whipped Cream: Beat ½ cup cold whipping cream, 2 tablespoons powdered sugar and ½ teaspoon vanilla extract in small bowl until stiff.

Ricotta Cheese Filling

1¾ cups (15 ounces) ricotta cheese*

¼ cup sugar

3 tablespoons Grand Marnier
   (orange-flavored liqueur) or
   orange juice concentrate,
   undiluted

¼ cup candied red or green cherries,
   coarsely chopped

⅓ cup HERSHEY'S MINICHIPS™
   Semi-Sweet Chocolate

*1 cup (½ pint) whipping cream may be substituted for ricotta cheese. Beat with sugar and liqueur until stiff. Fold in candied cherries and small chocolate chips.

Beat ricotta cheese, sugar and liqueur in large bowl until smooth. Fold in candied cherries and small chocolate chips.

Oven-Tested Tips

For better results when making whipped cream, place the bowl in the freezer to chill for a few minutes before beating.

Holiday Chocolate Cake

Festive Yule Loaf

2¾ cups all-purpose flour, divided
⅓ cup sugar
1 teaspoon salt
1 package active dry yeast
1 cup milk
½ cup butter or margarine
1 egg
½ cup golden raisins
½ cup chopped candied red and green cherries
½ cup chopped pecans
Vanilla Glaze (recipe follows, optional)

Combine 1½ cups flour, sugar, salt and yeast in large bowl. Heat milk and butter over medium heat until very warm (120° to 130°F). Gradually stir into flour mixture. Add egg. Mix with electric mixer on low speed 1 minute. Beat on high speed 3 minutes, scraping sides of bowl frequently. Toss raisins, cherries and pecans with ¼ cup flour in small bowl; stir into yeast mixture. Stir in enough of remaining 1 cup flour to make a soft dough. Turn out onto lightly floured surface. Knead about 10 minutes or until smooth and elastic. Place in greased bowl; turn to grease top of dough. Cover with towel. Let rise in warm, draft-free place about 1 hour or until double in volume.

Punch dough down. Divide in half. Roll out each half on lightly floured surface to form 8-inch circle. Fold in half; press only folded edge firmly. Place on ungreased cookie sheet. Cover with towel. Let rise in warm, draft-free place about 30 minutes or until double in volume.

Preheat oven to 375°F. Bake 20 to 25 minutes until golden brown. Remove from cookie sheet and cool completely on wire rack. Frost with Vanilla Glaze, if desired. Store in airtight containers.

Makes 2 loaves

Vanilla Glaze: Combine 1 cup sifted powdered sugar, 4 to 5 teaspoons light cream or half-and-half and ½ teaspoon vanilla in small bowl; stir until smooth.

Rum Fruitcake Cookies

1 cup sugar
¾ cup shortening
3 eggs
⅓ cup orange juice
1 tablespoon rum extract
3 cups all-purpose flour
2 teaspoons baking powder
1 teaspoon baking soda
1 teaspoon salt
2 cups (8 ounces) chopped candied mixed fruit
1 cup raisins
1 cup nuts, coarsely chopped

1. Preheat oven to 375°F. Lightly grease cookie sheets; set aside. Beat sugar and shortening in large bowl until fluffy. Add eggs, orange juice and rum extract; beat 2 minutes.

2. Combine flour, baking powder, baking soda and salt in medium bowl. Add candied fruit, raisins and nuts. Stir into creamed mixture. Drop dough by rounded teaspoonfuls 2 inches apart onto prepared cookie sheets. Bake 10 to 12 minutes or until golden. Let cookies stand on cookie sheets 2 minutes. Remove to wire racks; cool completely.

Makes about 6 dozen cookies

Gingerbread People

2¼ cups all-purpose flour

2 teaspoons ground cinnamon

2 teaspoons ground ginger

1 teaspoon baking powder

½ teaspoon salt

¼ teaspoon ground cloves

¼ teaspoon ground nutmeg

¾ cup butter, softened

½ cup packed light brown sugar

½ cup dark molasses

1 egg

Prepared creamy or gel-type tube frosting (optional)

Candies and other decorations (optional)

1. Combine flour, cinnamon, ginger, baking powder, salt, cloves and nutmeg in large bowl.

2. Beat butter and brown sugar in large bowl until light and fluffy. Beat in molasses and egg. Gradually add flour mixture; beat until well blended. Shape dough into 3 discs. Wrap well in plastic wrap; refrigerate 1 hour or until firm.

3. Preheat oven to 350°F. Working with 1 disc at a time, place on lightly floured surface. Roll out dough with lightly floured rolling pin to ³⁄₁₆-inch thickness. Cut out gingerbread people with floured 5-inch cookie cutters; place on ungreased cookie sheets. Press dough trimmings together gently; reroll and cut out more cookies.

4. Bake about 12 minutes or until edges are golden brown. Let cookies stand on cookie sheets 1 minute; remove to wire racks to cool completely.

5. Pipe icing onto cooled cookies. Decorate with candies, if desired. Let stand at room temperature 20 minutes or until set. Store tightly covered at room temperature or freeze up to 3 months.

Makes about 16 large cookies

Gingerbread People

Spicy Gingerbread with Cinnamon Pear Sauce

   2 cups all-purpose flour
   1 cup light molasses
   ¾ cup buttermilk
   ½ cup butter, softened
   ½ cup packed light brown sugar
   1 teaspoon baking soda
   1 teaspoon ground ginger
   1 teaspoon ground cinnamon
   ¼ teaspoon salt
   ¼ teaspoon ground cloves
      Cinnamon Pear Sauce (recipe follows)

1. Preheat oven to 325°F. Grease and lightly flour 9-inch square baking pan.

2. Combine all ingredients except Cinnamon Pear Sauce in large bowl. Beat with electric mixer at low speed until well blended, scraping side of bowl with rubber spatula frequently. Beat at high speed 2 minutes more. Pour into prepared pan.

3. Bake 50 to 55 minutes or until wooden toothpick inserted in center comes out clean. Cool in pan on wire rack about 30 minutes. Cut into squares; serve warm with Cinnamon Pear Sauce.

Makes 9 servings

Cinnamon Pear Sauce

   2 cans (16 ounces each) pear halves in syrup, undrained
   2 tablespoons granulated sugar
   1 teaspoon fresh lemon juice
   ½ teaspoon ground cinnamon

Drain pear halves, reserving ¼ cup syrup. Place pears, reserved syrup, granulated sugar, lemon juice and cinnamon in work bowl of food processor or blender; cover. Process until smooth. Just before serving, place pear sauce in medium saucepan; heat until warm.

Makes 2 cups sauce

Yuletide Linzer Bars

   1⅓ cups butter, softened
   ¾ cup sugar
   1 egg
   1 teaspoon grated lemon peel
   2½ cups all-purpose flour
   1½ cups whole almonds, ground
   1 teaspoon ground cinnamon
   ¾ cup raspberry preserves
      Powdered sugar

1. Preheat oven to 350°F. Grease 13×9-inch baking pan.

2. Beat butter and sugar in large bowl at medium speed of electric mixer until creamy. Beat in egg and lemon peel until blended. Mix in flour, almonds and cinnamon until well blended.

3. Press 2 cups dough onto bottom of prepared pan. Spread preserves over crust. Press remaining dough, a small amount at a time, evenly over preserves.

4. Bake 35 to 40 minutes until golden brown. Cool in pan on wire rack. Sprinkle with powdered sugar; cut into bars.

Makes 36 bars

Yule Tree Namesakes

Butter Cookie Dough (recipe follows)

Cookie Glaze (recipe follows)

Green food coloring

Powdered sugar

Assorted candies

3 packages (12 ounces each) semisweet chocolate chips, melted

1 cup flaked coconut, tinted green*

*Tinting coconut: Dilute few drops of food coloring with ½ teaspoon water in large plastic bag. Add flaked coconut. Close bag and shake well until the coconut is evenly coated. If deeper color is desired, add more diluted food color and shake again.

1. Preheat oven to 350°F. Roll dough on floured surface to ⅛-inch thickness. Cut out cookies using 3- to 4-inch tree-shaped cookie cutter. Place 2 inches apart on ungreased cookie sheets.

2. Bake 12 to 14 minutes until edges begin to brown. Remove to wire racks; cool.

3. Reserve ⅓ cup Cookie Glaze; color remaining glaze green with food coloring. Place cookies on wire rack set over waxed paper-lined cookie sheet. Spoon green glaze over cookies.

4. Add 1 to 2 tablespoons powdered sugar to reserved Cookie Glaze. Spoon into pastry bag fitted with small writing tip. Pipe names onto trees and decorate with assorted candies as shown in photo. Let stand until glaze is set.

5. Spoon melted chocolate into 1¾-inch paper baking cups, filling evenly. Let stand until chocolate is very thick and partially set. Place trees upright in chocolate. Sprinkle tinted coconut over chocolate.

Makes 24 place cards

Butter Cookie Dough

¾ cup butter, softened

¼ cup granulated sugar

¼ cup packed light brown sugar

1 egg yolk

1¾ cups all-purpose flour

¾ teaspoon baking powder

⅛ teaspoon salt

1. Combine butter, granulated sugar, brown sugar and egg yolk in medium bowl. Add flour, baking powder and salt; mix well.

2. Cover; refrigerate until firm, about 4 hours or overnight.

Makes about 2 dozen cookies

Cookie Glaze

4 cups powdered sugar

4 to 6 tablespoons milk

Combine powdered sugar and enough milk to make a medium-thick pourable glaze.

Makes about 4 cups glaze

Oven-Tested Tips

Heavy aluminum cookie sheets produce the most evenly baked and browned cookies. Dark sheets can cause overbrowning and burned bottoms. Cookies won't get as crisp if you bake them on insulated sheets—the ones with an air pocket—and may take slightly longer to cook.

Hanukkah Coin Cookies

1 cup (2 sticks) butter or margarine, softened

1 cup sugar

1 egg

1 teaspoon vanilla extract

1¾ cups all-purpose flour

½ cup HERSHEY'S Cocoa

1½ teaspoons baking powder

½ teaspoon salt

Buttercream Frosting (recipe follows)

1. Beat butter, sugar, egg and vanilla in large bowl until well blended. Stir together flour, cocoa, baking powder and salt; gradually add to butter mixture, beating until well blended. Divide dough in half; place each half on separate sheet of wax paper.

2. Shape each portion into log, about 7 inches long. Wrap each log in wax paper or plastic wrap. Refrigerate until firm, at least 8 hours.

3. Heat oven to 325°F. Cut logs into ¼-inch-thick slices. Place on ungreased cookie sheet.

4. Bake 8 to 10 minutes or until set. Cool slightly; remove from cookie sheet to wire rack. Cool completely. Prepare Buttercream Frosting; spread over tops of cookies.
Makes about 4½ dozen cookies

Buttercream Frosting

¼ cup (½ stick) butter, softened

1½ cups powdered sugar

1 to 2 tablespoons milk

½ teaspoon vanilla extract

Yellow food color

Beat butter until creamy. Gradually add powdered sugar and milk to butter, beating to desired consistency. Stir in vanilla and food color. *Makes about 1 cup frosting*

Holiday Pumpkin-Nut Muffins

2½ cups all-purpose flour

1 cup packed light brown sugar

1 tablespoon baking powder

1 teaspoon ground cinnamon

½ teaspoon ground nutmeg

½ teaspoon ground ginger

¼ teaspoon salt

1 cup solid pack pumpkin (not pumpkin pie filling)

¾ cup milk

2 eggs

6 tablespoons butter, melted

⅔ cup roasted, salted pepitas (pumpkin seeds), divided

½ cup golden raisins

1. Preheat oven to 400°F. Grease or paper-line 18 (2¾-inch) muffin cups.

2. Combine flour, brown sugar, baking powder, cinnamon, nutmeg, ginger and salt in large bowl. Stir pumpkin, milk, eggs and melted butter in medium bowl until well blended. Stir pumpkin mixture into flour mixture. Mix just until all ingredients are moistened. Stir in ⅓ cup pepitas and raisins. Spoon into prepared muffin cups, filling ⅔ full. Sprinkle remaining pepitas over muffin batter.

3. Bake 15 to 18 minutes or until wooden pick inserted in center comes out clean. Cool in pans 10 minutes. Remove from pans and cool completely on wire racks. Store in airtight container. *Makes 18 muffins*

Christmas Spritz Cookies

2¼ cups all-purpose flour

¼ teaspoon salt

1¼ cups powdered sugar

1 cup butter, softened

1 egg

1 teaspoon almond extract

1 teaspoon vanilla

Green food coloring (optional)

Candied red and green cherries and assorted decorative candies (optional)

Icing (recipe follows, optional)

Preheat oven to 375°F. Place flour and salt in medium bowl; stir to combine. Beat powdered sugar and butter in large bowl until light and fluffy. Beat in egg, almond extract and vanilla. Gradually add flour mixture. Beat until well blended.

Divide dough in half. If desired, tint half of dough with green food coloring. Fit cookie press with desired plate (or change plates for different shapes after first batch). Fill press with dough; press dough 1 inch apart onto ungreased cookie sheets. Decorate cookies with cherries and assorted candies, if desired.

Bake 10 to 12 minutes or until just set. Remove cookies to wire racks; cool completely.

Prepare Icing, if desired. Pipe or drizzle on cooled cookies. Decorate with cherries and assorted candies, if desired. Store tightly covered at room temperature or freeze up to 3 months.   *Makes about 5 dozen cookies*

Icing

1½ cups powdered sugar

2 tablespoons milk plus additional, if needed

⅛ teaspoon almond extract

Place all ingredients in medium bowl; stir until thick, but spreadable. (If icing is too thick, stir in 1 teaspoon additional milk.)

Oven-Tested Tips

If you're baking several batches of cookies, you can speed things up by placing the cookies onto sheets of foil or parchment paper ahead of time. That way they'll be ready to slide right onto cookie sheets and into the oven. Make sure that you let the cookie sheet cool before you bake another batch on the same one or the dough can melt and spread, changing the final shape and texture of the cookies. If you're baking two sheets of cookies at a time, rotate the cookie sheets from top to bottom and front to back halfway through to insure even browning.

Christmas Spritz Cookies

Holiday Rye Bread

    3 to 3½ cups all-purpose flour,
        divided
2½ cups rye flour
    ⅓ cup sugar
    2 envelopes FLEISCHMANN'S®
        RapidRise™ Yeast
2½ teaspoons salt
    1 tablespoon grated orange peel
    2 teaspoons fennel seed
    1 cup beer or malt liquor
    ½ cup water
    ¼ cup light molasses
    2 tablespoons butter or margarine
        Molasses Glaze (recipe follows)

In large bowl, combine 1½ cups all-purpose flour, rye flour, sugar, undissolved yeast, salt, orange peel and fennel seed. Heat beer, water, molasses and butter until very warm (120° to 130°F). Stir into dry ingredients. Beat 2 minutes at medium speed of electric mixer, scraping bowl occasionally. Stir in enough remaining flour to make soft dough. Knead on lightly floured surface until smooth and elastic, about 8 to 10 minutes. Cover; let rest 10 minutes.

Divide dough into 4 equal pieces. Roll each to 10×6-inch oval. Roll each up tightly from long side, as for jelly roll, tapering ends. Pinch seams to seal. Place on greased baking sheets. Cover; let rise in warm, draft-free place until doubled in size, about 1½ hours.

With sharp knife, make 3 diagonal cuts on top of each loaf. Brush with Molasses Glaze. Bake at 375°F for 15 minutes; brush loaves with Glaze. Bake additional 10 minutes or until done. Remove loaves from oven and brush again with Glaze. Cool on wire racks.

Makes 4 small loaves

Molasses Glaze: Combine 2 tablespoons molasses and 2 tablespoons water. Stir until well blended.

Snowman Cupcakes

    1 package (about 18 ounces) yellow
        or white cake mix plus
        ingredients to prepare mix
    2 containers (16 ounces each)
        vanilla frosting
    4 cups flaked coconut
15 large marshmallows
15 miniature chocolate covered
        peanut butter cups, unwrapped
    Small red candies and pretzel sticks
        for decoration
    Green and red decorating gel

1. Preheat oven to 350°F. Line 15 regular-size (2½-inch) muffin pan cups and 15 small (about 1-inch) muffin pan cups with paper muffin cup liners. Prepare cake mix according to package directions. Spoon batter into muffin cups.

2. Bake 10 to 15 minutes for small cupcakes and 15 to 20 minutes for large cupcakes or until cupcakes are golden and toothpick inserted into centers comes out clean. Cool in pans on wire racks 10 minutes. Remove from pans to racks; cool completely. Remove paper liners.

3. For each snowman, frost bottom and side of 1 large cupcake; coat with coconut. Repeat with 1 small cupcake. Attach small cupcake to large cupcake with frosting to form snowman body. Attach marshmallow to small cupcake with frosting to form snowman head. Attach inverted peanut butter cup to marshmallow with frosting to form snowman hat. Use pretzels for arms and small red candies for buttons as shown in photo. Pipe faces with decorating gel as shown. Repeat with remaining cupcakes.

Makes 15 snowmen

Snowman Cupcakes

Festive Holiday Rugelach

1½ cups (3 sticks) butter or margarine,
    softened
12 ounces cream cheese, softened
3½ cups all-purpose flour, divided
½ cup powdered sugar
¾ cup granulated sugar
1½ teaspoons ground cinnamon
1¾ cups "M&M's"® Chocolate Mini
    Baking Bits, divided
Powdered sugar

Preheat oven to 350°F. Lightly grease cookie sheets; set aside. In large bowl cream butter and cream cheese. Slowly work in 3 cups flour. Divide dough into 6 equal pieces and shape into squares. Lightly flour dough, wrap in waxed paper and refrigerate at least 1 hour. Combine remaining ½ cup flour and ½ cup powdered sugar. Remove one piece of dough at a time from refrigerator; roll out on surface dusted with flour-sugar mixture to 18×5×⅛-inch-thick strip. Combine granulated sugar and cinnamon. Sprinkle dough strip with 2 tablespoons cinnamon-sugar mixture. Sprinkle about ¼ cup "M&M's"® Chocolate Mini Baking Bits on wide end of each strip. Roll dough starting at wide end to completely enclose baking bits. Cut strip into 1½-inch lengths; place seam side down about 2 inches apart on prepared cookie sheets. Repeat with remaining ingredients. Bake 16 to 18 minutes or until golden. Cool completely on wire racks. Sprinkle with powdered sugar. Store in tightly covered container.

Makes about 6 dozen cookies

Variation: For crescent shapes, roll each piece of dough into 12-inch circle. Sprinkle with cinnamon-sugar mixture. Cut into 12 wedges. Place about ½ teaspoon "M&M's"® Chocolate Mini Baking Bits at wide end of each wedge and roll up to enclose baking bits. Place seam side down on prepared cookie sheets and proceed as directed.

Danish Cookie Rings (Vanillekranser)

½ cup blanched almonds
2 cups all-purpose flour
¾ cup sugar
¼ teaspoon baking powder
1 cup butter, cut into small pieces
1 egg
1 tablespoon milk
1 tablespoon vanilla
15 candied red cherries
15 candied green cherries

Grease cookie sheets; set aside. Process almonds in food processor until ground, but not pasty. Place almonds, flour, sugar and baking powder in large bowl. Cut butter into flour mixture with pastry blender or 2 knives until mixture is crumbly.

Beat egg, milk and vanilla in small bowl with fork until well blended. Add egg mixture to flour mixture; stir until soft dough forms.

Spoon dough into pastry bag fitted with medium star tip. Pipe 3-inch rings 2 inches apart on prepared cookie sheets. Refrigerate rings 15 minutes or until firm.

Preheat oven to 375°F. Cut red cherries into quarters. Cut green cherries into halves; cut each half into 4 slivers. Press red cherry quarter onto each ring where ends meet. Arrange 2 green cherry slivers on either side of red cherry to form leaves. Bake 8 to 10 minutes or until golden. Remove cookies to wire racks; cool completely. Store tightly covered at room temperature or freeze up to 3 months. *Makes about 5 dozen cookies*

Festive Holiday Rugelach

Poinsettia Pie

2 cups chocolate wafer crumbs

6 tablespoons butter, melted

⅛ teaspoon peppermint extract (optional)

¾ cup sugar, divided

1 envelope unflavored gelatin

⅓ cup cold water

3 eggs, separated*

⅓ cup crème de menthe

½ cup whipping cream, whipped

Chocolate curls or leaves (optional)

Use only grade A clean, uncracked eggs.

1. Preheat oven to 350°F. Combine cookie crumbs, butter and peppermint extract, if desired, in small bowl. Press onto bottom and up side of 9-inch pie plate. Bake 8 minutes. Cool on wire rack.

2. Combine ½ cup sugar and gelatin in small saucepan. Add cold water; let stand 1 minute. Stir over low heat until gelatin is completely dissolved.

3. Beat egg yolks in small bowl. Stir about ¼ cup gelatin mixture into egg yolks; return egg yolk mixture to saucepan. Cook over low heat, stirring constantly, until thick enough to coat back of spoon. Remove from heat; stir in liqueur. Cool to room temperature.

4. Beat egg whites until foamy. Gradually beat in remaining ¼ cup sugar; continue beating until soft peaks form. Fold into gelatin mixture. Gently fold in whipped cream. Pour into cooled crust. Refrigerate until firm, 8 hours or overnight.

5. Garnish with chocolate curls or leaves, if desired.   *Makes 1 (9-inch) pie*

Holiday Peppermint Slices

1 package (18 ounces) refrigerated sugar cookie dough

¼ teaspoon peppermint extract, divided

Red food coloring

Green food coloring

1. Remove dough from wrapper according to package directions. Cut dough into thirds.

2. Combine ⅓ of dough, ⅛ teaspoon peppermint extract and enough red food coloring to make dough desired shade of red. Knead dough until evenly tinted.

3. Repeat with second ⅓ of dough, remaining ⅛ teaspoon peppermint extract and green food coloring.

4. To assemble, shape each portion of dough into 8-inch roll. Place red roll beside green roll; press together slightly. Place plain roll on top. Press rolls together to form one tri-colored roll; wrap in plastic wrap. Refrigerate 2 hours or overnight.

5. Preheat oven to 350°F.

6. Cut dough into ¼-inch-thick slices. Place 2 inches apart on ungreased cookie sheets. Bake 8 to 9 minutes or until set but not browned. Cool 1 minute on cookie sheets. Cool completely on wire racks.

Makes 2½ dozen cookies

Classic Pumpkin Pie with Candied Pecan Topping

Crust

> **1 (9-inch) Classic CRISCO® Single Crust (recipe page 132)**

Filling

> **1 can (16 ounces) solid-pack pumpkin (not pumpkin pie filling)**
>
> **1 can (12 ounces or 1½ cups) evaporated milk**
>
> **2 eggs, lightly beaten**
>
> **½ cup granulated sugar**
>
> **¼ cup firmly packed light brown sugar**
>
> **1 teaspoon cinnamon**
>
> **½ teaspoon salt**
>
> **½ teaspoon ginger**
>
> **¼ teaspoon nutmeg**
>
> **⅛ teaspoon cloves**

Topping

> **¼ cup granulated sugar**
>
> **¼ cup water**
>
> **2 tablespoons butter or margarine**
>
> **1 cup pecan pieces**

1. Roll and press crust into 9-inch glass pie plate. Do not bake. Heat oven to 350°F.

2. For filling, combine pumpkin, evaporated milk, eggs, granulated sugar, brown sugar, cinnamon, salt, ginger, nutmeg and cloves in large bowl. Mix well. Pour into unbaked pie crust.

3. Bake at 350°F for 1 hour 10 minutes or until knife inserted in center comes out clean. *Do not overbake*. Cool completely.

4. Grease baking sheet lightly with shortening.

5. For topping, combine granulated sugar and water in small saucepan. Cook and stir on medium heat until sugar dissolves. Increase heat. Bring to a boil. Boil 7 to 8 minutes or until mixture becomes light golden brown, stirring frequently. Stir in butter and nuts. Stir briskly. Spread quickly in thin layer on greased baking sheet. Cool completely. Break into pieces. Sprinkle around edge of pie. (You might not use all of topping. Cover and store any extra for later use.) Refrigerate leftover pie.

Makes 1 (9-inch) pie (8 servings)

Oven-Tested Tips

To make a great pie, it's important to pick the right pie plate. Heat-resistant glass pie plates or dull-finished metal pie pans will give the best browning. A shiny metal pan reflects heat, so the bottom crust can turn out underbaked and soggy. The most common pie size is 9 inches, but different pie plates all labeled 9 inches can hold dramatically different amounts of filling. Make sure the one you choose will hold the amount of filling in the recipe (remember fruit fillings shrink quite a bit.) Finally, if you choose a nonstick pie pan be sure the crust is secured over the edge. The nonstick coating won't hold it in place as well and it could slide down the sides when the crust shrinks in the oven.

Classic Pumpkin Pie with Candied Pecan Topping

International Bake Shop

Travel the world without leaving your kitchen. The recipes for sweet and savory baked goods gathered here come from all over the globe—France, Italy, Norway, Jamaica, the Middle East and more. Try your hand at turning out homemade Bagels, Mocha Biscotti or Chocolate Madeleines. Wherever you decide to visit, you're sure to have a tasty trip.

Mocha Biscotti

2½ cups all-purpose flour
½ cup unsweetened cocoa
2 teaspoons baking powder
1¼ cups sugar
¾ cup egg substitute
¼ cup margarine or butter, melted
4 teaspoons instant coffee powder
½ teaspoon vanilla extract
⅓ cup PLANTERS® Slivered Almonds, chopped
   Powdered sugar, optional

1. Mix flour, cocoa and baking powder in small bowl; set aside.

2. Beat sugar, egg substitute, margarine, coffee powder and vanilla in large bowl with mixer at medium speed for 2 minutes. Stir in flour mixture and almonds. Divide dough in half. Shape each portion of dough with floured hands into 14×2-inch log on a greased baking sheet. (Dough will be sticky.) Bake in preheated 350°F oven for 25 minutes.

3. Remove from oven and cut each log on a diagonal into 16 (1-inch) slices. Place biscotti, cut side up, on baking sheets; return to oven and bake 10 to 15 minutes more on each side or until lightly toasted.

4. Remove from sheets. Cool completely on wire racks. Dust biscotti tops with powdered sugar, if desired. Store in airtight container. *Makes 32 biscotti*

Prep Time: 20 minutes
Cook Time: 35 minutes
Total Time: 1 hour and 5 minutes

St. Joseph's Ricotta Puffs (Sfince Di San Giuseppe)

Filling

    1 pound ricotta cheese, drained

    ½ cup confectioners' sugar

    4 ounces grated dark chocolate

    ¼ cup candied fruit, finely chopped

    1 teaspoon orange extract

    1 teaspoon vanilla

Puffs

    1 cup water

    ½ Butter Flavor CRISCO® Stick or ½ cup Butter Flavor CRISCO® all-vegetable shortening

    1 tablespoon granulated sugar

    ½ teaspoon salt

    1 cup sifted all-purpose flour

    4 large eggs, beaten

    1 teaspoon fresh grated lemon peel

    1 teaspoon fresh grated orange peel

    Confectioners' sugar

1. For filling, combine all filling ingredients in large bowl; mix well. Refrigerate while making puffs.

2. For puffs, heat oven to 450°F. Combine water, shortening, granulated sugar and salt in medium saucepan. Bring to a boil over medium-high heat; stir well. Add flour, stirring vigorously, until mixture leaves sides of pan. Remove from heat; let cool.

3. Slowly add eggs, beating vigorously, to cooled flour mixture. Add lemon and orange peel; mix well.

4. Spray baking sheets with CRISCO® No-Stick Cooking Spray. Drop tablespoonfuls of batter 2 inches apart onto baking sheets.

5. Bake at 450°F for 15 minutes. *Reduce oven temperature to 350°F.* Bake an additional 15 to 20 minutes or until golden. Cool completely on cooling rack.

6. To assemble, cut puffs in half horizontally. Spoon ricotta filling into bottom half. Cover with top half. Drizzle with melted chocolate, if desired.   *Makes about 18 puffs*

Tip: This dessert is traditionally made on March 19, the feast day of St. Joseph. They appear in bakeries weeks before and are still there weeks after March 19. These delightful treats are delicious any time of the year.

Norwegian Almond Squares

    1¾ cups all-purpose flour

    1 cup sugar

    ¼ cup ground almonds

    1 cup butter, softened

    1 egg

    1 teaspoon ground cinnamon

    ½ teaspoon salt

    1 egg white

    ¾ cup sliced almonds

Preheat oven to 350°F. Combine flour, sugar, ground almonds, butter, egg, cinnamon and salt in medium bowl. Beat at low speed of electric mixer, scraping bowl often, until well mixed, 2 to 3 minutes. Press dough onto ungreased cookie sheet to ¹⁄₁₆-inch thickness.

Beat egg white with fork in small bowl until foamy. Brush over dough; sprinkle with sliced almonds. Bake 12 to 15 minutes or until very lightly browned. Immediately cut into 2-inch squares and remove from pan. Cool; store in tightly covered container.

Makes about 3½ dozen squares

Focaccia

1½ cups water

1 package active dry yeast

1 teaspoon sugar

4 cups all-purpose flour, divided

7 tablespoons olive oil, divided

1 teaspoon salt

¼ cup bottled roasted red peppers, drained and cut into strips

¼ cup pitted black olives

To proof yeast, sprinkle yeast and sugar over warm (105° to 110°F) water in large bowl; stir until dissolved. Let stand 5 minutes or until mixture is bubbly. Add 3½ cups flour, 3 tablespoons oil and salt, stirring until soft dough forms. Turn out dough onto lightly floured surface. Knead 5 minutes or until smooth and elastic, gradually adding remaining flour to prevent sticking, if necessary. Shape dough into ball; place in large, lightly greased bowl. Turn dough over so top is greased. Cover with towel; let rise in warm place 1 hour or until doubled in bulk.

Brush 15½×10½-inch jelly-roll pan with 1 tablespoon oil. Punch down dough. Turn out dough onto lightly floured surface. Flatten into rectangle; roll out almost to size of pan. Place dough in pan; gently press dough to edges of pan. Poke surface of dough with end of wooden spoon handle, making indentations every 1 or 2 inches. Brush with remaining 3 tablespoons oil. Gently press peppers and olives into dough, forming decorative pattern. Cover with towel; let rise in warm place 30 minutes or until doubled in bulk.

Preheat oven to 450°F. Bake 12 to 15 minutes or until golden brown. Cut into squares or rectangles. Serve hot.

Makes 12 servings

Focaccia

Jamaican Cherry Bread

Jamaican Cherry Bread

2½ teaspoons active dry yeast

3¼ cups bread flour

1 tablespoon grated lime peel

2 teaspoons minced fresh ginger *or*
¾ teaspoon ground ginger

1 teaspoon salt

1 cup milk

¼ cup firmly packed brown sugar

¼ cup lime juice

3 tablespoons butter, melted

⅔ cup toasted coconut*

½ cup dried tart cherries

To toast coconut: spread coconut on ungreased pan. Bake in preheated 350°F oven 5 to 7 minutes, stirring occasionally, or until golden brown.

Bread Machine Directions

1. Measure carefully, placing all ingredients except coconut and cherries in bread machine pan in order specified by owner's manual.

2. Program desired cycle; press start. Add coconut and cherries at the beep or at the end of the first kneading cycle. Remove baked bread from pan; cool on wire rack. Serve at room temperature.

Makes 1 loaf, about 16 slices

Favorite recipe from **Cherry Marketing Institute**

Festive Lebkuchen

3 tablespoons butter
1 cup packed brown sugar
¼ cup honey
1 egg
   Grated peel and juice of 1 lemon
3 cups all-purpose flour
2 teaspoons ground allspice
½ teaspoon baking soda
½ teaspoon salt
   White decorator's frosting

1. Melt butter with brown sugar and honey in medium saucepan over low heat, stirring constantly. Pour into large bowl. Cool 30 minutes.

2. Add egg, lemon peel and juice; beat 2 minutes with electric mixer at high speed. Stir in flour, allspice, baking soda and salt until well blended. Cover; refrigerate overnight or up to 3 days.

3. Preheat oven to 350°F. Grease cookie sheets. Roll out dough to ½-inch thickness on lightly floured surface with lightly floured rolling pin. Cut out with 3-inch cookie cutters. Transfer to prepared cookie sheets.

4. Bake 15 to 18 minutes until edges are light brown. Cool 1 minute. Remove to wire racks; cool completely. Decorate with white frosting. Store in airtight container.

Makes 1 dozen cookies

Swedish Cookie Shells

1 cup butter, softened
⅔ cup sugar
1 large egg white
1 teaspoon vanilla
½ teaspoon almond extract
2 cups all-purpose flour, divided
¼ cup finely ground blanched almonds

1. Beat butter and sugar in large bowl until light and fluffy. Beat in egg white, vanilla and almond extract until well blended. Gradually add 1½ cups flour and almonds. Beat until well blended. Stir in enough remaining flour with spoon to form soft dough. Form dough into 1-inch-thick square; wrap in plastic wrap and refrigerate until firm, 1 hour or overnight.

2. Preheat oven to 375°F. Press rounded teaspoonfuls of dough into greased sandbakelser tins* or mini muffin pan cups. Place tins on baking sheet. Bake 8 to 10 minutes or until cookie shells are lightly browned. Cool cookies in tins 1 minute.

3. Carefully loosen cookies from tins with point of small knife. Invert tins over wire racks; tap lightly to release cookies; cool completely (cookies should be shell-side up). Repeat with remaining dough; cool cookie tins between batches.

4. Serve cookies shell-side up. Store tightly covered at room temperature or freeze up to 3 months.   *Makes about 10 dozen cookies*

Sandbakelser tins are little tart pans (2-3 inches in diameter) with fluted edges.

Viennese Chocolate Torte

¼ cup HERSHEY'S Cocoa
¼ cup boiling water
⅓ cup shortening
¾ cup sugar
½ teaspoon vanilla extract
 1 egg
 1 cup all-purpose flour
¾ teaspoon baking soda
¼ teaspoon salt
⅔ cup buttermilk or sour milk*
¼ cup seedless black raspberry
    preserves
    Cream Filling (recipe follows)
    Cocoa Glaze (recipe follows)
    MOUNDS® Coconut Flakes,
    toasted

*To sour milk: Use 2 teaspoons white vinegar plus milk to equal ⅔ cup.

1. Heat oven to 350°F. Lightly grease 15½×10½×1-inch jelly-roll pan; line pan with wax paper and lightly grease paper.

2. Stir together cocoa and boiling water in small bowl until smooth; set aside. Beat shortening, sugar and vanilla in medium bowl until creamy; beat in egg. Stir together flour, baking soda and salt; add alternately with buttermilk to shortening mixture. Add reserved cocoa mixture, beating just until blended. Spread batter into pan.

3. Bake 16 to 18 minutes or until wooden pick inserted in center comes out clean. Cool 10 minutes; remove from pan. Remove wax paper; cool completely. Cut cake crosswise into three equal pieces. Place one piece on serving plate; spread 2 tablespoons preserves evenly on top of cake. Spread half of Cream Filling over preserves. Repeat layering. Glaze top of torte with Cocoa Glaze, allowing some to drizzle down sides. Garnish with coconut. Refrigerate several hours. Cover; refrigerate leftover torte.

Makes 10 servings

Cream Filling: Beat 1 cup whipping cream, 2 tablespoons powdered sugar and 1 teaspoon vanilla extract in small bowl until stiff. Makes about 2 cups filling.

Cocoa Glaze

 2 tablespoons butter or margarine
 2 tablespoons HERSHEY'S Cocoa
 2 tablespoons water
 1 cup powdered sugar
½ teaspoon vanilla extract

Melt butter in saucepan. Stir in cocoa and water. Cook, stirring constantly, until mixture thickens. *Do not boil.* Remove from heat. Whisk in powdered sugar gradually. Add vanilla and beat with whisk until smooth. Add additional water ½ teaspoon at a time until desired consistency.

Oven-Tested Tips

When layer cakes come out with a dome in the center, it's because the edges of a thick cake batter cook first, letting the center continue to rise higher than the sides. To prevent it, try covering the pan lightly with foil. Remove it for the last 15 minutes of baking so the top can turn golden.

Viennese Chocolate Torte

Ma'moul
(Date Pastries)

Filling

> 1 pound chopped pitted dates
> ½ cup water
> ¼ cup granulated sugar
> 1 teaspoon almond extract
> 2 tablespoons fresh grated orange peel
> ½ teaspoon ground cinnamon

Pastry

> 1 Butter Flavor CRISCO® Stick or 1 cup Butter Flavor CRISCO® all-vegetable shortening
> ¼ cup granulated sugar
> 3 tablespoons milk
> 1 tablespoon rosewater* or water
> 2 cups all-purpose flour
> Confectioners' sugar

Rosewater is available at Middle Eastern markets.

1. For filling, combine dates, water, ¼ cup sugar and almond extract in small saucepan. Bring to boil over medium-high heat. Reduce heat to low; simmer 4 to 5 minutes, stirring often, until mixture becomes thick paste. Stir in orange peel and cinnamon. Remove from heat; cool.

2. Heat oven to 300°F.

3. For pastry, combine shortening and ¼ cup sugar in large bowl. Beat at medium speed with electric mixer until well blended. Beat in milk and rosewater. Beat in flour, ¼ cup at a time, until well blended. Knead dough in bowl until dough holds together and is easy to shape.

4. Pinch off walnut-size piece of dough. Roll into ball. Pinch sides up to form pot shape. Fill center with level tablespoonful of date filling. Pinch dough closed; press to seal.

Slightly flatten and smooth top. Place on ungreased baking sheets about 1 inch apart.

5. Bake at 300°F for 16 to 20 minutes or until firm and set. *Do not allow pastries to brown.* Cool on baking sheets 3 minutes; transfer to cooling racks. Sprinkle with confectioners' sugar while still warm. Cool completely.

Makes about 2½ dozen pastries

Background: These cookies are traditionally served in Syria during the Easter Holiday.

Georgian Baklava
(Pakhlava)

> 2 cups all-purpose flour
> ½ teaspoon baking soda
> 1 cup butter, cut into pieces
> 2 eggs, separated
> ½ cup sour cream
> 1 cup finely ground walnuts
> 1 cup dried fruit bits
> ¾ cup sugar
> ½ teaspoon ground cinnamon
> 2 teaspoons water

1. Place flour and baking soda in large bowl; stir to combine. Cut butter into flour mixture with pastry blender or 2 knives until mixture forms pea-sized pieces.

2. Reserve 1 egg yolk in cup; cover with plastic wrap. Add remaining yolk and sour cream to flour mixture; toss with fork until mixture holds together. Form dough into a ball; wrap in plastic wrap and refrigerate 2 hours or until firm.

3. Meanwhile, for filling, combine walnuts, dried fruit, sugar and cinnamon in medium bowl; set aside. Beat egg whites in large bowl with electric mixer until stiff peaks

form. Gently fold in fruit mixture until evenly combined.

4. Grease and lightly flour 9-inch square baking pan. Divide dough into 3 equal pieces. Shape each piece into 3-inch square about 1 inch thick. Place each square between two pieces of well-floured waxed paper. Roll dough into 9-inch squares.

5. Invert dough into bottom of baking pan; trim to fit pan. Remove second sheet of waxed paper.

6. Add water to reserved egg yolk; beat lightly with fork until foamy. Brush dough with egg yolk mixture. Spread half of fruit mixture on dough. Repeat procedure with second dough square, egg mixture and remaining fruit mixture. Cover with third dough square; turn edges under for neat appearance.

7. Preheat oven to 350°F. Score top of dough into diamonds by making lengthwise diagonal cuts, just through top layers of dough, every 1½ inches, with sharp knife. Make crosswise horizontal cuts, just through top layers of dough, to form diamond shapes.

8. Brush dough with remaining egg yolk mixture. Bake 45 minutes or until browned. Remove pan to wire rack; cool completely. Cut bars all the way through. Carefully lift bars out of pan. Store tightly covered in single layer. *Makes about 2½ dozen bars*

Ma'moul (Date Pastries)

English Thumbprint Cookies

English Thumbprint Cookies

1 cup pecan pieces
1¼ cups all-purpose flour
¼ teaspoon salt
½ cup butter, softened
½ cup packed light brown sugar
1 teaspoon vanilla
1 large egg, separated
2 to 3 tablespoons seedless raspberry or strawberry jam

1. Preheat oven to 350°F. To toast pecans, spread on ungreased baking sheet. Bake 8 to 10 minutes or until golden brown, stirring frequently. Remove pecans from baking sheet and cool. Process cooled pecans in food processor until finely chopped; transfer to shallow bowl.

2. Place flour and salt in medium bowl; stir to combine. Beat butter and brown sugar in large bowl with electric mixer at medium speed until light and fluffy. Beat in vanilla and egg yolk. Gradually beat in flour mixture. Beat egg white with fork until frothy.

3. Shape dough into 1-inch balls. Roll balls in egg white; roll in nuts to coat. Place balls on ungreased cookie sheets. Press deep indentation in center of each ball with thumb.

4. Bake 8 minutes or until set. Remove cookies from oven; fill each indentation with about ¼ teaspoon jam. Return filled cookies to oven; continue to bake 8 to 10 minutes or until lightly brown. Immediately remove cookies to wire racks; cool completely.

5. Store cookies tightly covered at room temperature or freeze up to 3 months.

Makes about 2½ dozen cookies

Classic Anise Biscotti

4 ounces whole blanched almonds
  (about ¾ cup)
2¼ cups all-purpose flour
1 teaspoon baking powder
¾ teaspoon salt
¾ cup sugar
½ cup unsalted butter, softened
3 eggs
2 tablespoons brandy
2 teaspoons grated lemon peel
1 tablespoon whole anise seeds

1. Preheat oven to 375°F. To toast almonds, spread almonds on baking sheet. Bake 6 to 8 minutes or until toasted and light brown; turn off oven. Remove almonds with spoon to cutting board; cool. Coarsely chop almonds.

2. Combine flour, baking powder and salt in small bowl. Beat sugar and butter in medium bowl with electric mixer at medium speed until light and fluffy. Add eggs, 1 at a time, beating well after each addition and scraping side of bowl often. Stir in brandy and lemon peel. Add flour mixture gradually; stir until smooth. Stir in chopped almonds and anise seeds. Cover and refrigerate dough 1 hour or until firm.

3. Preheat oven to 375°F. Grease large baking sheet. Divide dough in half. Shape ½ of dough into 12×2-inch log on lightly floured surface. (Dough will be fairly soft.) Pat smooth with lightly floured fingertips. Transfer to prepared baking sheet. Repeat with remaining ½ of dough to form second log. Bake 20 to 25 minutes or until logs are light golden brown. Remove baking sheet from oven to wire rack; turn off oven. Cool logs completely.

4. Preheat oven to 350°F. Cut logs diagonally with serrated knife into ½-inch-thick slices. Place slices flat in single layer on 2 ungreased baking sheets.

5. Bake 8 minutes. Turn slices over; bake 10 to 12 minutes or until cut surfaces are light brown and cookies are dry. Remove cookies to wire racks; cool completely. Store cookies in airtight container up to 2 weeks.

Makes about 4 dozen cookies

Classic Anise Biscotti

Homemade Pizza

½ tablespoon active dry yeast

1 teaspoon sugar, divided

½ cup warm water (105° to 115°F)

1¾ cups all-purpose flour, divided

¾ teaspoon salt, divided

2 tablespoons olive oil, divided

1 can (14½ ounces) whole peeled tomatoes, undrained

1 medium onion, chopped

1 clove garlic, minced

2 tablespoons tomato paste

1 teaspoon dried oregano leaves

½ teaspoon dried basil leaves

⅛ teaspoon black pepper

½ small red bell pepper, cored and seeded

½ small green bell pepper, cored and seeded

4 fresh medium mushrooms

1 can (2 ounces) flat anchovy fillets

1¾ cups (7 ounces) shredded mozzarella cheese

½ cup freshly grated Parmesan cheese

⅓ cup pitted ripe olives, halved

1. To proof yeast, sprinkle yeast and ½ teaspoon sugar over warm water in small bowl; stir until yeast is dissolved. Let stand 5 minutes or until mixture is bubbly.*

2. Place 1½ cups flour and ¼ teaspoon salt in medium bowl; stir in yeast mixture and 1 tablespoon oil, stirring until a smooth, soft dough forms. Place dough on lightly floured surface; flatten slightly. Knead dough, using as much of remaining flour as needed to form a stiff elastic dough.

3. Shape dough into a ball; place in large greased bowl. Turn to grease entire surface. Cover with clean kitchen towel and let dough rise in warm place 30 to 45 minutes until doubled in bulk. Press two fingertips about ½ inch into dough. Dough is ready if indentations remain when fingers are removed.

4. For sauce, finely chop tomatoes in can, reserving juice. Heat remaining 1 tablespoon oil in medium saucepan over medium heat. Add onion; cook 5 minutes or until soft. Add garlic; cook 30 seconds more. Add tomatoes with juice, tomato paste, oregano, basil, remaining ½ teaspoon sugar, ½ teaspoon salt and black pepper. Bring to a boil over high heat; reduce heat to medium-low. Simmer, uncovered, 10 to 15 minutes until sauce thickens, stirring occasionally. Pour into small bowl; cool.

5. Punch dough down. Knead briefly on lightly floured surface to distribute air bubbles; let dough stand 5 minutes more. Flatten dough into circle on lightly floured surface. Roll out dough, starting at center and rolling to edges, into 10-inch circle. Place circle in greased 12-inch pizza pan; stretch and pat dough out to edges of pan. Cover and let stand 15 minutes.

6. Preheat oven to 450°F. Cut bell peppers into ¾-inch pieces. Trim mushroom stems; wipe clean with damp kitchen towel and thinly slice. Drain anchovies. Mix mozzarella and Parmesan cheeses in small bowl. Spread sauce evenly over pizza dough. Sprinkle with ⅔ of cheeses. Arrange bell peppers, mushrooms, anchovies and olives over cheeses.

7. Sprinkle remaining cheeses on top of pizza. Bake 20 minutes or until crust is golden brown. To serve, cut into wedges.

Makes 4 to 6 servings

If yeast does not bubble, it is no longer active. Always check expiration date on yeast packet. Also, water that is too hot will kill yeast; it is best to use a thermometer.

Almond Brioches

1 package active dry yeast
⅓ cup sugar plus 1 teaspoon, divided
½ cup warm water (105° to 115°F)
½ cup butter or margarine, softened
3 eggs
½ teaspoon almond extract
3½ cups all-purpose flour, divided
¾ teaspoon salt
¼ cup packed almond paste (about 2 ounces), cut into 16 pieces and flattened into nickel-size discs
1 egg yolk
1 tablespoon half-and-half or milk
¼ cup sliced almonds
Additional sugar (optional)

1. To proof yeast, sprinkle yeast and 1 teaspoon sugar over warm water in small bowl; stir until yeast is dissolved. Let stand 5 minutes or until mixture is bubbly.

2. Beat butter and remaining ⅓ cup sugar in large bowl with electric mixer at medium speed until light and fluffy. Add eggs, 1 at a time, beating well after each addition. Beat in almond extract. Reduce speed to low; beat in yeast mixture, 1½ cups flour and salt. Beat at medium speed 2 minutes.

3. Remove beater and insert dough hook.* Add remaining 2 cups flour. Beat at low speed briefly. Beat at medium speed 3 minutes. Dough will be sticky.

4. Cover with towel; let rise in warm place about 1½ hours or until doubled in bulk. Stir down dough. Cover with plastic wrap; refrigerate 2 hours or overnight.

5. Punch down dough. Turn out onto lightly floured surface; flatten slightly. Knead dough 2 minutes. Cut dough into 16 pieces. Cover with towel; let rest 10 minutes. Grease 16 (3¾×1½-inch) brioche pans or 16 (2½-inch) muffin pan cups; set aside.

6. To form brioches, reserve about 1 teaspoon dough from each piece, shaping larger pieces of dough into balls.

7. Place almond paste discs in center of large pieces of dough by pulling edges of dough over and around almond paste, making smooth round top. Place in prepared pans. (If dough becomes too soft and sticky, refrigerate 10 minutes.)

8. To form top knot, make deep depression in each dough ball with greased end of wooden spoon. Shape small dough piece into teardrop-shaped ball; place pointed end of ball into hole. Repeat with remaining dough. Place brioche pans on jelly-roll pan.

9. Cover brioches with towel; let rise in warm place 45 minutes or until almost doubled in bulk. Preheat oven to 375°F.

10. Combine egg yolk and half-and-half in small bowl. Brush brioches with egg yolk mixture. Sprinkle with almonds and additional sugar, if desired. Bake 20 minutes or until golden and sound hollow when lightly tapped. Remove from pans; cool on wire racks 10 minutes. Serve warm.

Makes 16 brioches

To finish mixing without dough hook, stir in remaining 2 cups flour, ½ cup at a time, with wooden spoon. Continue stirring about 5 minutes. Proceed with step 4.

Oven-Tested Tips

Brioche is a French-created yeast bread made light and rich by the addition of butter and eggs. The classic shape with a top knot is easiest to make in the fluted mold called a brioche pan. These can be purchased at most cooking supply stores.

Almond Brioche

Bagels

6 Bagels

    1 cup plus 3 tablespoons water

    2 tablespoons sugar

    1½ teaspoons salt

    3 cups bread flour

    2 teaspoons rapid-rise active dry yeast

9 Bagels

    1½ cups water

    3 tablespoons sugar

    2 teaspoons salt

    4 cups bread flour

    2 teaspoons rapid-rise active dry yeast

For Boiling and Baking

    3 quarts water

    1 tablespoon sugar

    2 to 3 tablespoons cornmeal

    1 egg, beaten

    1 to 2 tablespoons sesame seeds, poppy seeds, caraway seeds or cinnamon sugar (optional)

Bread Machine Directions

1. Measuring carefully, place all ingredients except those required for boiling and baking in bread machine pan in order specified by owner's manual. Program dough cycle setting; press start.

2. Turn out dough onto floured surface; knead briefly. Cut into 6 pieces for small batch or 9 pieces for large batch. Shape into balls. Place on floured surface; let rest 10 minutes. Poke thumb through center of each ball to make hole. Stretch into doughnut shapes. Place back on floured surface. Let rise, uncovered, 15 minutes or until puffy. *Do not overproof bagels.*

3. For boiling and baking, preheat oven to 400°F. Bring water and sugar to a boil in large, deep skillet. Spray 2 baking sheets with nonstick cooking spray; sprinkle with cornmeal. Lower bagels, 3 at a time, into boiling water. Boil 5 minutes, turning often. Remove bagels using slotted spoon; drain briefly on paper towels. Place 2 inches apart on prepared baking sheets. Brush with beaten egg and sprinkle with sesame seeds, if desired. Bake 25 to 30 minutes or until golden brown. Remove and cool on wire racks. *Makes 6 or 9 bagels*

European Kolacky

    1 cup butter or margarine, softened

    1 package (8 ounces) cream cheese, softened

    1 tablespoon milk

    1 tablespoon sugar

    1 egg yolk

    1½ cups all-purpose flour

    ½ teaspoon baking powder

    1 can SOLO® or 1 jar BAKER® Filling (any flavor)

    Powdered sugar

Cream butter, cream cheese, milk and sugar in medium bowl with electric mixer until thoroughly blended. Beat in egg yolk. Sift together flour and baking powder; stir into butter mixture to make stiff dough. Cover and refrigerate several hours or overnight.

Preheat oven to 400°F. Roll out dough on lightly floured surface to ¼-inch thickness. Cut dough with floured 2-inch cookie cutter. Place cookies on ungreased cookie sheets about 1 inch apart. Make depression in centers of cookies with thumb or back of spoon. Spoon ½ teaspoon filling into centers of cookies.

Bake 10 to 12 minutes or until lightly browned. Remove from baking sheets and cool completely on wire racks. Sprinkle with powdered sugar just before serving.

Makes about 3 dozen cookies

Lemon Semolina Syrup Cake

2 cups farina or semolina flour

1 cup sugar

1½ teaspoons baking powder

¼ teaspoon salt

2 cups plain low-fat yogurt

2 tablespoons FILIPPO BERIO®
    Extra Light Tasting Olive Oil

Finely grated peel of 1 lemon

12 to 15 walnut halves

1 cup light corn syrup

2 tablespoons lemon juice

Fresh strawberries (optional)

Preheat oven to 350°F. Grease 9-inch springform pan with olive oil.

In large bowl, combine farina, sugar, baking powder and salt. With wooden spoon or spatula, mix in yogurt, olive oil and lemon peel until well blended. *Do not use electric mixer.* Pour batter into prepared pan. Score top of batter with tip of sharp knife, making 12 to 15 squares or diamond shapes, about ½ inch deep. (Marks will not remain completely visible before baking, but will show slightly when baked.) Place walnut half in center of each square or diamond shape.

Bake 45 minutes or until golden brown and toothpick inserted in center comes out clean. Meanwhile, in small saucepan, combine corn syrup and lemon juice. Heat over medium heat, stirring frequently, until mixture is hot.

When cake tests done, remove from oven. Make ½-inch-deep cuts through scored portions, cleaning knife after each cut. Immediately pour hot syrup over cake in pan. Let stand 1 to 2 hours or until syrup is absorbed and cake is cool. Remove side of pan; serve garnished with strawberries, if desired. Cover; refrigerate any remaining cake.   *Makes 10 to 12 servings*

Lemon Semolina Syrup Cake

Raspberry-Filled Chocolate Ravioli

1 cup butter, softened
½ cup granulated sugar
2 squares (1 ounce each) bittersweet or semisweet chocolate, melted and cooled
1 egg
1 teaspoon vanilla
½ teaspoon chocolate extract (optional)
¼ teaspoon baking soda
  Dash salt
2½ cups all-purpose flour
1 cup seedless raspberry jam
  Powdered sugar

Mix butter and granulated sugar in large bowl until blended. Add melted chocolate, egg, vanilla, chocolate extract, if desired, baking soda and salt; beat until light. Blend in flour to make stiff dough. Divide dough in half. Cover; refrigerate until firm.

Preheat oven to 350°F. Lightly grease cookie sheets or line with parchment paper. Roll out dough, half at a time, ⅛ inch thick between two sheets of plastic wrap. Remove top sheet of plastic. (If dough gets too soft and sticks to plastic, refrigerate until firm.) Cut dough into 1½-inch squares. Place half the squares, 2 inches apart, on prepared cookie sheets. Place about ½ teaspoon jam on center of each square; top with another square. Using fork, press edges of squares together to seal, then pierce center of each square. Bake 10 minutes or just until edges are browned. Remove to wire racks to cool. Dust lightly with powdered sugar.

Makes about 6 dozen ravioli

Raspberry-Filled Chocolate Ravioli

Bolivian Almond Cookies (Alfajores de Almendras)

4 cups natural almonds
1 cup all-purpose flour
¼ teaspoon salt
1 cup sugar
¾ cup butter, softened
1 teaspoon vanilla
½ teaspoon almond extract
2 eggs
2 tablespoons milk
1 tablespoon grated lemon peel
1 cup sliced natural almonds

1. Place 4 cups almonds in food processor. Process using on/off pulsing action until almonds are ground, but not pasty.

2. Preheat oven to 350°F. Grease cookie sheets; set aside.

3. Place ground almonds, flour and salt in medium bowl; stir to combine.

4. Beat sugar, butter, vanilla and almond extract in large bowl with electric mixer at medium speed until light and fluffy. Beat in eggs and milk. Gradually add ½ of flour mixture. Beat at low speed until well blended. Stir in lemon peel and remaining flour mixture.

5. Drop rounded teaspoonfuls of dough 2 inches apart onto prepared cookie sheets. Flatten slightly with spoon; top with sliced almonds.

6. Bake 10 to 12 minutes or until edges are lightly browned. Remove cookies with spatula to wire racks; cool completely.

Makes about 3 dozen cookies

Three-Berry Kuchen

1¾ cups all-purpose flour, divided
2 teaspoons baking powder
½ teaspoon baking soda
½ teaspoon salt
⅔ cup MOTT'S® Apple Sauce
4 egg whites
¼ cup nonfat plain yogurt
2 tablespoons granulated sugar
1 teaspoon grated lemon peel
2 cups assorted fresh or thawed, frozen blueberries, raspberries or blackberries
¼ cup firmly packed light brown sugar
2 tablespoons margarine

1. Preheat oven to 350°F. Spray 10-inch round cake pan with nonstick cooking spray.

2. In small bowl, combine 1½ cups flour, baking powder, baking soda and salt.

3. In large bowl, whisk together apple sauce, egg whites, yogurt, granulated sugar and lemon peel.

4. Add flour mixture to apple sauce mixture; stir until well blended. Spread batter into prepared pan.

5. Sprinkle berries over batter. Combine remaining ¼ cup flour and brown sugar in small bowl. Cut in margarine with pastry blender or fork until mixture resembles coarse crumbs. Sprinkle over berries.

6. Bake 50 to 55 minutes or until lightly browned. Cool on wire rack 20 minutes. Serve warm or cool completely. Cut into 9 slices. *Makes 9 servings*

Chocolate-Gilded Danish Sugar Cones

½ cup butter, softened
½ cup sugar
½ cup all-purpose flour
2 egg whites
1 teaspoon vanilla
3 ounces bittersweet chocolate *or*
   ½ cup semisweet chocolate chips

1. Preheat oven to 400°F. Generously grease 4 cookie sheets. Beat butter and sugar in large bowl until light and fluffy. Blend in flour. In clean, dry bowl, beat egg whites until foamy. Blend into butter mixture. Add vanilla.

2. Using teaspoon, place 4 mounds of dough 4 inches apart on each prepared cookie sheet. Spread mounds to 3-inch diameter with small spatula dipped in water.

3. Bake 1 sheet at a time, 5 to 6 minutes or until edges are just barely golden. *Do not overbake, or cookies will become crisp too quickly and will be difficult to shape.*

4. Remove from oven and quickly loosen each cookie from cookie sheet with thin spatula. Shape each cookie into cone; cones will become firm as they cool. (If cookies become too firm to shape, return to oven for few seconds to soften.)

5. Melt chocolate in small bowl over hot water. Stir until smooth. When all cookies are baked and cooled, dip wide ends into melted chocolate; let stand until chocolate is set.   *Makes about 16 cookies*

Tarte au Sucre (Sugar Tart)

1 unbaked 9-inch Classic CRISCO® Single Crust* (recipe page 132)
¾ cup firmly packed brown sugar
¾ cup granulated sugar
½ cup ground almonds
2 large eggs, beaten
1½ tablespoons all-purpose flour
½ teaspoon fresh grated nutmeg
½ cup plus 1 tablespoon heavy cream
½ teaspoon almond extract
½ teaspoon vanilla
2 tablespoons unsalted butter, cut into small pieces

Prepare pie crust using Butter Flavor CRISCO® all-vegetable shortening.

1. Heat oven to 350°F. Lightly spray 9-inch removable bottom tart pan with CRISCO® No-Stick Cooking Spray. Press pie crust onto bottom and up side of pan; refrigerate.

2. Combine brown sugar, granulated sugar, almonds, eggs, flour and nutmeg in large bowl until well blended. Add cream, almond extract and vanilla until well blended. Place tart pan on baking sheet; pour in filling. Dot evenly with butter.

3. Bake at 350°F for 25 to 30 minutes or until filling is a light golden color, puffs up and is just set. Cool on cooling rack. Serve at room temperature.   *Makes 8 servings*

Tip: This tart is a favorite for home entertaining in Belgium.

Apple and Walnut Strudel

1 package (about 17 ounces) frozen puff pastry

1 cup sour cream

1 egg, separated

1 tablespoon water

1 can (21 ounces) apple pie filling

1 cup coarsely chopped walnuts

1. Thaw the puff pastry according to package directions.

2. Preheat oven to 375°F. Spray 2 baking sheets with nonstick cooking spray.

3. Combine sour cream and egg yolk in small bowl; set aside. In separate small bowl, mix egg white and water; set aside.

4. On lightly floured board, roll 1 sheet pastry into 12×10-inch rectangle. Spread ½ can pie filling vertically down center ⅓ of pastry. Spread ½ cup sour cream mixture over apples; sprinkle with ½ cup walnuts.

5. Fold one long side of pastry over apple mixture then fold the other side over filling overlapping edges. Press edges together to seal. Place on baking sheet, seam side down, tucking under ends. Using a sharp knife, make 7 diagonal slits on the top, then brush with egg white mixture. Repeat with remaining pastry, apple filling, sour cream mixture and walnuts. Bake for 30 to 35 minutes or until golden brown.

Makes 16 servings

Dutch Chocolate Meringues

¼ cup finely chopped pecans

2½ tablespoons unsweetened cocoa powder (preferably Dutch process)

3 egg whites

¼ teaspoon salt

¾ cup granulated sugar

Powdered sugar (optional)

1. Preheat oven to 200°F. Line cookie sheets with foil; grease well. Set aside.

2. Place pecans and cocoa in medium bowl; stir to combine.

3. Beat egg whites and salt in clean large bowl with electric mixer at high speed until light and foamy. Gradually beat in granulated sugar until stiff peaks form.

4. Gently fold pecan mixture into egg white mixture with rubber spatula by gently cutting down to bottom of bowl, scraping up side of bowl, then folding over top of mixture. Repeat until pecan mixture is evenly incorporated.

5. Spoon batter into pastry bag fitted with large plain tip. Pipe 1-inch mounds 2 inches apart on prepared cookie sheets. Bake 1 hour. Turn oven off. *Do not open oven door;* let stand in oven until set, 2 hours or overnight.

6. When cookies are firm, carefully peel cookies from foil. Dust with powdered sugar, if desired. Store loosely covered at room temperature up to 2 days.

Makes about 6 dozen cookies

Meringue Mushrooms: Pipe same number of 1-inch-tall "stems" as mounds. Bake as directed in step 5. When cookies are firm, attach "stems" to "caps" with melted chocolate. Dust with sifted unsweetened cocoa powder.

Almond Chinese Chews

1 cup granulated sugar
3 eggs, lightly beaten
1 can SOLO® or 1 jar BAKER®
    Almond Filling
¾ cup all-purpose flour
1 teaspoon baking powder
¼ teaspoon salt
    Powdered sugar

Preheat oven to 300°F. Grease 13×9-inch baking pan; set aside.

Beat granulated sugar and beaten eggs in medium-size bowl with electric mixer until thoroughly blended. Add almond filling; beat until blended. Sift together flour, baking powder and salt; fold into almond mixture. Spread batter evenly in prepared pan.

Bake 40 to 45 minutes or until wooden toothpick inserted in center comes out clean. Cool completely in pan on wire rack. Cut into 2×1½-inch bars; dust with powdered sugar. *Makes about 3 dozen bars*

Chocolate Madeleines

1¼ cups all-purpose flour
1 cup sugar
⅛ teaspoon salt
¾ cup (1½ sticks) butter, melted (no substitutes)
⅓ cup HERSHEY'S Cocoa
3 eggs
2 egg yolks
½ teaspoon vanilla extract
    Chocolate Frosting (recipe follows)

1. Heat oven to 350°F. Lightly grease indentations of madeleine mold pan (each shell is 3×2 inches).

2. Stir together flour, sugar and salt in medium saucepan. Combine melted butter and cocoa; stir into dry ingredients. In small bowl, lightly beat eggs, egg yolks and vanilla with fork until well blended; stir into chocolate mixture, blending well. Cook over very low heat, stirring constantly, until mixture is warm. *Do not simmer or boil.* Remove from heat. Fill each mold half full with batter. (Do not overfill).

3. Bake 8 to 10 minutes or until wooden toothpick inserted in center comes out clean. Invert onto wire rack; cool completely. Prepare Chocolate Frosting; frost flat sides of cookies. Press frosted sides together, forming shells.
Makes about 1½ dozen filled cookies

Chocolate Frosting

1¼ cups powdered sugar
2 tablespoons HERSHEY'S Cocoa
2 tablespoons butter, softened (no substitutes)
2 to 2½ tablespoons milk
½ teaspoon vanilla extract

Stir together powdered sugar and cocoa in small bowl. In another small bowl, beat butter and ¼ cup of the cocoa mixture until fluffy. Gradually add remaining cocoa mixture alternately with milk, beating to spreading consistency. Stir in vanilla.

Acknowledgments

The publisher would like to thank the companies and organizations listed below for the use of their recipes and photographs in this publication.

Birds Eye®

Bob Evans®

California Dried Plum Board

Cherry Marketing Institute

ConAgra Foods®

Del Monte Corporation

Dole Food Company, Inc.

Duncan Hines® and Moist Deluxe® are registered trademarks of Aurora Foods Inc.

Eagle® Brand

Egg Beaters®

Filippo Berio® Olive Oil

Fleischmann's® Yeast

General Mills, Inc.

Grandma's® is a registered trademark of Mott's, Inc.

Hershey Foods Corporation

The Hidden Valley® Food Products Company

Hormel Foods, LLC

Kahlúa® Liqueur

Kraft Foods Holdings

©Mars, Incorporated 2002

McIlhenny Company (TABASCO® brand Pepper Sauce)

Minnesota Cultivated Wild Rice Council

Mott's® is a registered trademark of Mott's, Inc.

National Honey Board

National Onion Association

Nestlé USA

New York Apple Association, Inc.

Norseland, Inc. / Lucini Italia Co.

North Dakota Wheat Commission

OREO® Chocolate Sandwich Cookies

Peanut Advisory Board

PLANTERS® Nuts

The Quaker® Oatmeal Kitchens

Reckitt Benckiser Inc.

RED STAR® Yeast, a product of Lasaffre Yeast Corporation

Sargento® Foods Inc.

The J.M. Smucker Company

Sokol and Company

Unilever Bestfoods North America

Washington Apple Commission

Wisconsin Milk Marketing Board

Index

A

Almond
Almond Amaretto Loaf, 152
Almond Brioches, 358
Almond Chinese Chews, 370
Bolivian Almond Cookies (Alfajores de Almendras), 364
Cherry and Almond Coffee Cake, 44
Chocolate Almond Frosting, 182
Chocolate Almond Pear Torte, 124
Chocolate Almond Torte, 182
Dried Cherry-Almond Bread, 160
Fabulous Blonde Brownies, 259
Norwegian Almond Squares, 344
White Chocolate & Almond Brownies, 244
Yuletide Linzer Bars, 327
Amaretto Glaze, 152
Anadama Bread, 18
Angel Biscuits, 70
Angel Food Cake, 172
Angel Food Roll with Strawberry Sauce, 194

Apples
Apple and Walnut Strudel, 368
Apple Cheddar Scones, 72
Apple Cranberry Pie, 110
Apple-Gingerbread Mini Cakes, 212
Apple Ring Coffee Cake, 40
Autumn Apple Bars, 236
Cheddar and Apple Muffins, 190
Cider Apple Pie in Cheddar Crust, 114
Golden Apple Buttermilk Bread, 96
Peanut Butter Crumble Topped Apple Pie, 131
Scrumptious Apple Cake, 167
Walnut Cheddar Apple Bread, 98

Applesauce
Cocoa Applesauce Raisin Muffins, 74
Lots o' Chocolate Bread, 94
Raspberry-Applesauce Coffee Cake, 60
Scrumptious Apple Cake, 167
Apple Sauce Cinnamon Rolls, 54

Apricot
Apricot Carrot Bread, 104
Apricot-Filled Coffee Cakes, 56
Chewy Oatmeal-Apricot-Date Bars, 231
Autumn Apple Bars, 236

B

Bacon-Cheese Muffins, 38
Bagels, 360
Baked Doughnuts with Cinnamon Glaze, 43
Baker's® Premium Chocolate Chunk Cookies, 228

Bananas
Banana Bread, 108
Banana-Chocolate Chip Bread, 140
Banana Crescents, 318
Banana Split Cupcakes, 296
Good Morning Bread, 63
Peanut Butter Chip & Banana Mini Muffins, 210
Tropical Fruit Coconut Tart, 128
Upside-Down Hot Fudge Sundae Pie, 118
Basic White Bread, 26
Bayou Yam Muffins, 68
Best Cherry Pie, The, 118
Bird's Nest Cookies, 298

Biscuits
Angel Biscuits, 70
Biscuits, 70
Cherry-Up Biscuits, 66
Chive Whole Wheat Drop Biscuits, 85
Country Recipe Biscuits, 79
Freezer Buttermilk Biscuits, 80
Green Onion Cream Cheese Breakfast Biscuits, 58
Herb Biscuits, 82
Zesty Parmesan Biscuits, 76
Bittersweet Pecan Brownies with Caramel Sauce, 256
Black & White Cheesecake, 275
Black & White Pistachio Cake, 206
Black Pepper-Onion Bread, 142

Blueberry
Blueberry Coffeecake, 42
Minnesota's Fresh Blueberry Cream Cheese Pie, 120
Peach Blueberry Cheesecake, 280
Streusel-Topped Blueberry Muffins, 86
Three-Berry Kuchen, 364
Bolivian Almond Cookies (Alfajores de Almendras), 364
Boston Brown Bread, 103

Bran
Bran and Honey Rye Breadsticks, 32
Grandma's® Bran Muffins, 74
Peachy Oat Bran Muffins, 77
Brandy Glaze, 184
Brandy Pecan Cake, 184

Bread Machine Recipes, 136–161
  Bagels, 360
  Good Morning Bread, 63
  Jamaican Cherry Bread, 347
Breadsticks
  Breadstick Sampler, 104
  Pizza Breadsticks, 140
  Poppy Seed Breadsticks, 14
  Roasted Garlic Breadsticks, 34
  Rosemary Breadsticks, 108
  Sugar-and-Spice Twists, 294
Breakfast Cookies, 48
Broccoli & Cheddar Muffins, 78
Broiled Topping, 164
Brownie Berry Parfaits, 260
Brownie Cake Delight, 244
Brownie Fudge, 262
Brownie Pizza, 254
Brownies (*see pages 242-267*): Chocolate
    Brownie Pie, 114
Brunchtime Sour Cream Cupcakes, 42
Buckwheat: Onion Buckwheat Bread, 22
Butter Cookie Dough, 292, 328
Buttercream Frosting, 330
Buttermilk
  Angel Biscuits, 70
  Boston Brown Bread, 103
  Buttermilk Corn Bread Loaf, 90
  Dilled Buttermilk Bread, 160
  Freezer Buttermilk Biscuits, 80
  Golden Apple Buttermilk Bread, 96
  Grandma's® Bran Muffins, 74
  Herb Biscuits, 82
  Holiday Chocolate Cake, 322
  Irish Soda Bread, 107
  Peanut Butter Chocolate Chip Loaves,
    102
  Spiced Brown Bread Muffins, 79
  White Chocolate Chunk Muffins, 76
Butterscotch
  Butterscotch Blondies, 219
  Butterscotch Brownies, 258
  Choco-Scutterbotch, 214

C
Cajun Hot Tomato Bread, 24
Cakes, 162–189 (*see also* **Coffee Cakes;**
    Cupcakes; Tube and Bundt Cakes)
  Apple-Gingerbread Mini Cakes, 212
  Black and White Pistachio Cake, 206
  Brownie Cake Delight, 244
  Chocolate-Chocolate Cake, 192

Cakes (*continued*)
  Chocolate Toffee Cream Cake, 212
  Della Robbia Cake, 196
  Dump Cake, 205
  Enchanted Castle, 298
  Holiday Chocolate Cake, 322
  Ice Cream Cone Cakes, 308
  Kahlúa® Black Forest Cake, 202
  Lemon Semolina Syrup Cake, 362
  Three-Berry Kuchen, 364
Cappuccino Cupcakes, 210
Caramel
  Bittersweet Pecan Brownies with Caramel
    Sauce, 256
  Caramel Topping, 271
  Chocolate Caramel Sugar Cookies, 220
  Chocolate Squares with Nutty Caramel
    Sauce, 162
Carrots
  Apricot Carrot Bread, 104
  Carrot Cake, 180
  Carrot-Raisin-Nut Bread, 153
  Hikers' Bar Cookies, 230
  Morning Glory Bread, 90
  Spiced Kahlúa® Loaf, 100
Cashew: Cashew-Lemon Shortbread Cookies,
    220
Celia's Flat Fruit Pie, 128
Cereal
  Banana Bread, 108
  Cinnamon Trail Mix, 306
  "Everything but the Kitchen Sink" Bar
    Cookies, 295
  Fruity Cookie Rings and Twists, 296
  Grandma's® Bran Muffins, 74
  Tomato-Peppercorn-Cheese Bread, 20
  Tropical Fruit Coconut Tart, 128
Cheddar and Apple Muffins, 190
Cheery Cheesecake Cookie Bars, 286
Cheese Twists, 301
Cherry
  Banana Split Cupcakes, 296
  Best Cherry Pie, The, 118
  Cherry and Almond Coffee Cake, 44
  Cherry Cream Filling, 267
  Cherry-Up Biscuits, 66
  Danish Cookie Rings (Vanillekranser),
    336
  Dried Cherry-Almond Bread, 160
  Dump Cake, 205
  Golden Cherry Granola Bread, 142
  Jamaican Cherry Bread, 347

Cherry (*continued*)

Kahlúa® Black Forest Cake, 202

Marbled Cherry Brownies, 266

Sour Cream Coffee Cake with Brandy-Soaked Cherries, 46

Chewy Oatmeal-Apricot-Date Bars, 231

Chili Cheese Bread, 138

Chive Whole Wheat Drop Biscuits, 85

Chocolate (*see also* **Chocolate Chips, Cocoa**)

Baker's® Premium Chocolate Chunk Cookies, 228

Bird's Nest Cookies, 298

Brownie Fudge, 262

Cappuccino Cupcakes, 210

Cheery Cheesecake Cookie Bars, 286

Chocolate Almond Frosting, 182

Chocolate Almond Pear Torte, 124

Chocolate Almond Torte, 182

Chocolate-Berry Cheesecake, 271

Chocolate Brownie Pie, 114

Chocolate-Caramel Sugar Cookies, 220

Chocolate-Chocolate Cake, 192

Chocolate Chunk Cinnamon Coffee Cake, 48

Chocolate Chunk Sour Cream Muffins, 82

Chocolate-Dipped Cinnamon Thins, 234

Chocolate-Gilded Danish Sugar Cones, 366

Chocolate-Orange Bavarian Torte, 200

Chocolate Peanut Butter Cups, 197

Chocolate Popovers, 72

Chocolate Raspberry Avalanche Cake, 164

Chocolate Squares with Nutty Caramel Sauce, 162

Chocolate Strawberry Whipped Cream Cake, 186

Chocolate Sugar Cookies, 220

Chocolate Toffee Cream Cake, 212

Chocolate Topping, 271

Chocolate Truffle Tart, 116

Chocolate Turtle Cheesecake, 280

Choco-Scutterbotch, 214

Coconutty "M&M'S"® Brownies, 266

Crispy's Irresistible Peanut Butter Marbles, 218

Decadent Pie, 122

Decadent Turtle Cheesecake, 271

Devil's Fudge Brownies, 250

Espresso Swirl Cheesecake, 284

Festive Holiday Rugelach, 336

Flourless Chocolate Cake with Raspberry Sauce, 181

Fudge Topping, 262

Jam-Filled Chocolate Sugar Cookies, 220

Chocolate (*continued*)

Jeweled Brownie Cheesecake, 282

Kahlúa® Black Forest Cake, 202

Kahlúa® Chocolate Decadence, 168

Oreo® Brownie Treats, 206

PB & J Cookie Sandwiches, 302

Philadelphia® 3-Step® Tiramisu Cheesecake, 276

Raspberry Chocolate Mousse Pie, 127

Raspberry-Filled Chocolate Ravioli, 363

Triple Chocolate Sticky Buns, 156

Upside-Down Hot Fudge Sundae Pie, 118

Chocolate Chips

Banana-Chocolate Chip Bread, 140

Banana Split Cupcakes, 296

Black & White Cheesecake, 275

Butterscotch Brownies, 258

Chocolate-Berry Cheesecake, 271

Chocolate Chip Cheesecake, 283

Chocolate Chip Lemon Loaf, 96

Chocolate Chip Shortbread, 224

Chocolate-Chocolate Chip Bread, 106

Chocolate Glaze, 200, 275

Chocolate Mini Cheesecakes, 270

Coffee Walnut Chocolate Chip Muffins, 44

"Everything but the Kitchen Sink" Bar Cookies, 295

Fudge Nut Glaze, 314

Hershey's® Milk Chocolate Chip Giant Cookies, 300

Lots o' Chocolate Bread, 94

Mini Chip Glaze, 249

Nancy's Dishpan Cookies, 226

Orange Cappuccino Brownies, 264

Orange Chocolate Chip Bread, 199

Peanut Butter Chocolate Chip Loaves, 102

Raspberry Fudge Brownies, 248

Refreshing Choco-Orange Cheesecake, 278

Rocky Road Brownies, 262

Royal Glaze, 186

Yule Tree Namesakes, 328

Chocolate-Chocolate Cake, 192

Chocolate-Chocolate Chip Bread, 106

Chocolate Chunk Cinnamon Coffee Cake, 48

Chocolate Chunk Sour Cream Muffins, 82

Chocolate-Dipped Cinnamon Thins, 234

Chocolate Espresso Brownies, 246

Chocolate Frosting, 370

Chocolate-Gilded Danish Sugar Cones, 366

Chocolate Glaze, 200, 275

Chocolate Madeleines, 370

Chocolate Mini Cheesecakes, 270

Chocolate-Orange Bavarian Torte, 200
Chocolate Peanut Butter Cups, 197
Chocolate Popovers, 72
Chocolate Raspberry Avalanche Cake, 164
Chocolate Squares with Nutty Caramel Sauce, 162
Chocolate Strawberry Whipped Cream Cake, 186
Chocolate Sugar Cookies, 220
Chocolate Toffee Cream Cake, 212
Chocolate Topping, 271
Chocolate Truffle Tart, 116
Chocolate Turtle Cheesecake, 280
Chocolate Whipped Cream, 322
Choco-Scutterbotch, 214
Christmas Spritz Cookies, 332
Cider Apple Pie in Cheddar Crust, 114
Cinnamon
    Apple Sauce Cinnamon Rolls, 54
    Baked Doughnuts with Cinnamon Glaze, 43
    Chocolate Chunk Cinnamon Coffee Cake, 48
    Chocolate-Dipped Cinnamon Thins, 234
    Cinnamon Butter, 74
    Cinnamon Chip Filled Crescents, 40
    Cinnamon Pear Sauce, 327
    Cinnamon-Pecan Pull-Apart Bread, 143
    Cinnamon-Raisin Bread, 30
    Cinnamon-Raisin Rolls, 192
    Cinnamon Twists, 16
    Oven-Baked French Toast, 52
    Quick Cinnamon Sticky Buns, 204
    Yeasty Cinnamon Loaves, 16
Classic Anise Biscotti, 355
Classic Crisco® Crust, 132
Classic Pumpkin Pie with Candied Pecan Topping, 340
Classic Refrigerator Sugar Cookies, 225
Cocoa
    Chocolate Frosting, 370
    Chocolate Madeleines, 370
    Chocolate Whipped Cream, 322
    Cocoa Applesauce Raisin Muffins, 74
    Cocoa Glaze, 350
    Cocoa Pecan Crescents, 236
    Cocoa Streusel, 52
    Cocoa-Walnut Crescents, 216
    Crunchy-Topped Cocoa Cake, 164
    Dutch Chocolate Meringues, 368
    Glazed Cocoa Batter Bread, 13
    Hershey®s "Perfectly Chocolate" Chocolate Cake, 176
    Holiday Chocolate Cake, 322

Cocoa (continued)
    Holiday Fudge Torte, 314
    Ooey Gooey Peanut Butter and Fudge Brownies, 253
    "Perfectly Chocolate" Chocolate Frosting, 176
    Sensational Peppermint Pattie Brownies, 256
    Viennese Chocolate Torte, 350
Coconut
    Bird's Nest Cookies, 298
    Coconut Date Nut Quick Bread, 98
    Coconut-Topped Brownies, 244
    Coconut Topping, 266
    Coconutty "M&M'S"® Brownies, 266
    Decadent Pie, 122
    Marvelous Macaroons, 228
    Orange Coconut Muffins, 87
    Snowman Cupcakes, 334
    Tropical Chunk Cookies, 238
    Tropical Fruit Coconut Tart, 128
    Wisconsin Ricotta Tart with Kiwi and Raspberry Sauce, 130
    Yule Tree Namesakes, 328
Coconutty "M&M'S"® Brownies, 266
Coffee Cakes
    Apple Ring Coffee Cake, 40
    Apricot-Filled Coffee Cakes, 56
    Blueberry Coffeecake, 42
    Cherry and Almond Coffee Cake, 44
    Chocolate Chunk Cinnamon Coffee Cake, 48
    Cranberry Streusel Coffee Cake, 55
    Orange Streusel Coffeecake, 52
    Quick Crumb Coffee Cake, 60
    Raspberry-Applesauce Coffee Cake, 60
    Sour Cream Coffee Cake with Brandy-Soaked Cherries, 46
Coffee Walnut Chocolate Chip Muffins, 44
Cookie Canvases, 308
Cookie Glaze, 308, 316, 328
Cookies, 214–241
    Almond Chinese Chews, 370
    Banana Crescents, 318
    Bird's Nest Cookies, 298
    Bolivian Almond Cookies (Alfajores de Almendras), 364
    Breakfast Cookies, 48
    Butter Cookie Dough, 292, 328
    Cheery Cheesecake Cookie Bars, 286
    Chocolate-Gilded Danish Sugar Cones, 366
    Chocolate Madeleines, 370
    Christmas Spritz Cookies, 332
    Classic Anise Biscotti, 355
    Cookie Canvases, 308

Index ◆ 375

Cookies (continued)

Currant Cheesecake Bars, 274
Danish Cookie Rings (Vanillekranser), 336
Dutch Chocolate Meringues, 368
Easy Lemon Pudding Cookies, 202
English Thumbprint Cookies, 354
European Kolacky, 360
"Everything but the Kitchen Sink" Bar Cookies, 295
Festive Holiday Rugelach, 336
Festive Lebkuchen, 348
Fruity Cookie Rings and Twists, 296
Gingerbread People, 326
Handprints, 310
Hanukkah Coin Cookies, 330
Hershey®s Milk Chocolate Chip Giant Cookies, 300
Holiday Peppermint Slices, 338
Hot Dog Cookies, 292
Meringue Mushrooms, 368
Mocha Biscotti, 342
Norwegian Almond Squares, 344
PB & J Cookie Sandwiches, 302
Peanut Butter S'Mores, 302
Peanut Butter Surprise Cookies, 198
Puzzle Cookie, 310
Rum Fruitcake Cookies, 324
Scottish Shortbread, 314
Strawberry Streusel Squares, 198
Swedish Cookie Shells, 348
Toffee Chunk Brownie Cookies, 250
Yuletide Linzer Bars, 327
Yule Tree Namesakes, 328

Cornmeal

Anadama Bread, 18
Bayou Yam Muffins, 68
Buttermilk Corn Bread Loaf, 90
Southern Spoon Bread, 93

Country Pecan Pie, 116
Country Recipe Biscuits, 79

Cranberry

Apple Cranberry Pie, 110
Cranberry Scones, 80
Cranberry Streusel Coffee Cake, 55
Peanutty Cranberry Bars, 234

Cream Cheese

Apple Cranberry Pie, 110
Brownie Pizza, 254
Cheery Cheesecake Cookie Bars, 286
Cherry and Almond Coffee Cake, 44
Chocolate-Berry Cheesecake, 271
Chocolate Chip Cheesecake, 283
Chocolate-Chocolate Cake, 192

Cream Cheese (continued)

Chocolate Mini Cheesecakes, 270
Chocolate Turtle Cheesecake, 280
Creamy Baked Cheesecake, 288
Creamy Lemon Cheesecake, 278
Currant Cheesecake Bars, 274
Decadent Turtle Cheesecake, 271
Easy Raspberry Chiffon Pie, 110
Espresso Swirl Cheesecake, 284
European Kolacky, 360
Fabulous Fruit Tart, 119
Festive Holiday Rugelach, 336
Green Onion Cream Cheese Breakfast Biscuits, 58
Heavenly Cheesecake, 277
Holiday Cheesecake Presents, 312
Jeweled Brownie Cheesecake, 282
Lemon Cheesecake, 272
Mini Cheesecakes, 270
Minnesota's Fresh Blueberry Cream Cheese Pie, 120
New York Cheesecake, 268
New York Style Cheesecake, 288
Peach Blueberry Cheesecake, 280
Philadelphia® Cheesecake Brownies, 246
Philadelphia® 3-Step® Tiramisu Cheesecake, 276
Refreshing Choco-Orange Cheesecake, 278
White Chocolate Cheesecake with Orange Sauce, 276

Cream Filling, 350
Creamy Baked Cheesecake, 288
Creamy Filled Brownies, 249
Creamy Filling, 249
Creamy Lemon Cheesecake, 278
Crisp Cheese Popovers, 85
Crispy's Irresistible Peanut Butter Marbles, 218
Crunchy-Topped Cocoa Cake, 164
Crusty Rye Bread, 136

Cupcakes

Banana Split Cupcakes, 296
Brunchtime Sour Cream Cupcakes, 42
Cappuccino Cupcakes, 210
Chocolate Peanut Butter Cups, 197
Play Ball, 306
Pretty-in-Pink Peppermint Cupcakes, 209
Snowman Cupcakes, 334

D

Dates

Chewy Oatmeal-Apricot-Date Bars, 231
Coconut Date Nut Quick Bread, 98

Dates (continued)
  Date Nut Bread, 88
    Good Morning Bread, 63
    Ma'moul Date Pastries, 352
Decadent Pie, 122
Decadent Turtle Cheesecake, 271
Della Robbia Cake, 196
Devil's Fudge Brownies, 250
Dilled Buttermilk Bread, 160
Dinner Rolls, 36
Double-Decker Confetti Brownies, 252
Dried Cherry-Almond Bread, 160
Dried Tomato and Rosemary Bread, 148
Dump Cake, 205
Dutch Chocolate Meringues, 368

E
Easy Lemon Pudding Cookies, 202
Easy Microwave Brownies, 248
Easy Raspberry Chiffon Pie, 134
Egg and Sausage Breakfast Strudel, 62
Egg Twist, 22
Enchanted Castle, 298
English Muffin Bread, 146
English-Style Scones, 64
English Thumbprint Cookies, 354
Espresso Swirl Cheesecake, 284
European Kolacky, 360
"Everything but the Kitchen Sink" Bar Cookies,
  295

F
Fabulous Blonde Brownies, 259
Fabulous Fruit Tart, 119
Farmer-Style Sour Cream Bread, 31
Festive Holiday Rugelach, 336
Festive Lebkuchen, 348
Festive Yule Loaf, 324
Flaky Pastry, 118
Flourless Chocolate Cake with Raspberry Sauce,
  181
Focaccia, 346
Freezer Buttermilk Biscuits, 80
Freezer White Bread, 26
French Bread, 28
Fresh Nectarine Pie with Strawberry Topping,
  126
Frostings, Fillings & Glazes
  Amaretto Glaze, 152
  Brandy Glaze, 184
  Buttercream Frosting, 330
  Cherry Cream Filling, 267

Frostings, Fillings & Glazes (continued)
  Chocolate Almond Frosting, 182
  Chocolate Frosting, 370
  Chocolate Glaze, 275
  Chocolate Topping, 271
  Chocolate Whipped Cream, 322
  Cocoa Glaze, 350
  Cookie Glaze, 308, 316, 328
  Cream Filling, 350
  Creamy Filling, 249
  Filling, 188
  Fudge Nut Glaze, 314
  Fudgy Mocha Frosting, 258
  Icing, 332
  Irish Cream Frosting, 254
  Kahlúa® Glaze, 100
  Mini Chip Glaze, 249
  Mocha Yogurt Glaze, 189
  Molasses Glaze, 334
  Orange Baba Syrup, 174
  "Perfectly Chocolate" Chocolate Frosting, 176
  Powdered Sugar Frosting, 13
  Powdered Sugar Glaze, 216
  Quick Glaze, 210
  Raspberry Tortoni Filling, 170
  Ricotta Cheese Filling, 322
  Royal Glaze, 186
  Royal Icing, 304, 321
  Strawberry Whipped Cream Filling, 186
  Vanilla Glaze, 324
  Vanilla Whipped Cream, 322
  Yogurt Glaze, 167
Fruit (see also individual listings)
  Celia's Flat Fruit Pie, 128
  Fabulous Fruit Tart, 119
  Georgian Baklava (Pakhlava), 352
  Rum Fruitcake Cookies, 324
  Strawberry Rhubarb Pie, 122
  Tropical Fruit Coconut Tart, 120
  Tropical Treat Muffins, 86
Fruity Cookie Rings and Twists, 296
Fudge Nut Glaze, 314
Fudge Topping, 262
Fudgy Mocha Brownies with a Crust, 258
Fudgy Mocha Frosting, 258

G
Georgian Baklava (Pakhlava), 352
Gingerbread Farm Animals in Corral, 304
Gingerbread House Dough, 304
Gingerbread Log Cabin, 320
Gingerbread People, 326

Gingerbread Streusel Raisin Muffins, 66
Ginger-Peach Blossoms, 159
Glazed Cocoa Batter Bread, 13
Golden Apple Buttermilk Bread, 96
Golden Cheese Bread, 18
Golden Cherry Granola Bread, 142
Golden Chiffon Cake, 174
Good Morning Bread, 63
Grandma's Gingerbread, 92
Grandma's® Bran Muffins, 74
Green Onion Cream Cheese Breakfast Biscuits, 58

H
Ham-Broccoli Quiche, 47
Handprints, 310
Hanukkah Coin Cookies, 330
Heavenly Cheesecake, 277
Heavenly Lemon Muffins, 208
Heavenly Strawberry Muffins, 208
Herb Biscuits, 82
Hershey's Best Brownies, 242
Hershey's Milk Chocolate Chip Giant Cookies, 300
Hershey's "Perfectly Chocolate" Chocolate Cake, 176
Hikers' Bar Cookies, 230
Holiday Cheesecake Presents, 312
Holiday Chocolate Cake, 322
Holiday Fudge Torte, 314
Holiday Peppermint Slices, 338
Holiday Pumpkin-Nut Muffins, 330
Holiday Rye Bread, 334
Homemade Pizza, 356
Honey
    Blueberry Coffeecake, 42
    Bran and Honey Rye Breadsticks, 32
    Honey Currant Scones, 69
    Honey Ginger Snaps, 232
    Honey-Orange Spicecake, 178
    Honey Shortbread, 222
    Honey Wheat Bread, 145
    Honey Wheat Brown-and-Serve Rolls, 20
    Honey Whole-Grain Bread, 10
Hot Dog Cookies, 292

I
Ice Cream Cone Cakes, 308
Icing, 332
Irish Brownies, 254
Irish Cream Frosting, 254
Irish Soda Bread, 107

J
Jamaican Cherry Bread, 347
Jam-Filled Chocolate Sugar Cookies, 220
Jeweled Brownie Cheesecake, 282

K
Kahlúa® Black Forest Cake, 202
Kahlúa® Chocolate Decadence, 168
Kahlúa® Glaze, 100
Kiwi: Wisconsin Ricotta Tart with Kiwi and Raspberry Sauce, 130

L
Lady Baltimore Cake, 188
Lemon
    Cashew-Lemon Shortbread Cookies, 220
    Chocolate Chip Lemon Loaf, 96
    Creamy Lemon Cheesecake, 278
    Easy Lemon Pudding Cookies, 202
    Heavenly Lemon Muffins, 208
    Lemon Cheesecake, 272
    Lemon Meringue Pie, 120
    Lemon Poppy Seed Bundt Cake, 173
    Lemon Poppy Seed Muffins, 84
    Lemon Poppy Seed Tea Loaf, 92
    Lemon Semolina Syrup Cake, 362
    Luscious Lemon Bars, 216
    Sunny Lemon Cake, 182
Liqueurs & Spirits
    Almond Amaretto Loaf, 152
    Amaretto Glaze, 152
    Brandy Glaze, 184
    Brandy Pecan Cake, 184
    Irish Brownies, 254
    Irish Cream Frosting, 254
    Kahlúa® Black Forest Cake, 202
    Kahlúa® Chocolate Decadence, 168
    Kahlúa® Glaze, 100
    Rum Fruitcake Cookies, 324
    Sour Cream Coffee Cake with Brandy-Soaked Cherries, 46
    Spiced Kahlúa® Loaf, 100
Lots o' Chocolate Bread, 94
Luscious Lemon Bars, 216

M
Macadamia Nuts
    Mocha-Macadamia Nut Muffins, 83
    Tropical Chunk Cookies, 238
Ma'moul Date Pastries, 352
Maple Butter, 62
Maple-Walnut Bread, 158

Marbled Cherry Brownies, 266
Marble Swirl Bread, 37
Marshmallow
    Banana Split Cupcakes, 296
    "Everything but the Kitchen Sink" Bar
        Cookies, 295
    Fudge Topping, 262
    Peanut Butter S'Mores, 302
    Rocky Road Brownies, 262
    Snowman Cupcakes, 334
Marvelous Macaroons, 228
Meringue Mushrooms, 368
Miniature Brownie Cups, 260
Mini Cheesecakes, 270
Mini Chip Glaze, 249
Minnesota's Fresh Blueberry Cream Cheese Pie,
    120
Mocha Biscotti, 342
Mocha-Macadamia Nut Muffins, 83
Mocha Marble Pound Cake, 189
Mocha Yogurt Glaze, 189
Molasses
    Anadama Bread, 18
    Gingerbread Streusel Raisin Muffins, 66
    Grandma's Gingerbread, 92
    Grandma's® Bran Muffins, 74
    Molasses Glaze, 334
    Pennsylvania Shoo-Fly Pie, 132
    Soft Molasses Spice Cookies, 222
    Spicy Gingerbread with Cinnamon Pear
        Sauce, 327
Mom's Favorite White Cake, 166
Morning Glory Bread, 90
Muffins
    Bacon-Cheese Muffins, 38
    Bayou Yam Muffins, 68
    Broccoli & Cheddar Muffins, 78
    Cheddar and Apple Muffins, 190
    Chocolate Chunk Sour Cream Muffins,
        82
    Cocoa Applesauce Raisin Muffins, 74
    Gingerbread Streusel Raisin Muffins, 66
    Grandma's® Bran Muffins, 74
    Heavenly Lemon Muffins, 208
    Heavenly Strawberry Muffins, 208
    Holiday Pumpkin-Nut Muffins, 330
    Lemon Poppy Seed Muffins, 84
    Mocha-Macadamia Nut Muffins, 83
    Orange Brunch Muffins, 50
    Orange Coconut Muffins, 87
    Oreo® Muffins, 290
    Peachy Oat Bran Muffins, 77

Muffins (*continued*)
    Peanut Butter Chip & Banana Mini Muffins,
        210
    Pesto Surprise Muffins, 71
    Southwestern Corn Muffins, 78
    Spiced Brown Bread Muffins, 79
    Streusel-Topped Blueberry Muffins, 86
    Tropical Treat Muffins, 86
    White Chocolate Chunk Muffins, 76
Multigrain Bread, 150

N
Nancy's Dishpan Cookies, 226
Nectarines: Fresh Nectarine Pie with Strawberry
    Topping, 126
New York Cheesecake, 268
New York Style Cheesecake, 288
Norwegian Almond Squares, 344
Nuts (*see also* **Almond; Cashew; Macadamia
    Nuts; Pecans; Pistachio; Walnuts**)
    Chocolate Chunk Cinnamon Coffee Cake, 48
    Creamy Filled Brownies, 249
    Fudge Nut Glaze, 314
    Holiday Pumpkin-Nut Muffins, 330
    Rum Fruitcake Cookies, 324

O
Oatmeal Bread, 138
Oatmeal-Raisin Bread, 149
Oatmeal Toffee Bars, 232
Oats
    Breakfast Cookies, 48
    Chewy Oatmeal-Apricot-Date Bars, 231
    Nancy's Dishpan Cookies, 226
    Oatmeal Bread, 138
    Oatmeal-Raisin Bread, 149
    Oatmeal Toffee Bars, 232
    Peachy Oat Bran Muffins, 77
    Peanut Butter Crumble Topped Apple Pie,
        131
    Peanutty Cranberry Bars, 234
    Savory Summertime Oat Bread, 48
Onion Buckwheat Bread, 22
Onion-Wheat Pan Bread, 100
Ooey Gooey Peanut Butter and Fudge Brownies,
    253
Orange
    Chocolate-Orange Bavarian Torte, 200
    Honey-Orange Spicecake, 178
    Orange Baba Cake, 174
    Orange Baba Syrup, 174
    Orange Bavarian, 200

Orange (*continued*)
  Orange Brunch Muffins, 50
  Orange Cappuccino Brownies, 264
  Orange Chocolate Chip Bread, 199
  Orange Coconut Muffins, 87
  Orange Pecan Pie, 319
  Orange Sauce, 276
  Orange Streusel Coffeecake, 52
  Refreshing Choco-Orange Cheesecake, 278
  White Chocolate Cheesecake with Orange Sauce, 276
Oreo® Brownie Treats, 206
Oreo® Muffins, 290
Oven-Baked French Toast, 52

P
P.B. Chips Brownie Cups, 264
PB & J Cookie Sandwiches, 302
Peach
  Ginger-Peach Blossoms, 159
  Peach Blueberry Cheesecake, 280
  Peach Delight Pie, 134
  Peachy Oat Bran Muffins, 77
Peachy Oat Bran Muffins, 77
Peanut Butter
  Breakfast Cookies, 48
  Chocolate Peanut Butter Cups, 197
  Crispy's Irresistible Peanut Butter Marbles, 218
  Ooey Gooey Peanut Butter and Fudge Brownies, 253
  PB & J Cookie Sandwiches, 302
  Peanut Butter Chip & Banana Mini Muffins, 210
  P.B. Chips Brownie Cups, 264
  Peanut Butter Chocolate Chip Loaves, 102
  Peanut Butter Crumble Topped Apple Pie, 131
  Peanut Butter S'Mores, 302
  Peanut Butter Surprise Cookies, 198
  Peanutty Cranberry Bars, 234
  Tiny Mini Kisses Peanut Blossoms, 226
  Triple Layer Peanut Butter Bars, 240
  "Ultimate" Peanut Butter Whoopee Pie, The, 112
Peanutty Cranberry Bars, 234
Pear-Ginger Upside-Down Cake, 178
Pears
  Chocolate Almond Pear Torte, 124
  Cinnamon Pear Sauce, 327
  Pear-Ginger Upside-Down Cake, 178

Pecans
  Bittersweet Pecan Brownies with Caramel Sauce, 256
  Brandy Pecan Cake, 184
  Chocolate Squares with Nutty Caramel Sauce, 162
  Cinnamon-Pecan Pull-Apart Bread, 143
  Classic Pumpkin Pie with Candied Pecan Topping, 340
  Cocoa Pecan Crescents, 236
  Country Pecan Pie, 116
  Decadent Pie, 122
  Decadent Turtle Cheesecake, 271
  Devil's Fudge Brownies, 250
  Dump Cake, 205
  English Thumbprint Cookies, 354
  Glazed Cocoa Batter Bread, 13
  Nancy's Dishpan Cookies, 226
  Orange Pecan Pie, 319
  Pumpkin-Nut Bread, 35
  Raspberry Pecan Thumbprints, 238
Pennsylvania Shoo-Fly Pie, 132
Peppermint
  Holiday Peppermint Slices, 338
  Pretty-in-Pink Peppermint Cupcakes, 209
  Sensational Peppermint Pattie Brownies, 256
"Perfectly Chocolate" Chocolate Frosting, 176
Pesto Surprise Muffins, 71
Philadelphia® Cheesecake Brownies, 246
Philadelphia® 3-Step® Tiramisu Cheesecake, 276
Pie and Pastry Crusts
  Classic Crisco® Crust, 132
  Flaky Pastry, 128
  Pie Crust, 126
  Reduced-Fat Pie Pastry, 118
Pie Crust, 126
Pies, 110–135
  Classic Pumpkin Pie with Candied Pecan Topping, 340
  Orange Pecan Pie, 319
  Poinsettia Pie, 338
Pineapple
  Carrot Cake, 180
  Dump Cake, 205
  Marvelous Macaroons, 228
  Pineapple Sweet Potato Pie, 131
  Tropical Fruit Coconut Tart, 128
  White Chocolate Pound Cake, 168
Pistachio: Black and White Pistachio Cake, 206
Pizza Breadsticks, 140
Play Ball, 306
Plum Purée, 106

Poinsettia Pie, 338
Poppy Seeds
    Lemon Poppy Seed Bundt Cake, 173
    Lemon Poppy Seed Muffins, 84
    Lemon Poppy Seed Tea Loaf, 92
    Poppy Seed Breadsticks, 14
Potato Bread, 154
Powdered Sugar Frosting, 13
Powdered Sugar Glaze, 216
Pretty-in-Pink Peppermint Cupcakes, 209
Puff Pastry
    Apple and Walnut Strudel, 368
    Cherry and Almond Coffee Cake, 44
Pumpernickel Bread, 144
Pumpkin
    Classic Pumpkin Pie with Candied Pecan
      Topping, 340
    Holiday Pumpkin-Nut Muffins, 330
    Pumpkin Cheesecake, 286
    Pumpkin-Ginger Scones, 78
    Pumpkin-Nut Bread, 35
    Quick Pumpkin Bread, 106
Puzzle Cookie, 310

Q
Quiche
    Ham Broccoli Quiche, 47
    Spinach Quiche, 50
Quick Cinnamon Sticky Buns, 204
Quick Crumb Coffee Cake, 60
Quick Glaze, 210
Quick Pumpkin Bread, 106

R
Raisins
    Breakfast Cookies, 48
    Carrot-Raisin-Nut Bread, 153
    Cinnamon-Raisin Bread, 30
    Cinnamon-Raisin Rolls, 192
    Cocoa Applesauce Raisin Muffins, 74
    Filling, 188
    Gingerbread Streusel Raisin Muffins, 66
    Grandma's® Bran Muffins, 74
    Irish Soda Bread, 107
    Oatmeal-Raisin Bread, 149
    Rum Fruitcake Cookies, 324
Raspberry
    Brownie Berry Parfaits, 260
    Chocolate Raspberry Avalanche Cake, 164
    Easy Raspberry Chiffon Pie, 134
    Flourless Chocolate Cake with Raspberry
      Sauce, 181

Raspberry (*continued*)
    Raspberry-Applesauce Coffee Cake, 60
    Raspberry Chocolate Mousse Pie, 127
    Raspberry-Filled Chocolate Ravioli, 363
    Raspberry Fudge Brownies, 248
    Raspberry Pecan Thumbprints, 238
    Raspberry Topping, 288
    Raspberry Tortoni Cake Roll, 170
    Raspberry Tortoni Filling, 170
    Three-Berry Kuchen, 364
    Wisconsin Ricotta Tart with Kiwi and
      Raspberry Sauce, 130
Reduced-Fat Pie Pastry, 118
Refreshing Choco-Orange Cheesecake, 278
Refrigerator White Bread, 26
Ricotta Cheese Filling, 322
Roasted Garlic Breadsticks, 34
Roasted Pepper-Olive Loaf, 158
Rocky Road Brownies, 262
Rolls and Buns
    Apple Sauce Cinnamon Rolls, 54
    Cinnamon Chip Filled Crescents, 40
    Cinnamon-Raisin Rolls, 192
    Dinner Rolls, 36
    Ginger-Peach Blossoms, 159
    Honey Wheat Brown-and-Serve Rolls, 20
    Quick Cinnamon Sticky Buns, 204
    Sage Buns, 14
    Triple Chocolate Sticky Buns, 156
Rosemary Breadsticks, 108
Royal Glaze, 186
Royal Icing, 304, 321
Rum Fruitcake Cookies, 324
Rye Flour
    Bran and Honey Rye Breadsticks, 32
    Crusty Rye Bread, 136
    Holiday Rye Bread, 334
    Marble Swirl Bread, 37

S
Sage Buns, 14
St. Joseph's Ricotta Puffs, 344
Santa Lucia Bread Wreath, 316
Savory Summertime Oat Bread, 12
Scones
    Apple Cheddar Scones, 72
    Cranberry Scones, 80
    English-Style Scones, 64
    Honey Currant Scones, 69
    Pumpkin-Ginger Scones, 78
Scottish Shortbread, 314
Scrumptious Apple Cake, 167

Sensational Peppermint Pattie Brownies, 256
Shortcut "Sourdough" Corn Bread, 150
Slow Cooker Recipes
    Boston Brown Bread, 103
    Chocolate Chip Lemon Loaf, 96
    Honey Whole-Grain Bread, 10
Snowman Cupcakes, 334
Soft Molasses Spice Cookies, 222
Soft Pretzels, 301
Sour Cream
    Apple and Walnut Strudel, 368
    Brandy Pecan Cake, 184
    Brunchtime Sour Cream Cupcakes, 42
    Chocolate Chip Cheesecake, 283
    Chocolate-Chocolate Cake, 192
    Chocolate Chunk Cinnamon Coffee Cake,
      48
    Chocolate Chunk Sour Cream Muffins, 82
    Creamy Baked Cheesecake, 288
    Farmer-Style Sour Cream Bread, 31
    New York Cheesecake, 268
    Orange Baba Cake, 174
    Orange Coconut Muffins, 87
    Peach Blueberry Cheesecake, 280
    Peanut Butter Crumble Topped Apple Pie,
      131
    Refreshing Choco-Orange Cheesecake, 278
    Sour Cream Coffee Cake with Brandy-Soaked
      Cherries, 46
    Traditional Ricotta Cheesecake, 272
    Walnut Cheddar Apple Bread, 98
    White Chocolate Cheesecake with Orange
      Sauce, 276
    White Chocolate Pound Cake, 168
Southern Spoon Bread, 93
Southwestern Corn Muffins, 78
Spiced Brown Bread Muffins, 79
Spiced Kahlúa® Loaf, 100
Spicy Cheese Bread, 32
Spicy Gingerbread with Cinnamon Pear Sauce,
    327
Spinach Quiche, 50
State Fair Cracked Wheat Bread, 146
Strawberry
    Angel Food Roll with Strawberry Sauce, 194
    Chocolate-Berry Cheesecake, 271
    Chocolate Strawberry Whipped Cream Cake,
      186
    Fresh Nectarine Pie with Strawberry Topping,
      126
    Fruit Filling, 166
    Heavenly Strawberry Muffins, 208

Strawberry (*continued*)
    Lemon Cheesecake, 272
    Strawberry Frosting, 166
    Strawberry Rhubarb Pie, 122
    Strawberry Streusel Squares, 198
    Strawberry Whipped Cream Filling, 186
Streusel
    Cocoa Streusel, 52
    Cranberry Streusel Coffee Cake, 55
    Gingerbread Streusel Raisin Muffins, 66
    Orange Streusel Coffeecake, 52
    Strawberry Streusel Squares, 198
    Streusel-Topped Blueberry Muffins, 86
    Streusel Topping, 46
Sugar-and-Spice Twists, 294
Sunny Lemon Cake, 182
Swedish Cookie Shells, 348
Sweet Potatoes and Yams
    Bayou Yam Muffins, 68
    Pineapple Sweet Potato Pie, 131

T
Tarte au Sucre (Sugar Tart), 366
Tarts and Tortes
    Chocolate Almond Pear Torte, 124
    Chocolate Almond Torte, 182
    Chocolate-Orange Bavarian Torte, 200
    Chocolate Truffle Tart, 116
    Fabulous Fruit Tart, 119
    Holiday Fudge Torte, 314
    Tarte au Sucre (Sugar Tart), 366
    Tropical Fruit Coconut Tart, 128
    Tuscan Brunch Torta, 58
    Viennese Chocolate Torte, 350
    Wisconsin Ricotta Tart with Kiwi and
      Raspberry Sauce, 130
Tex-Mex Quick Bread, 94
Three-Berry Kuchen, 364
Thyme-Cheese Bubble Loaf, 144
Tiny Mini Kisses Peanut Blossoms, 226
Toffee
    Chocolate Toffee Cream Cake, 212
    Oatmeal Toffee Bars, 232
    Toffee Chunk Brownie Cookies, 250
Tomato Cheese Bread, 194
Tomato-Peppercorn-Cheese Bread, 20
Traditional Ricotta Cheesecake, 272
Triple Chocolate Sticky Buns, 156
Triple Layer Peanut Butter Bars, 240
Tropical Chunk Cookies, 238
Tropical Fruit Coconut Tart, 128
Tropical Treat Muffins, 86

Tube and Bundt Cakes
  Brandy Pecan Cake, 184
  Chocolate Raspberry Avalanche Cake, 164
  Golden Chiffon Cake, 174
  Lemon Poppy Seed Bundt Cake, 173
  Orange Baba Cake, 174
  White Chocolate Pound Cake, 168
Tuscan Brunch Torta, 58

U
"Ultimate" Peanut Butter Whoopie Pie, The, 112
Upside-Down Hot Fudge Sundae Pie, 118

V
Vanilla Glaze, 324
Vanilla Whipped Cream, 322
Viennese Chocolate Torte, 350

W
Walnuts
  Apple and Walnut Strudel, 368
  Apple Ring Coffee Cake, 40
  Brownie Fudge, 262
  Brunchtime Sour Cream Cupcakes, 42
  Carrot-Raisin-Nut Bread, 153
  Chewy Oatmeal-Apricot-Date Bars, 231
  Cocoa-Walnut Crescents, 216
  Coconut Date Nut Quick Bread, 98
  Coffee Walnut Chocolate Chip Muffins, 44
  Date Nut Bread, 88
  Fudge Topping, 262
  Georgian Baklava (Pakhlava), 352
  Kahlúa® Chocolate Decadence, 168
  Maple-Walnut Bread, 158
  Rocky Road Brownies, 262
  Streusel Topping, 46
  Walnut Cheddar Apple Bread, 98
Whipped Topping
  Chocolate Toffee Cream Cake, 212
  Decadent Pie, 122
  Philadelphia® 3-Step® Tiramisu Cheesecake, 276
  Raspberry Chocolate Mousse Pie, 127
White Chocolate
  Fabulous Blonde Brownies, 259
  Orange Brunch Muffins, 50
  Strawberry Frosting, 166
  Tropical Chunk Cookies, 238
  White Chocolate & Almond Brownies, 244
  White Chocolate Cheesecake with Orange Sauce, 276

White Chocolate (continued)
  White Chocolate Chunk Muffins, 76
  White Chocolate Pound Cake, 168
Whole Wheat Flour
  Carrot Cake, 180
  Chive Whole Wheat Drop Biscuits, 85
  Golden Apple Buttermilk Bread, 96
  Golden Cherry Granola Bread, 142
  Good Morning Bread, 63
  Honey Wheat Bread, 145
  Honey Wheat Brown-and-Serve Rolls, 20
  Honey Whole-Grain Bread, 10
  Orange Coconut Muffins, 87
  Savory Summertime Oat Bread, 12
  Spiced Brown Bread Muffins, 79
  Spiced Kahlúa® Loaf, 100
  Whole Wheat Herb Bread, 24
  Whole Wheat Loaves, 149
Wild Rice
  Wild Rice Breakfast Bread, 62
  Wild Rice-Spinach-Feta Bread, 154
  Wild Rice Three Grain Bread, 28
Wisconsin Ricotta Tart with Kiwi and Raspberry Sauce, 130

Y
Yeast Breads, 10–37
  Almond Brioches, 358
  Angel Biscuits, 70
  Festive Yule Loaf, 324
  Focaccia, 346
  Herb Biscuits, 82
  Holiday Rye Bread, 334
  Jamaican Cherry Bread, 347
  Santa Lucia Bread Wreath, 316
Yeasty Cinnamon Loaves, 16
Yogurt Glaze, 167
Yuletide Linzer Bars, 327
Yule Tree Namesakes, 328

Z
Zesty Parmesan Biscuits, 76

METRIC CONVERSION CHART

VOLUME MEASUREMENTS (dry)

⅛ teaspoon = 0.5 mL
¼ teaspoon = 1 mL
½ teaspoon = 2 mL
¾ teaspoon = 4 mL
1 teaspoon = 5 mL
1 tablespoon = 15 mL
2 tablespoons = 30 mL
¼ cup = 60 mL
⅓ cup = 75 mL
½ cup = 125 mL
⅔ cup = 150 mL
¾ cup = 175 mL
1 cup = 250 mL
2 cups = 1 pint = 500 mL
3 cups = 750 mL
4 cups = 1 quart = 1 L

VOLUME MEASUREMENTS (fluid)

1 fluid ounce (2 tablespoons) = 30 mL
4 fluid ounces (½ cup) = 125 mL
8 fluid ounces (1 cup) = 250 mL
12 fluid ounces (1½ cups) = 375 mL
16 fluid ounces (2 cups) = 500 mL

WEIGHTS (mass)

½ ounce = 15 g
1 ounce = 30 g
3 ounces = 90 g
4 ounces = 120 g
8 ounces = 225 g
10 ounces = 285 g
12 ounces = 360 g
16 ounces = 1 pound = 450 g

DIMENSIONS

1/16 inch = 2 mm
⅛ inch = 3 mm
¼ inch = 6 mm
½ inch = 1.5 cm
¾ inch = 2 cm
1 inch = 2.5 cm

OVEN TEMPERATURES

250°F = 120°C
275°F = 140°C
300°F = 150°C
325°F = 160°C
350°F = 180°C
375°F = 190°C
400°F = 200°C
425°F = 220°C
450°F = 230°C

BAKING PAN SIZES

Utensil	Size in Inches/Quarts	Metric Volume	Size in Centimeters
Baking or Cake Pan (square or rectangular)	8×8×2	2 L	20×20×5
	9×9×2	2.5 L	23×23×5
	12×8×2	3 L	30×20×5
	13×9×2	3.5 L	33×23×5
Loaf Pan	8×4×3	1.5 L	20×10×7
	9×5×3	2 L	23×13×7
Round Layer Cake Pan	8×1½	1.2 L	20×4
	9×1½	1.5 L	23×4
Pie Plate	8×1¼	750 mL	20×3
	9×1¼	1 L	23×3
Baking Dish or Casserole	1 quart	1 L	—
	1½ quart	1.5 L	—
	2 quart	2 L	—